Gregory S. Feltenberger, MBA, FACMPE, FACHE, CPHIMS
David N. Gans, MHSA, FACMPE

BENCHMARKING
SUCCESS

The Essential Guide
for Group Practices

MGMA®

Defining Your Profession™

Production Credits

Editorial Director: Marilee E. Aust
Project Editor: Anne Serrano, MA
Book Production: Glacier Publishing Services, Inc.
Reviewer: Matt Groenig, FACMPE

Library of Congress Cataloging-in-Publication Data

Feltenberger, Gregory S.
  Benchmarking success : the essential guide for medical practice managers / by Gregory S. Feltenberger, David N. Gans.
    p. ; cm.
  Includes bibliographical references and index.
  Summary: "Benchmarking and use of medical practice data are necessities in today's health care environment. Administrators and physician-owners must ask (and answer) questions such as how the practice compares with others, how profitable and productive it is, what ratios and formulas to make comparisons. This book answers these and other questions"--Provided by publisher.
  ISBN 978-1-56829-289-2
  1. Medicine--Practice. 2. Benchmarking (Management) I. Gans, David N. II. Medical Group Management Association. III. Title.
  [DNLM: 1. Practice Management, Medical--organization & administration. 2. Benchmarking--organization & administration. W 80 F325b 2008]
  R728.F45 2008
  610.68--dc22
                                                                    2007050986

Item #6711
ISBN: 978-1-56829-289-2

Key Private Bank

This book is dedicated to my children,
Brittany, Aaron and Taylor, for always making
me proud. To my wife, Denise, for her love and support,
to my mother, Linda, for her strength and inspiration,
and to my father, Ron, for his drive and focus.
And finally, to all the outstanding members of the
U.S. Air Force Medical Service.

Greg

This book is dedicated to my parents,
Hope and Harry, who instilled a love of learning,
and to my spouse, Joan, who encouraged me
to pursue my dreams.

David

Contents

Preface

Benchmarking and the use of medical practice data have become a necessity in today's health care environment. To lead a successful practice, administrators and physician–owners must ask (and answer) several questions. For instance, how does my practice compare with others and what ratios and formulas should I use for comparison? How profitable and productive is my practice, and what performance metrics should I look at? This book will help answer these and many other questions. Also, many of the calculations are presented with a goal (for example, "higher the better" or "lower the better"). In general, the goals presented are typical across all practices; however, and in most cases, practice-specific factors (context) will determine the right goal for your practice.

The idea for this book originated from research and development of the Medical Group Management Association's (MGMA's) Web-based Virtual Medical Practice and the need for a user-friendly "how-to" guide for medical practice benchmarking, complete with standardized medical practice terms, ratios and formulas. The examples used in this book were developed to illustrate and explain benchmarking methods and are not representative of actual medical practices.

Users of medical practice data should pay careful attention to the first few chapters because the true value of benchmarking can only be realized by understanding the process and interpreting and communicating the findings. In addition, the implications of improperly using data or making decisions based on erroneous interpretations can result in serious and costly mistakes — perhaps negatively affecting your job or the practice's financial health.

To help users with many of the benchmarking tools presented in this book, most of the practice factors presented can be associated with line items from a sample accounts receivable (A/R) aging report, operational report, balance sheet, or income statement found in Appendix A, "Example Practice: Description, Reports and Financial Statements."

In addition, as you read through and use this book, if you have suggestions for improving the content or you know of (or use) other formulas, ratios or methods of measurement that should be included, the authors would greatly appreciate the input.

Chapter 1: Why Benchmark?

This chapter answers the question "Why Benchmark?"and addresses the reasons for benchmarking — or "if you don't measure it, you can't manage it" and "if you don't value it, you won't change it."

Chapter 2: Benchmarking Fundamentals

This chapter explains the importance of and need for standards and describes techniques for determining baseline and current status of a practice. In addition, this chapter presents factors that can be changed to improve a practice. And finally, this chapter describes similarities and differences of small and solo practices in comparison to larger practices.

Chapter 3: Measurement and Benchmarking

This chapter defines measurement, associated terms, the art and science of benchmarking and several benchmarking methods. In addition, this chapter describes common mistakes to avoid when interpreting measurements and benchmarks.

Chapter 4: Management by the Numbers

This chapter presents methods of describing and presenting data in meaningful ways, changing it into information, and using it to help make management decisions.

Chapter 5: How to Show the Bank a Creditworthy Practice

This chapter explains differences in medical practice financial accounting, what financial indicators banks want to see and how to demonstrate practice creditworthiness.

Chapter 6: Measuring Practice Operations

This chapter provides several techniques for measuring practice operations at the patient, provider and staffing levels.

Chapter 7: Tools for Measuring Practice Finances

This chapter describes tools for measuring practice finances, calculating financial ratios and using financial statements.

Chapter 8: Hospital and Inpatient Metrics

This chapter presents common hospital and inpatient metrics for determining market share, occupancy rates, length of stay, payer mix, expense and revenue per discharge, full-time equivalents per bed and other measures.

Chapter 9: Talking Numbers to Physicians

This chapter describes methods for communicating with physicians using executive summaries, presentations, graphs, charts and tables. It also presents considerations regarding audience, formatting and writing style.

Chapter 10: Performance and Practices of Successful Medical Groups

This chapter describes traits of successful groups to include profitability and operating costs; productivity, capacity and staffing; accounts receivable and collections; patient satisfaction; managed care operations; and other formulas.

Chapter 11: Conclusion and Future Implications

This section summarizes, highlights, and presents possible future implications and uses of benchmarking in health care.

Appendix A: Example Practice: Description, Reports and Financial Statements

This section presents a description, an A/R aging and operational report, a balance sheet and an income statement for a sample practice. Many of the factors presented in the formulas and ratios throughout this book can be referenced in this section to assist users with finding numbers and performing calculations.

Appendix B: Group Practice Measures in Military Health Care

This section describes unique measures used in the military health care environment to include Military Health System metrics, business planning and use of civilian measures in the military.

Appendix C: Four Methodologies to Improve Healthcare Demand Forecasting

This section is a reprint of an article that originally appeared in *Healthcare Financial Management* by Murray J. Côté and Stephen J. Tucker that presents four methods of forecasting, the pros and cons of each method, and an explanation of how to apply each method.

Appendix D: Benchmarking Guidance

This section contains an article from MGMA's *Performance and Practices of Successful Medical Groups* report on general benchmarking topics.

Appendix E: Profitability and Operating Costs

This section contains articles and data from the MGMA *Performance and Practices of Successful Medical Group*s reports on profitability and operating costs.

Appendix F: Productivity, Capacity and Staffing

This section contains articles and data from the MGMA *Performance and Practices of Successful Medical Groups* reports on productivity, capacity, and staffing.

Appendix G: Accounts Receivable and Collections

This section contains articles and data from the MGMA *Performance and Practices of Successful Medical Groups* reports on accounts receivable and collections.

Appendix H: Patient Satisfaction

This section contains articles and data from the MGMA *Performance and Practices of Successful Medical Group*s reports on patient satisfaction.

Appendix I: Managed Care

This section contains articles and data from the MGMA *Performance and Practices of Successful Medical Groups* reports on managed care.

Appendix J: Sources of Benchmarking and Operations Improvement Information

This section presents resources on measurement and benchmarking and identifies many sources of benchmarking data that can be applied to actual medical practices.

Glossary

This section provides terms and definitions used throughout this book.

Acronyms and Geographic Sections

This section provides many common acronyms and geographic sections used throughout this book and in MGMA surveys and other publications.

Physician Categories

This section lists most of the typical physician categories (specialties) used throughout this book and in the MGMA surveys and other publications.

Acknowledgments

We would like to thank Marilee Aust and the staff at MGMA for their patience, support and invaluable guidance. In addition, we would like to thank Lee Ann Webster, CPA, FACMPE, for her suggestions and review of the entire book and James Margolis, MPA, FACMPE, for his recommendations and attention to detail in review of several chapters and appendices. Furthermore, we would also like to thank Maj. Jerry Harvey, U.S. Air Force fellow in residence at MGMA, for his comments and recommendations for Appendix B. And we'd like to thank Lt. Col. Jerome "John" Hyzy, chief of data modeling & analysis at the Office of the Air Force Surgeon General, for his tireless support, invaluable insights and guidance.

And finally, we would like to thank Ronald L. Stoudt, senior vice president, and Greg Staab, area banking executive, both of Key Bank, for writing Chapter 5: "How to Show the Bank a Creditworthy Practice." And we would like to thank Maj. Ted Woolley, chief of performance improvement at the Office of the Air Force Surgeon General, for authoring Chapter 8: "Hospital and Inpatient Metrics."

CHAPTER 1

Why Benchmark?

"That which we persist in doing becomes easier, not that the task itself has become easier, but that our ability to perform it has improved."

— *Ralph Waldo Emerson*

There are many reasons for benchmarking, and most are related to a specific purpose (usually improvement). For example, a practice may want to determine how the billing office performance or physician productivity compares to other like practices. But in general, practices benchmark to gain a deeper understanding of where they are, where they want to go and how to get there. The current state of health care — constantly changing and growing in complexity — dictates more elaborate and accurate methods of measurement, analysis, comparison and improvement. Because long-term success is directly related to a practice's ability to identify, predict and adjust for changes, benchmarking, when used properly, is the best tool for overcoming these challenges.

This book is meant to be a desktop reference for medical practice benchmarking. And within these pages, several methods are presented and explained for practical use. In addition, a more subtle purpose of this book is to "set the standard" by eliminating ambiguity in health care measurement and benchmarking.

Two key principles of benchmarking are: (1) if you don't measure it, you can't manage it, and (2) if you don't value it, you won't change it. These principles have been applied to non-health care industries for many years and are ideally suited for use in health care. It has been said, health care is the only service industry that doesn't treat itself like one. And although the health care industry appears to have gone to great lengths to separate itself from other business sectors, there are many more similarities than differences. In the MBA classroom, students are taught, managers manage process and leaders lead people. The same can be said of the health care field — there are processes to be managed and people to be led. In addition, other service industries provide customers with services while health care also has customers (patients) that expect services (procedures and treatments).

Exhibit 1.1　Questions to Help Answer "How It Got There"

- How important are the supplies to the providers?
- How long has the practice done business with the supply company?
- How competitive is the local supply market?
- How was the practice's business arrangement with the supply company set up?
- Does the practice have a contractual agreement with the supply company? If yes, when does it expire?
- What internal controls are in place to manage costs for purchasing and inventory functions?
- What factors could be causing high supply costs (for example, theft, waste, disorganization, spoilage [pharmaceutical inventory], obsolescence or kickbacks between the supply company and clinic personnel)?

If You Don't Measure It, You Can't Manage It

In order to manage something, it's necessary to know what it is (description), where it is (comparison) and how it got there (context). This can be accomplished through measurement and benchmarking (see Exhibit 1.1). Proper practice management requires the use of subjective and objective measurement, analysis, comparison and improvement.

For example, if you want to manage (reduce) supply costs, first you would identify what it is. In this case, supply costs consist of any disposable medical item used to provide clinical services to patients. Its current cost can be calculated using a formula for average daily cost of supplies per provider and per patient (description). Using historical data, it is possible to determine whether costs are increasing and to what degree (comparison). And finally, to determine whether the situation needs to be changed, you would have to explore the current state and background of the issue (context).

If You Don't Value It, You Won't Change It

Driving change in a practice will affect every member of the organization, and many will resist; therefore, the value (benefit) of instituting a change must outweigh the status quo or leaving things "as is." Measurement and benchmarking are not the final step in the process — they simply enable the process to evolve toward action. It is completely appropriate to measure and benchmark; however, this activity is in vain if something isn't done with the findings. Ideally, the results should be used to support change; however, they may be used to validate past changes or support the current status. And once a benchmarking process is finished, the practice can "pick-and-choose" the areas to focus its efforts, create buy-in (sell the change) and start the process of improvement (or repeat the entire benchmarking exercise — that is, continuous process improvement).

What can be done with the findings? There are many options: (1) drive and/or support change; (2) educate staff; (3) validate the past; (4) build buy-in; (5) conduct performance reviews; and (6) plan for the future.

Exhibit 1.2   Relationship Between Key Benchmarking Principles

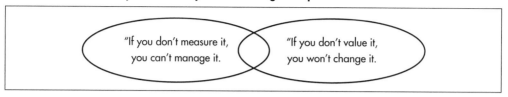

When using the key benchmarking principles — "if you don't measure it, you can't manage it" and "if you don't value it, you won't change it" — it is necessary you recognize the interrelationship (see Exhibit 1.2). First, proper management requires some degree of measurement to ensure the attribute of interest is fully understood (for example, is a full-time-equivalent [FTE] clearly defined?). Second, once measurement has taken place, management must decide whether the value of pursuing change is worth disrupting the practice in the quest for improvement. And third, if management feels the measures dictate a need to change, and value can be realized by making the change, the most important step is to instill a sense of value in making the change with physicians and staff; without buy-in, the value (benefit) of change will never be fully realized.

Of special note, processes can easily be changed, but it's only with the support and buy-in of physicians and staff that real improvement can be achieved (see Exhibit 1.3). It has been said, "If you take care of your people, your people will take care of you, but if you don't take care of your people, your people will take care of you." This is certainly true when making changes.

People naturally resist change and there are several reasons for this behavior. For example, they may feel a loss of control or discomfort from uncertainty.[1] If the change wasn't anticipated or staff felt surprised, they will either resist or undermine any changes. Some staff may be emotionally invested in a current process or may consider change a threat to their abilities or competence. And finally, change can often be interpreted as a disruption to the status quo that will create more work or reduce staff positions or personnel.[1]

Organizational commitment is necessary to drive change. That is, the organization must feel strongly that change is needed, is focused on discovering what it wants (or needs) to change and has developed a vision and expectations for the organization's future state.[2] In addition, acceptance of the benefits, ability of the organization to change and a commitment to improve can be demonstrated best by showing disbelievers (a field trip) an organization that has already implemented the proposed change.[2]

Exhibit 1.3   Methods of Facilitating Change[1]

- Involve providers and staff in the process.
- Communicate, communicate, communicate.
- Communicate early and regularly.
- Explain purpose.
- Establish expectations.
- Ask for comments, suggestions and involvement in process.
- Dissect into manageable parts and implement change.
- Be patient.
- Identify "star performers" and recognize them publicly.
- Ensure resources and training are available to achieve goal.
- Remain flexible.
- Focus on the future; don't dwell on the past.

The importance of creating buy-in and facilitating change must be seriously considered and built into the improvement process. For instance, the change driver (administrator) must understand staff will have strong emotional reactions toward change and will perceive it as a threat.[1] Therefore, the administrator must fully explore the underlying feelings and perceptions of providers and staff. To maximize acceptance, the administrator should (1) solicit providers and staff for feedback and suggestions; (2) explain the reasons behind the need for change; and (3) involve all members in the process as much as is reasonable based on the planned timeline.[1]

Notes

1. D. Balestracci and J. Barlow, *Quality Improvement, Practical Applications for Medical Group Practice,* 2nd ed. (Englewood, CO: Center for Research in Ambulatory Health Care Administration, 1998).

2. R. Camp, "Best Practice Benchmarking: The Path to Excellence." *CMA Magazine* 72, no. 6 (1998): 10.

Chapter 2

Benchmarking Fundamentals

"To compare is to improve."

— Unknown

Simply put, benchmarking is measurement and comparison for the purpose of improvement. In particular, medical practice benchmarking is a systematic, logical and common-sense approach to measurement, analysis, comparison and improvement (see Exhibit 2.1). Therefore, benchmarking is comparison to a standard. Benchmarking improves understanding of processes and clinical and administrative characteristics at a single point in time (snapshot) or over time (trend).[1]

In addition, benchmarking is the continuous process of measuring and comparing performance internally (over time) and externally (against other organizations and industries). Finally, benchmarking is determining how the "best in class" achieve their performance levels. This consists of analyzing and comparing best practices to uncover what they did, how they did it and what must be done to adapt it to your practice (process benchmarking).[2]

Who Set the Standard? The importance of having a standard is to ensure consistency, a common understanding and continuity over time. To date, a true standard has not been set for medical practice benchmarking. Therefore, this book is an attempt to rectify this void. In addition, the Medical Group Management

Exhibit 2.1 What Is Benchmarking?

- A systematic, logical and common-sense approach to measurement, comparison and improvement.
- Copying the best, closing gaps and differences, and achieving superiority.[3]
- "A positive, proactive process to change operations in a structured fashion to achieve superior performance. The purpose is to gain a competitive advantage."[3]
- Comparing organizational performance to the performance of other organizations.[1]
- Continuous process of comparison with the best[1] or "the toughest competitors or companies renowned as leaders."[4]
- A method for identifying processes to new goals with full support of management.[1]

Association (MGMA) has a long history of surveying and providing medical practices with valuable benchmarking information. Therefore, survey reports from MGMA are excellent standard-setting (benchmarking) tools because they amass several decades of medical practice data and provide the foundation for building true standards.

Reasons for Benchmarking

There are many reasons for benchmarking.[2] First, benchmarks can be used to objectively evaluate performance to aid in understanding a practice's strengths and weaknesses. Second, benchmarks can be used to observe where a practice has been and predict where it is going. Third, benchmarks can be used to analyze what others have done (best in class) and learn from their experiences (lessons learned). Fourth, benchmarks can be used to determine how the best in class achieve their performance levels and what methods they used to implement their processes. Fifth, benchmarks can be used to convince physicians and staff of the need for change. And sixth, benchmarking can help identify areas for improving practice operations and the bottom line.

In addition, when instituting process improvement, benchmarking can uncover areas with the most potential for improvement. In most instances, benchmarking can be considered a method for comparing similar or best practices. In addition, benchmarking is an excellent tool for uncovering different processes and clinical and administrative activities and factors. Also, benchmarking provides valuable, and in most cases, quantitative support to aid in communication, decision-making and developing buy-in. And in summary, benchmarking can be used to evaluate, observe, analyze, determine best in class, and convince others of a need for change.[2]

The benefits and reasons for benchmarking are to:[2]

- Increase understanding of practice operations;
- Learn about industry leaders, competitors and best practices;
- Incorporate best practices;
- Gain or maintain a competitive advantage and industry superiority;
- Adopt best practices from any industry into organizational processes (learn and compare against others);
- Break down reluctance to change;
- Uncover new concepts, ideas and technologies;
- Objectively evaluate performance strengths and weaknesses;
- Observe where you have been and predict where you are going;
- Analyze what others do, to learn from their experiences;

- Determine how the best in class achieve their performance levels so you can implement their processes; and
- Convince internal audiences of the need for change.

The "Value" of Benchmarking

Proper benchmarking consists of more than simple comparison of two numbers. The true value of benchmarking lies in the numbers combined with an understanding of the current state of the practice, calculation of the difference between the current state and a new value or benchmark, knowing the context and background of the practice values when interpreting the results, deciding on a course of action and goal, and determining when the goal is achieved. For example, a comparison of average number of procedures per patient visit per physician to a known benchmark will only permit a mathematical analysis. However, what if one physician in the practice has been focusing on patients with simple medical issues that don't generate multiple procedures? The numbers alone would indicate this physician is underperforming and is below the others in procedural productivity; whereas, knowing the background, context, or other measures permit for a more detailed analysis. Perhaps this physician's focus is on acute care services and his/her average number of patient encounters per day is almost twice that of other physicians in the practice?

Sources of Benchmarks

Benchmarks are available from many sources. The most common benchmarking measures are averages (means) and medians of health care performance measures derived from surveys, reports, or data files. For example, the *MGMA Physician Compensation and Production Survey* and *Cost Survey for Single-Specialty and Multispecialty Practices* are excellent sources for benchmarks. Another source is measures and processes from better-performing practices, which are modeled on organizations that have achieved a particular goal or attained a certain level of success or performance. For instance, the *MGMA Performance and Practices of Successful Medical Groups* is an ideal source for better-performing practice benchmarks. In addition, benchmarks from "best in industry" practices are excellent sources for measures and processes. These benchmarks are taken from organizations inside and outside health care. Of note, benchmarks from outside the health care industry are excellent sources that are often overlooked. For example, the Disney Corporation is a gerat resource for customer service, and Wal-Mart is ideal for supply-chain management and cost containment.

How to Benchmark

There are several methods of benchmarking.[2] A simple 10-step process might consist of the following:

1. Determine what is critical to your organization's success.

2. Identify metrics that measure the critical factors.

3. Identify a source for internal and external benchmarking data.

4. Measure your practice's performance.

5. Compare your practice's performance to the benchmark.

6. Determine if action is necessary based on the comparison.

7. If action is needed, identify the best practice and process used to implement it.

8. Adapt the process used by others in the context of your practice.

9. Implement new process, reassess objectives, evaluate benchmarking standards and recalibrate measures.

10. Do it again — benchmarking is an ongoing process, and tracking over time allows for continuous improvement

Standardizing Data for Comparison

Because the primary purpose of benchmarking is comparison, it is necessary to standardize data so organizations of different sizes can be compared.[5] A common method for standardizing data is to convert measures to percentages, per unit of input or per unit of output. For example, per unit of input can be presented as per full-time-equivalent (FTE) physician, per FTE provider, or per square foot; whereas, per unit of output can be presented on a per patient, per resource-based relative value scale unit or per procedure level.

What's Our Baseline?

Like any activity involving comparison, benchmarking requires an understanding of "where you are" — this is known as your baseline. The baseline represents where you are today or where you've been and provides a point of origin or starting point. In addition, a baseline is an initial state that forms a logical basis for comparison.[6] For example, to determine whether physicians have increased the average number of procedures per patient visit, it is necessary to have two measurements: the old value, or baseline, and the new value. To calculate the delta (or difference) between the two values, a simple formula can be used: new value minus old value. Without the baseline, it would not be possible to perform this or many other calculations such as percent change.

How Are We Doing?

This question can be answered by asking the question: "What is the difference between the baseline and your current state (or where we are today)?" The baseline can be an internal benchmark (historical measure) from inside the practice, a benchmark across like practices from an MGMA survey report, or a benchmark from outside the industry such as Disney or Wal-Mart. Additional insights can also be assessed by calculating the difference between your current state and an established benchmark or industry average or median. To determine the difference, there are several methods

Exhibit 2.2   What Is the Difference?

Mathematical difference (delta)

- New value minus old value;

- Current state minus initial state; and

- Benchmark or industry value minus current state.

Percent change

Inferential statistical methods

- Independent T-test

  — Difference between two independent averages;

- Mann-Whitney U-test

  — Difference between two independent medians;

- Paired T-test

  — Difference between two averages; and

  — Comparison of (1) case and matched control or (2) repeated measures.

- Wilcoxon Matched Pairs Test

  — Difference between two medians;

- One-Way ANOVA

  — Difference between three or more averages;

- Kruskal-Wallis H-test

  — Difference between three or more medians.

and statistical tools. For instance, the mathematical difference or delta consists of subtracting the baseline value from the current value, whereas percent change is a method for assessing changes over time or the proportion of one value in comparison to another. In addition to these methods, there are more statistically intense methods for determining difference that can be generalized across a group (see Exhibit 2.2).

More complex inferential methods are available to determine the statistical significance of the difference between two or more averages or medians: Independent T-test, Mann-Whitney U-test, Paired T-test, Wilcoxon Matched Pairs Test, One-Way ANOVA and Kruskal-Wallis H-test. However, these methods require greater understanding of the use, limitations, requirements, analysis and interpretation of each technique, and are outside the scope of this book. For information on these methods, see Exhibit 2.3 for a short list of resources.

Exhibit 2.3   Sources of Statistics Information

- Bluman, A.G., *Elementary Statistics: A Step by Step Approach*, 4th ed. Boston: McGraw-Hill, 2001.

- Daniel, W.W., *Biostatistics: A Foundation for Analysis in the Health Sciences*, 7th ed. New York: John Wiley & Sons, 1999.

- Kelley, L.D., *Measurement Made Accessible: A Research Approach Using Qualitative, Quantitative, and Quality Improvement Methods*. Thousand Oaks, CA: SAGE Publications, 1999.

- Rosner, B., *Fundamentals of Biostatistics*, 3rd ed. Boston: PWS-Kent Publishing Company, 1990.

- Rothstein, J.M., and J.L. Echternach, *Primer on Measurement: An Introductory Guide to Measurement Issues*. Alexandria, VA: American Physical Therapy Association, 1993.

- Tabachnick, B.G., and L.S. Fidell, *Using Multivariate Statistics*, 4th ed. Boston: Allyn and Bacon, 2001.

Exhibit 2.4   Difference Between Delta and Percent Change

Is the Result Positive or Negative?	Delta	Percent Change
Positive value	New value (or benchmark) is *greater* than the old value. For example, $214,377 minus $145,000 equals a delta of $69,377.	New value has *increased.* For example, $145,000 divided by $214,377 equals 0.67 and when multiplied by 100 equals 67 percent.
Negative value	New value is *less.*	New value has *decreased.*

Interpretation of the difference is dependent on the method used. When using the delta, the difference will be a raw number, because the method consists of simple subtraction. Determining whether the difference is good or bad depends on the context, background and what the values represent. For example, if medical revenue after operating cost per FTE family practice physician is $145,000 and the MGMA benchmark indicates a median of $214,377, then the delta is $69,377 ($214,377 minus $145,000). A delta of $69,377 may suggest poor practice performance, reduced physician productivity, a capital investment or other practice deficiencies or large expenses. On the other hand, the percent change method indicates this practice is only generating 67 percent of the median for similar types of practices (see Exhibit 2.4). Therefore, the result is different between delta and percent change, and the interpretation may also be different.

Getting from Here to There   Once the difference between baseline and current state or current state and benchmark is known, the next step is to determine first, whether there is a desire to change and, second, what factors (practice measures) can be influenced in the preferred direction. Therefore, it is imperative a

Exhibit 2.5   Resources for Best Practices and Lessons Learned

• MGMA's EBSCO (Elton B. Stephens Company) database*	• *The McKinsey Quarterly* (www.mckinseyquarterly.com)
• MGMA e-mail forums*	• *Harvard Business Review* (www.hbr.org)
• MGMA assemblies and societies*	• *Six Sigma* (www.isixsigma.com)

* Require MGMA membership

desire to change be established throughout the organization. In addition, it should be grown and nurtured by involving physicians and staff in the entire process.

Best Practices and Lessons Learned

Knowing the best method for completing a task and mistakes to avoid would result in quicker and less costly improvements. Lessons learned are suggested techniques or efficiencies for overcoming errors or avoiding mistakes. They can be tips, tricks or cautions from those who have already tried and succeeded (or failed). And best practices are specific characteristics, measures or processes considered to be best in class by subjective (personal opinion) or objective criteria (for example, a measure at or above the 90th percentile). Exhibit 2.5 presents a short list of resources for finding best practices and lessons learned.

Methods and Checklists

Failing to plan, it has been said, is planning to fail. Therefore, an integral component of the benchmarking process is the proper use of systematic methods, checklists, scales and comparable measures. Systematic methods consist of formulas and ratios as found in this book. Checklists are a planning tool to ensure all variables and methods are used and considered — checklists ensure attention to detail and minimize the chance of missing steps in a process (see Exhibit 2.6). Scales provide the measuring stick — meaning they indicate whether your measures are high or low, good or bad, or where they are in comparison to others. And comparable measures are key to the heart and soul of benchmarking and provide a means for determining how your practice compares to others.

Small and Solo Practice Benchmarking

Small and solo practices share many similarities with their larger counterparts; however, the benefits and risks associated with the differences can have significant impact on a small practice's longevity and financial success.

Similarities with Larger Practices

All medical practices must operate in the same health care environment and deal with the same health care legislation, malpractice insurance,

Exhibit 2.6   Example Checklist [7]

The following checklist items can be used to increase the likelihood that a claim will be processed and paid when first submitted:

☐ Patient information is complete.

☐ Patient's name and address matches the insurer's records.

☐ Patient's group number and/or subscriber number is correct.

☐ Physician's Social Security number, provider number, or tax identification number is completed and correct.

☐ Claim is signed by the physician.

☐ All necessary dates are completed.

☐ Dates for care given are chronological and correct. For example, is the discharge date listed as before the admission date?

☐ Dates for care given are in agreement with the claims information from other providers such as the hospital, etc.

☐ Diagnosis is complete.

☐ Diagnosis is correct for the services or procedures provided.

☐ Diagnostic codes are correct for the services or procedures provided.

☐ CPT® and ICD-9 codes are accurate.

☐ Diagnosis is coded using ICD-9-CM to the highest level of specificity.

☐ Fee column is itemized and totaled.

☐ All necessary information about prescription drugs or durable medical equipment prescribed by the physician is included.

☐ The claim is legible.

payers, collection challenges, patient needs and expectations, delivery and standards of care and processes — just to name a few. Also, the benchmarking methods used by large organizations are identical to those used by small and solo practices (see Exhibit 2.7). And the use of standardized metrics permits comparison regardless of organizational size. Common examples available in most benchmarking datasets consist of measures per FTE physician/provider, per square foot, per patient, per procedure and per relative value unit (RVU).[5]

What's the Difference?

Small and solo practices are different from larger groups in several ways, some of which are beneficial, while others are not. For instance, smaller organizations are generally more flexible, can adapt and change quickly, and, in general, tend to be more efficient. However, small and solo practices are more sensitive to the risks associated with costly mistakes, lack of alternative revenue-generating methods and the absence of (or antiquated

Exhibit 2.7   Similarities Regardless of Size or Type[5]

- Legislation can change payment (for example, Medicare/Medicaid reimbursement rates are determined through legislation).

- Costs are increasing greater than inflation (for example, medical supplies and equipment costs are increasing at a greater percentage than reimbursement rates).

- Expenses change.

- Increases in physician compensation are from production (for example, much of physician compensation is based on physician production, or the number of patients seen and the procedures performed).

- Health savings accounts will change patient behavior (for example, patients will treat medical care more like a product or service they pay for using funds in their account).

- Hospitals are purchasing physician practices (again).

- Advances in medical care are changing care delivery.

- Physicians are publicly rated for quality and outcomes.

- Physicians are publicly rated for patient satisfaction.

condition of) robust information systems. For example, with only one or two physicians in a practice, what impact would a poor decision or loss of a physician (due to sickness or some other unforeseen event) have on the practice? Can a small practice afford to retain adequate earnings for contingencies? Does the existing information system complement and add to the efficiency of the practice? And does it interface (communicate) with the information systems used by payers, hospitals and other medical practices such as referring practices and physicians?

Ultimately, the goals of smaller practices mirror those of larger groups — to have more satisfied patients, more fulfilling work environments for physicians and staff, and better economic outcomes.[5] However, the additional sensitivities of small and solo practices must be considered to ensure surprise events don't adversely impact the practice.

Notes

1. R. Camp, "Benchmarking: The Search for Best Practices that Lead to Superior Performance, Part 1." *Quality Progress* 22, no. 1 (1989): 61.

2. D. Gans, "Benchmarking Successful Medical Groups to Improve Your Practice Performance." Presentation at MGMA Conference, Ohio, September 2006.

3. R. Camp, "Best Practice Benchmarking: The Path to Excellence." *CMA Magazine* 72, no. 6 (1998): 10.

4. R. Camp, "A Bible for Benchmarking by Xerox." *Financial Executive*, July/August, 9, 4, (1993): 23.

5. D. Gans and G. Feltenberger, "Benchmarking Military Performance Using Civilian Metrics." Presentation at American College of Healthcare Executives Annual Conference, March 2007.

6. Wikipedia, "Baseline (configuration management)," http://en.wikipedia.org (2006).

7. M. Zairi and J. Whymark, "The Transfer of Best Practices: How to Build a Culture of Benchmarking and Continuous Learning, Part 2." *Benchmarking* 7, no. 2 (2000): 146.

Chapter 3

Measurement and Benchmarking

"There are two possible outcomes: If the result confirms the hypothesis, then you've made a measurement. If the result is contrary to the hypothesis, then you've made a discovery."

— *Enrico Fermi*

Measurement is the collection and organization of data. In many cases, measurement is a method of converting an array, group, list or set of data into a single variable that describes the entire dataset. A mean or average is a calculation that summarizes the central tendency or mathematical center of many data points, provided all data is of the same unit of measurement. In general, an average is the most common calculation used to analyze and compare data, because most people understand the concept of an average and how to calculate it.

For example, if we count the number of patients seen per month for the last 10 months for an eight-provider family medical practice located in the suburbs, we have an array of data with 10 data points— one data point for each month (see Exhibit 3.1). If we also list the number of patients seen per month for the last 10 months for an eight-provider family medical practice located in a rural community, how can we easily compare these two practices? We can line up and organize the data points in ascending order, but what does this tell us? We might conclude the suburban practice sees a greater number of patients per month, but we can't accurately describe the difference or make a comparison. All we've done so far is arrange the data and assume there was a difference by looking at or "eyeballing" the data — not the most accurate method. However, by calculating the average number of patients seen per month for the last 10 months for each practice, a single and accurate measure can be used to describe and compare the two groups.

Comparing these practices, the suburban practice on average sees more patients per month than the rural practice — 111 more (average number of patients seen per month in the suburban practice minus average number of patients seen per month in the rural practice; 2,773 minus 2,662 = 111).

Exhibit 3.1   Example of Measurement: Number of Patients Seen per Month

Month	Suburban Practice	Rural Practice
January	2,620	2,650
February	2,231	2,660
March	2,264	2,266
April	2,650	2,067
May	2,657	1,687
June	2,670	3,690
July	3,067	3,070
August	2,690	2,071
September	3,171	2,731
October	3,710	3,730
Sum of number of patients seen per month	27,730	26,622
Number of data points (months)	10	10
Average (sum divided by number of months)	2,773	2,662

Exhibit 3.2   Examples of Benchmarks[1]

	Mean	Standard Deviation	25th Percentile	Median	75th Percentile	90th Percentile
Encounters per FTE physician	6,341	3,006	4,759	5,891	7,612	9,159
Total procedures per FTE physician	10,797	3,006	4,759	5,891	7,612	9,159
Physician work RVUs* per FTE physician	4,751	4,412	7,506	5,123	5,622	6,809
Physician compensation	$170,059	$64,046	$129,662	$156,011	$196,945	$250,741

* Relative value units

Art and Science of Benchmarking

Benchmarking, as it's related to measurement, is the art and science of comparison. The "art" takes place during the data gathering and interpretation phases and requires a method with some common sense, whereas the "science" is the systematic and logical process of analysis. Once interpretation and analysis have occurred, data is considered transformed into information that can be used for comparison and decision-making. That is, it is possible to determine whether the data is similar or different and by how much. Exhibit 3.2 represents several examples of metrics and associated benchmarks.

Other topics associated with benchmarking are (1) continuous improvement and (2) evaluation and assessment.[2] Continuous improvement

Exhibit 3.3   Common Benchmarking Methods

Transfer Model[3]
1. Identify and document best practices.
2. Validate and reach consensus for focus and true best practices.
3. Transfer and develop buy-in; sell ideas to management and get commitment to performance assessments, identification of priorities and establishment of a plan.
4. Implement plan, using team champions, and select critical practices to support strategic initiatives.

Five Stages of Benchmarking[4]
1. Plan and select the processes to benchmark and identify customer expectations and critical success factors.
2. Form the benchmarking team from across the organization.
3. Collect the data from best-practice organizations and identify own processes.
4. Analyze data for gaps.
5. Take action, identify what needs to be done to match best practice and implement change.

Five Steps of Benchmarking[5]
1. Plan what to benchmark and what organization to benchmark against.
2. Analyze performance gaps and project future performance.
3. Set targets for change and communicate to all levels.
4. Develop action plans, implement plans and adjust as necessary.
5. Achieve a state of maturity by integrating best practices into organization.

Ten Steps to Benchmarking[6]
1. Determine what is critical to your organization's success.
2. Identify metrics that measure the critical factors.
3. Identify a source for internal and external benchmarking data.
4. Measure your practice's performance.
5. Compare your practice's performance to the benchmark.
6. Determine if action is necessary based on the comparison.
7. If action is needed, identify the best practice and process used to implement it.
8. Adapt the process used by others in the context of your practice.
9. Implement new process, reassess objectives, evaluate benchmarking standards and recalibrate measures.
10. Do it again—benchmarking is an ongoing process, and tracking over time allows for continuous improvement.

refers to the need for repeated analysis using the same measures over time (trend). An evaluation is a subjective, personal judgment of the value (or worth) of something, whereas an assessment is objective and quantifiable (or assigned a numeric value).[2]

Benchmarking Methods   Because effective benchmarking consists of a systematic process, several methods have been developed to ensure the process is efficient (see Exhibit 3.3).

Proper measurement begins with selecting the right practice attribute, characteristic, property, dimension or variable to be assessed.[2] In other words, what do we want to measure? For example, encounters per FTE physician, total procedures per FTE physician and physician work RVUs per FTE physician are common examples of benchmarks and practice measures (see Exhibit 3.2). This book presents many practice attributes that have been operationally defined; that is, the attribute and measurement process have been clearly described in practice and literature as generally accepted. However, there may be practice attributes that are not typically measured or found in the literature. In these cases, it would be necessary to fully explore the characteristic before moving to the next step; this type of attribute could be called "homegrown." Of note, there are probably few instances when "homegrown" attributes are needed because the health care management field is sufficiently mature to have identified most, if not all, key practice characteristics.

Once a practice variable is selected, the next step is to decide on the appropriate method of measurement (or what metric should be used) and the intended purpose. There are two general categories of metrics: (1) informational and (2) actionable. Informational metrics provide a simple description and, unlike actionable metrics, don't clearly suggest ways of affecting change. For example, if we decide to measure the average number of patients seen per month in a suburban practice as a metric to describe monthly practice productivity, then this metric simply tells us the arithmetic mean; it doesn't suggest anything more. Actionable metrics, however, are usually more complex, require an understanding of the context and are compared to a benchmark or baseline. For instance, the formula to calculate the average number of patients seen per month (for the last 10 months) per provider for an eight-provider family medical practice is the sum of the number of patients seen per month for the last 10 months divided by the number of months divided by the number of providers (see Exhibit 3.1). If we use this formula as a metric to assess monthly practice productivity per provider and we want to improve productivity per provider, then this metric used in this context suggests, for example, that we can affect change by working with individual providers whose average is below the practice's overall average to increase the number of patients seen per month by the provider of interest.

Several questions should be asked as part of preliminary measurement steps. For instance, what do you want to measure? Is it a generally accepted practice characteristic (typical practice factor) or is it a homegrown practice attribute (custom or self-defined factor or metric)? What metric should be used? What is the appropriate method for measurement? And finally, what type of metric do you want to use and what is your intended purpose (information or action)?

Interpretation Pitfalls

Reliability is defined as repeatability and consistency. If given the same dataset and using the same measure, someone else should be able to calculate, describe and compare the data in the same way. For instance, if given the number of patients seen per month for the last 10 months in a suburban and rural practice and asked for the average number of patients seen per month for both practices, you would find the same average with the same comparison for each practice. Note that the same unit of measurement must be used; that is, all the data in your dataset or data array should be the same unit of measurement (in the example given, all numbers are based on number of patients seen). Reliability cannot be achieved if the unit of measurement is different in any of the data used in the measurement. For example, you cannot calculate an average using 2,650 patients seen in January; 2,264 seen in February; 3,265 seen in March; 2,166 seen in April; 3,167 seen in May; 1,869 seen in June; 2,771 seen in July; and 3,171 appointments booked in August without first changing appointments booked to the number of patients seen in August.

Validity is meaningfulness within a generally accepted theoretical basis (see Exhibit 3.4).[2] Or simply stated, does it really mean what it's expected to mean or is it being interpreted accurately? How you interpret your data and measurements are as important as ensuring you have used a reliable method. Understanding what a particular measure is meant to describe is paramount to using data properly to support good decisions. For instance, averages (means) represent the mathematical center of an array of data or central tendency, whereas the median is the "actual" center point of the array. In some cases, the average and median can be the same, but oftentimes there is a difference. Therefore, knowing how a measure is used, collected and calculated will assist in supporting your decisions; that is, your conclusions and analysis will be more valid and meaningful. This is particularly important when presenting your findings to others, because the better you understand the measures, why you selected them and how to explain them to others, the value and usefulness of your results will add significant credibility to your recommendations and/or decisions.

Another common mistake to avoid is averaging averages. Because any array of data points can be averaged (or measured using other methods), it's important to understand the limitations or implications of measuring calculated measures. The validity of the interpretation may be suspect (see Exhibit 3.5). The extremely low and high values in all the practices are minimized or diluted (their effect is almost eliminated). The effects of the low productivity and high productivity practices almost eliminate one another, which is why the average of the averages is near the average of the more balanced array (Family Practice 1).

Strength is related to validity and is the power, magnitude or accuracy of your interpretation or how confident you are in your interpretation. For

Exhibit 3.4   Example of Meaningfulness

It is important to understand the formulas used for measurement and how the measurement is collected and calculated. Using the data array from Exhibit 3.1 (Suburban Practice):

2,620 (January); 2,231 (February); 2,264 (March); 2,650 (April); 2,657 (May); 2,670 (June); 3,067 (July); 2,690 (August); 3,171 (September); 3,710 (October)

Average (mean) = sum of all data divided by the number of data points:

Sum of all data = 2,620 + 2,231 + 2,264 + 2,650 + 2,657 + 2,670 + 3,067 + 2,690 + 3,171 + 3,710 = 27,730

Number of data points = 10

Average = 2,773

Median = The data point in the center of the array (when arranged in order)

Data array = 2,231, 2,264, 2,620, 2,650, 2,657, 2,670, 2,690, 3,067, 3,171, 3,710

Center of array are two data points = 2,657 and 2,670

Median = 2,657 + 2,670 divided by 2 = 2664

Note: If the data array consisted of an odd number of data points, the median would be the true center data point.

Exhibit 3.5   Example of Averaging Averages Problem

Month	Number of Patients		
	Family Practice 1	Family Practice 2	Family Practice 3
January	2,231	1,687	2,159
February	2,264	2,067	2,353
March	2,620	2,071	2,520
April	2,650	2,266	2,564
May	2,657	2,650	2,660
June	2,670	2,660	2,961
July	2,690	2,731	3,162
August	3,067	3,070	3,259
September	3,171	3,690	3,359
October	3,710	3,730	3,763
Average (mean)	2,773	2,662	2,876
	(normal productivity practice)	(low productivity practice)	(high productivity practice)
Average of the averages for Practices 1, 2 and 3 = 2,770			

instance, if you want to describe the number of patients seen per month for three months (2,231, 2,264 and 2,620), a mean is an ideal descriptive statistic (mean = 2,372). This figure is somewhat descriptive of the lower months of 2,231 and 2,264, but a mean of 2,372 is not descriptive of the higher month when 2,620 patients were seen. Therefore, your confidence in a mean of 2,372 patients seen per month provides a less accurate description of the average number of patients seen per month. However, if this array consisted of a large number of months; that is, a large dataset with many data points, the accuracy of this metric and your confidence in the descriptive power of the mean may be much higher.

A final interpretation issue is related to the mutually exclusive and exhaustive nature of data. *Mutually exclusive* refers to a data point fitting into only one category.[2] For example, we decide months with 3,600 or more patients are categorized as high productivity, months with between 2,401 and 3,599 patients are medium or normal, and months with 2,400 or fewer patients are low. Therefore, each month "fits" into only one category — that's mutually exclusive — and a single month cannot be categorized as "high" and "medium." If a single month could be assigned to multiple categories, it would be difficult to accurately describe each month or interpret your findings. *Exhaustive* refers to the description of the attribute; that is, does the definition encompass all collected attributes?[2] For example, because all the measurements taken consisted of the number of patients seen per month, this attribute was defined to be actual patient encounters with a provider and all collected measures were based on this definition; that is, patients seen only by a nurse were not included because these encounters didn't "fit" the definition (or criteria).

Notes

1. MGMA, *Cost Survey for Single-Specialty Practices: 2005 Report Based on 2004 Data* and *Physician Compensation and Production Survey: 2005 Report Based on 2004 Data* (Englewood, CO: Medical Group Management Association, 2005).

2. J. Rothstein and J. Echternach, *Primer on Measurement: An Introductory Guide to Measurement Issues* (Alexandria, VA: American Physical Therapy Association, 1993).

3. M. Zairi and J. Whymark, "The Transfer of Best Practices: How to Build a Culture of Benchmarking and Continuous Learning, Part 2." *Benchmarking* 7, no. 2 (2000): 146.

4. D. Elmuti and Y. Kathawala, "An Overview of Benchmarking Process: A Tool for Continuous Improvement and Competitive Advantage." *Benchmarking for Quality Management & Technology* 4, no. 4 (1997): 229.

5. R. Camp, "Benchmarking: The Search for Best Practices that Lead to Superior Performance, Part 1." *Quality Progress* 22, no. 2 (1989): 70.

6. D. Gans, "Benchmarking Successful Medical Groups to Improve Your Practice Performance." Presentation at Medical Group Management Association Conference, Ohio, September 2006.

Chapter 4

Management by the Numbers

"If I had to sum up in one word what makes a good manager, I'd say decisiveness. You can use the fanciest computers to gather the numbers, but in the end you have to set a timetable and act."
— Lee Iacocca

Management can use numbers to diagnose and treat practice deficiencies, plan improvements, and examine practice activities and processes. And because numbers are less susceptible to the effects of human variation (feelings and emotions), they are more appropriate for decision-making. The beauty of numbers comes from their brevity, clarity and precision. For example, using the example array (list) of patient no-shows, which shows the number of no-shows per day from last month, it is possible to quickly summarize the week or entire month regarding no-show activity (see Exhibit 4.1). These averages and totals provide a brief, clear and precise picture describing no-show activity during each week or the entire month. There's little room for misinterpretation or confusion, provided a no-show is clearly defined, that is, a no-show is a patient who fails to show up within 15 minutes of an appointment rather than someone who fails to cancel 24 hours prior to his/her appointment.

Exhibit 4.1   Example Array of Data

Number of No-Shows per Day Last Month:						
Monday	Tuesday	Wednesday	Thursday	Friday	Weekly Average	Weekly Total
2	1	3	6	4	3.2	16
4	0	1	5	3	2.6	13
2	3	2	2	3	2.4	12
1	2	2	4	5	2.8	14
Monthly total = 55						
Monthly average = 2.75						

Exhibit 4.2   Measurement and Benchmarking Statistics

• Average (mean)	• Quartile
• Median	• Standard deviation
• Percentile	• Percent change

Exhibit 4.3   Types of Data and Examples

Data	Example
Nominal	Gender, marital status, ethnicity/race, blood type
Ordinal (categorical)	Likert scale score (small, medium, or large)
Interval	Temperature (Celsius), SAT score, IQ score
Ratio	Pulse rate, white blood cell count, height, weight, age

Organizing a group of numbers is the cornerstone in the benchmarking process. An array or group of numbers only become valuable once it is organized, whereas statistical methods and proper interpretation of the findings are necessary to uncover the useful information behind the numbers. A systematic approach is necessary and has been established through the use of averages (or means), medians, standard deviations, percentiles, quartiles and percent change (see Exhibit 4.2). These techniques can be used to measure and benchmark all practice attributes. In addition, these methods are easy to use, understand and communicate; most people are familiar with some, if not all methods.

Types of Data   There are four categories for classifying data (see Exhibit 4.3):

1. Nominal data is defined as data that is mutually exclusive (non-overlapping) and exhaustive, in which no order or ranking can be assigned.[1]

2. Ordinal data can be classified into categories and can be ranked but without precise differences between data; for example, using a Likert scale (small, medium, large; never, sometimes, usually, always; and poor, fair, good, very good, excellent).[2]

3. Interval data is rank ordered with precise differences between data but without a meaningful zero point.[2]

4. Ratio data is equal to interval data but with a true zero.[2]

Organizing Data   In order to describe and interpret an array of data, it must be organized. The most common method of organizing data is to build a frequency distribution table. A frequency distribution is defined as the organization of data into table form by category or group with frequencies and percentages).[2] When constructing a frequency distribution table, it's important to follow these guidelines: (1) each group is equal in width (see Exhibit 4.4); (2) there are no more than 12 categories or groups; (3) categories or groups are mutually exclusive; and (4) all categories or groups are all-inclusive.[2] Mutually exclusive means each data point can "fit" in one and only one category or group, whereas inclusive means each data point is included in a category or group.[3]

The type of data will dictate whether it should be categorized or grouped. Data such as gender or perceived level of pain is nominal and ordinal data and should be categorized, whereas interval and ratio data should be grouped. For example, the data in Exhibit 4.1, which is ratio level data, should be organized into groups. The formula in Exhibit 4.4 can be used to adhere to the guidelines previously mentioned and group the data.[3]

Once the group size is determined, a frequency distribution table, such as Exhibit 4.5, can be constructed and loaded with data from the array. Frequency (or number represented using "n") is representative of the tally or number of occurrences within each group, whereas relative frequency is

Exhibit 4.4 Grouping Data

Formula for grouping data = [(maximum value + 1) − (minimum value)] / (number of groups desired)

  Example:

    Maximum value = 6

    Minimum value = 0

    Number of groups desired = 4

    [(6 + 1) − (0)] / 4 = 1.75

    Rounded up = 2

  Therefore, the groups are:

- 0–2 no-shows (Group 1)
- 3–4 no-shows (Group 2)
- 5–6 no-shows (Group 3)

Reminder: When constructing a frequency distribution table, it's important to follow these guidelines:[2]

- Each group is equal in width (that is, there is an equal number of values/variables per category or group).

- There are no more than 12 categories or groups; however, this isn't a requirement, rather it's a "good-rule-of-thumb" to keep the frequency distribution tables and any charts and graphs from getting too lengthy or busy (obviously, if fewer categories or groups are used, the more concise the tables and illustrations but some degree of detail may be lost in too few categories or groups).

- Categories or groups are mutually exclusive.

- All categories or groups are all-inclusive (exhaustive).

Exhibit 4.5 Example of Frequency Distribution Table

Groups (Group No.)	Frequency (n)	Relative Frequency	Cumulative Frequency
0–2 (1)	13	54%	54%
3–4 (2)	8	33%	87%
5–6 (3)	3	13%	100%

Exhibit 4.6 Example of Bar Chart (average number of patient encounters per physician per month)

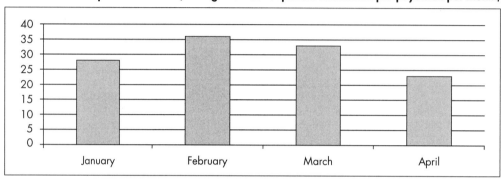

indicative of the percentage each group composes in relation to the total. And cumulative frequency is the relative frequency plus previous group percentages that totals to 100 percent when constructed appropriately.

Another method of organizing data is through graphing. Graphs, much like frequency tables, can be used to summarize, identify patterns and visually display large amounts of data.[3] For example, the average number of patient encounters per physician per month is ideally suited for display using a bar chart (Exhibit 4.6; data is fictitious).

Continuous data is ideally suited for display in a histogram.[3] For example, the distribution or list of patient ages is perfect for display using a histogram (see Exhibit 4.7; data is fictitious).

Relative frequency is perfectly suited for display in a pie chart. For example, the no-show groupings and relative frequency are perfect for presentation using a pie chart. Exhibit 4.8 displays groups of no-shows from one month (see data from Exhibit 4.1). That is, Group 1 consists of zero to two no-shows, Group 2 of three or four no-shows and Group 3 of five or six no-shows. The chart and legend in Exhibit 4.8 indicate 54 percent of the days per month were in Group 1 with zero to two no-shows, 33 percent were in Group 2 and 13 percent were in Group 3 (see Exhibits 4.1 and 4.5; data is fictitious).

Exhibit 4.7   Example of Histogram with Normal Curve (distribution of patient ages)

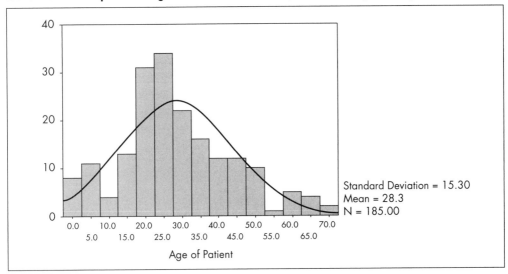

Exhibit 4.8   Example of Pie Chart (relative frequency data from Exhibit 4.5)

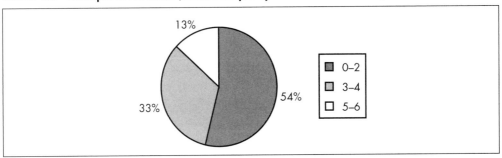

Continuous data showing trends can be graphed using a line chart (see Exhibit 4.9).[3]

And a scatter plot is the best format to show relationships between two variables located on the *x*-axis and *y*-axis (see Exhibit 4.10).[3]

Averages (Means) and Medians

Averages (or means) and medians are measures of central tendency. That is, they represent the center or middle point of all the data[4] and are a single value that is descriptive of the dataset.[3] The average is calculated by adding all data points and dividing by the number of data points (Exhibit 4.11).

Exhibit 4.9   Example of Line Chart (number of RVUs per provider per month)

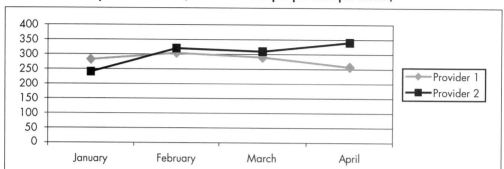

Exhibit 4.10   Example of Scatter Plot

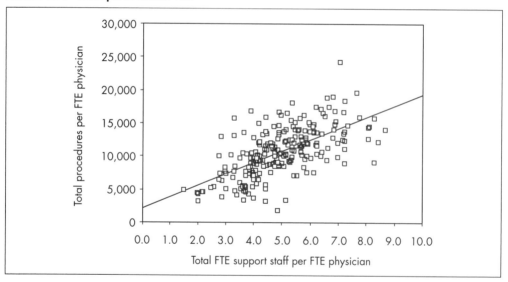

Exhibit 4.11   Formula for Calculating the Average (mean)

Average (mean) = sum of all data points / number of data points

    Example

        Data points = 101, 145, 167, 189, 192, 201

        Number of data points = 6

        (101 + 145 + 167 + 189 + 192 + 201) / 6

        Average (mean) = 995 / 6 = 165.8

Exhibit 4.12   Formula for Calculating the Median

If odd number of data points

    Median = center data point

    The data point located at the center position in the dataset when placed in ascending order; located at = [(number of data points + 1) / 2]

    Example

        Data points = 101, 145, 167, 189, 192, 201, 213

        Number of data points = 7

        Location of median = [(7 + 1) / 2] = 4th position

        Median = 189

If even number of data points

    Median = (2 center data points) / 2

    The two data points located at the center positions in the dataset when placed in ascending order; located at = (number of data points / 2) and [(number of data points / 2) + 1]

    Example

        Data points = 101, 145, 167, 189, 192, 201

        Number of data points = 6

        Location of median, point 1 = (6 / 2) = 3rd position

        Location of median, point 2 = [(6 / 2) +1] = 4th position

        Median = (167 + 189) / 2 = 178

The median is the data point in the true center of the dataset. An equal number of data points should be above as below; however, if the number of data points in the dataset is an even number, the median is the average of the two data points in the center (Exhibit 4.12).

Special care should be taken when rounding. In particular, rounding should be reserved for use with the final calculation.[2] If rounding is performed prior to the final calculation of the average or median, the difference between the calculated answer and the true answer may be significant, and accuracy will be lessened. In addition, and when possible, the average or median should be rounded to one more decimal place than is found in the dataset.[2] For instance, if the values in the dataset are in whole numbers (for example, 1, 2, 3, 4 and 6), the average or median should be shown with the 10th decimal place; that is, the average is 3.2 and the median is 3.0.

Standard Deviation The standard deviation is a measure of variation or dispersion. That is, it represents the spread of the data around the mean: Does the data cluster or spread out from the average? Exhibit 4.13 represents the probabilities associated with the standard distribution for a normally distributed array of data, which follows the bell-curve when graphed as a histogram (see

Exhibit 4.13   Distribution of Data by Standard Deviation

- 68% of data fall within ± 1 standard deviation
- 95% of data fall within ± 2 standard deviations
- 99.7% of data fall within ± 3 standard deviations
- 99.99% of data fall within ± 4 standard deviations
- 99.9999% of data fall within ± 5 standard deviations

Exhibit 4.14   Standard Deviation Example

Average = 28.3 years
Standard deviation = 15.3 years
68% = ± 1 standard deviation
28.3 + 15.3 = 44 years
28.3 – 15.3 = 13 years
96% = ± 2 standard deviations
28.3 + (15.3 × 2) = 59 years
28.3 – (15.3 × 2) = –2.3 = 0 years

Exhibit 4.7). However, there is a theorem that generally holds true and states 75 percent or more of data will fall within two standard deviations of the mean regardless of the distribution (normal or not normal) of the data.[2]

For example, a dataset containing all the ages of every established and new patient seen for the past year can be graphed using a histogram (a bar chart without gaps between bars). In Exhibit 4.7, it is possible to see the distribution of the ages in relation to the normal curve. In addition, since the bars of this histogram approximately match the normal curve line, the data (bars) can be considered normally distributed — this is the "art" of measurement and benchmarking. Because this data is normally distributed, the probabilities from Exhibit 4.13 can be applied to draw conclusions from the data. Because the distribution is normally distributed and the average age is 28.3 years and the standard deviation is 15.3 years, using the probabilities from Exhibit 4.13, it is possible to conclude that 68 percent of the practice's patients are between the ages of 13 and 44 and 96 percent of patients are between the ages of 0 and 59 (Exhibit 4.14).

Percentiles and Quartiles

Percentiles and quartiles provide some indication of the relative position with respect to the other data points. That is, a percentile is a value indicating the percent of values less than or equal to the percentile (see example in

Exhibit 4.15   Formula for Calculating Percentile

Percentile = [(number of values below a specific value) + 0.5] / total number of values × 100%

  Example

    An administrator collects the number of established patients seen per month for the past 12 months. What is the percentile rank of seeing 265 patients?

    Data points = 201, 211, 245, 251, 265, 267, 273, 275, 289, 292, 301, 313

    Percentile = [(4) + 0.5] / 12 × 100% = 38th percentile

  Therefore, any month where 265 established patients were seen was 38% better than all the months considered.

Exhibit 4.16   Percent Change

Percent change = (new value – old value) / old value

  Example: What is the percent change in the number of no-shows from last month to this month?

    New value (number of no-shows this month) = 18

    Old value (number of no-shows last month) = 26

    (18 – 26) / 26 = –31%

  Therefore, we can conclude from this analysis that no-shows have dropped by 31% this month vs. last month.

Exhibit 4.15).[2] Quartiles are simply the 25th (25 percent), 50th (50 percent or median) and 75th (75 percent) percentiles.[2]

Percent Change Percent change is a valuable method for assessing changes over time because it compares a new value with an old value. To calculate percent change, use the formula in Exhibit 4.16.

Averages (means), medians, percentiles, quartiles, standard deviations and percent change are tools needed to thoroughly assess, measure and benchmark a practice. These methods, when used properly, are very powerful because they are easy to calculate, communicate and understand; the strength of these methods lies in their simplicity.

Notes 1. A. Bluman, *Elementary Statistics, A Step by Step Approach*, 4th ed. (Boston: McGraw-Hill, 2001).

2. D.L. Kelley, *Measurement Made Accessible, A Research Approach Using Qualitative, Quantitative, and Quality Improvement Methods* (Thousand Oaks, CA: SAGE Publications, 1999).

3. W. Daniel, *Biostatistics: A Foundation for Analysis in the Health Sciences*, 7th ed. (New York: John Wiley & Sons, 1999).

4. B. Rosner, *Fundamentals of Biostatistics*, 3rd ed. (Boston: PWS-Kent Publishing, 1990).

Chapter 5

How to Show the Bank a Creditworthy Practice

"Capital as such is not evil; it is its wrong use that is evil. Capital in some form or other will always be needed."
— *Mahatma Gandhi*

It's bound to happen sooner or later — your practice will need to go to the bank for a loan. And the more you know about what the bank will be looking for, the better the chances of successfully borrowing needed capital; however, the reverse is also true. This is where measurement and benchmarking can play a key part in showing the financial, operational and clinical health of the practice — these are the vital signs of the practice. In addition, the more the bank knows about your practice, the type and nature of work, the local market, and the management, leadership and operations of the practice, the better your relationship with the bank will be and will include fewer surprises for both parties.

When approaching a bank, ask questions and educate them on your practice and the health care environment. Find out how well they understand the challenges facing medical practices. Determine how much they know about changes and the speed of those changes in the medical practice industry. In addition, don't underestimate the importance of examining the bank as closely as it will examine your practice.

The right banking partner will be the one that not only cares about your practice's success but actively works to help you achieve it. With so many banks to choose from, be certain to choose the most informed and most sincere and caring.

Differences in Medical Practice Financial Accounting

Today, the majority of medical groups are legally organized as limited liability companies (LLCs) or professional corporations (PCs). As members or partners, the physicians are not personally liable for the entity's debts and obligations. The bank's review of an LLC's (or PC's) operating agreement is important because the operating agreement may allocate respective rights, obligations, funding requirements, tax liabilities and other matters to LLC (or PC) members in different ways. Reimbursements may be affected by government regulation and by the practice's financial reporting.

What Banks Want to See The bank's primary concern will be the amount of risk the loan represents — the healthier the practice, the less risky a loan. That is, if the bank feels the practice is in good condition, it is more likely to consider the practice a safe risk and will grant the loan.

Qualities of a Successful Medical Practice

The bank will assess the overall condition of the practice — not just its finances. The following list will help when looking at the current state of the practice before the bank does. A lender may not be familiar with every type of practice measure, but a bank that will work as a partner in the practice's success should be asking questions that help the bank (and the practice) determine how well the practice is planning for its future. A successful practice performs well against these critical measurements:

- The practice manages operating costs with detailed cost accounting.

- Productivity is strong. Revenue and physician ratios are high, and cost ratios are low.

- The practice has timely billing and collections. Claims are submitted within 48 hours of a patient visit and filed electronically, and coding is complete, timely and accurate.

- Quality standards are established and adhered to, and quality is measured regularly.

- The practice has a quality medical information system from a reputable vendor, which is updated regularly. Business office procedures for patient records and coding should be centralized and automated to enhance the day-to-day productivity of the practice.

- The practice understands its competition and community demographics. The practice management team must regularly conduct demographic studies to identify any changes such as age of local population, household size, income levels, employments trends, insurance companies in the area and practice competition. The business plan should include a section to monitor and analyze this information.

- The practice has good relationships with the provider community.

- A low debt ratio shows a strong financial position.

- The practice delivers streamlined service by staffing at appropriate levels, designed to cater to patient perceptions of convenience, waiting time, staff friendliness and professionalism.

- The practice understands and adapts to the changing health care environment.

- The practice employs experienced administration that knows how to assess and negotiate with managed care companies. Administration must determine the financial impact of entering into managed care contracts to limit financial risk by fully understanding the terms of the contract.

- The practice's physicians are leaders in the community. To help shape the image of the practice in the community, physician involvement might include participation in speakers' bureaus, sponsorship of community events, wellness and prevention seminars, and charity events.

- The practice attracts, retains and appropriately compensates a mix of physicians. Physician compensation should reward both efficiency and effectiveness. In doing so, the practice minimizes both the risk of turnover and retention of underperforming physicians.

Areas the Bank Will Focus On Once a specific bank is selected and an application for a loan is submitted, the practice will find its operations are under a microscope. The bank will carefully examine five broad areas: (1) the way your business is legally organized; (2) financial controls and reporting; (3) practice management; (4) market position; and (5) creditworthiness.

Business Organization

Each type of business organization has advantages and disadvantages that may affect the risks of lending. A loan to one type of business organization may be structured differently from a loan in the same amount to a different type of business organization.

Financial Controls and Reporting

The bank will be interested in the contractual agreements the practice has with various payers. These contractual agreements often specify allowances for certain types of patient care. In addition, these agreements are typically negotiated or the practice accepts the allowances "as-is." Generally, adjustments to the contract result from the payer reimbursing the practice for less than what was billed. In particular, the bank will want to see that:

- Operational functions such as billing, accounts receivable, monitoring, collections and financial reporting are automated.

- The practice is collecting at least 95 percent of gross billings after any contractual adjustments. This is important because cash flow from operations is the primary source of repayment for a loan.

- Reimbursement rates are based on contractual allowances from third-party payers that are predictable and incorporated into the management of the practice's finances. If this is not the case, collections for receivables may be overstated.

- The practice has a diverse mix of payers. A practice that relies too heavily on one payer for reimbursement is considered more risky than a practice with several payers.

- Accounts receivable (A/R) information should be accurate and complete, because A/R is the practice's largest "asset." Sorted by payer, A/R should be reported net of contractual allowance (such as Medicare, Medicaid, managed care and commercial insurance, and bad debts). The bank will use the A/R figure to determine an appropriate amount for working capital loans. And this information helps the bank select the right loan for the practice.

- A/R more than 90 days past due compare favorably to industry standards.

- Medicare and Medicaid receivables represent less than 50 percent of total A/R. The practice's A/R mix should be diverse.

- A plan is in place to mitigate the impact of potential financial commitments, such as obligations to buy-out retiring or withdrawing partners so they will not create undue financial stress on the practice.

- Copays are collected at the time of service.

Practice Management

The bank will assess the management and market position of the practice. Due diligence by the bank's credit officer will include an analysis of the practice's strategic plans, management capabilities, service areas, competition and negotiations of third-party contracts. The credit officer must be comfortable with the results of all analyses and the findings from performing due diligence.

In addition, the bank will look closely at the day-to-day management of the practice. For example, if the practice is managed internally, the management team must be financially astute. Some practices contract with a physician practice management (PPM) company or an independent practice association (IPA) to handle all nonmedical-related business. This is done for efficiency and is an acceptable alternative to managing these functions internally.

The bank will want to see that each physician in the practice is financially responsible. The physician's personal leverage and cash flows should fall within acceptable ranges. These ranges may vary slightly from bank to bank. And this may be necessary whether or not the physicians have pledged guarantees on the loan. The physicians in the practice should not be financially overextended. The practice and physicians should not be contingently liable for financial obligations outside of the practice or its related entities. Contingent liability is an obligation of a person who signs a promissory note as an accommodation endorser, co-maker or guarantor, becoming liable for payment in the event the original borrower defaults. If it is contingently liable, the bank will want assurances the liability will not damage the practice if recourse were sought. If there are contingent liabilities, it's crucial the physicians fully understand the extent of their liability and how it might affect the practice. The bank will thoroughly assess this risk as part of the credit underwriting process. However, medical malpractice claims against the practice should be inconsequential. In addition, the practice must demonstrate that all required licensing to practice medicine and dispense prescriptions has been continually maintained and is current. And the practice must show that every physician in the practice carries adequate malpractice, life and disability insurance.

Market Position

The bank will want to see if the practice is part of a successful hospital network or has long-term or ongoing contracts with several hospitals or managed care companies (for example, health maintenance organizations (HMOs) and preferred provider organizations [PPOs]). The practice should have a strong reputation and demonstrated market power to withstand competition.

Creditworthiness

When banks consider lending, they follow established criteria for granting credit. Four guidelines, or "core factors," are considered when the bank is deciding whether to approve a loan request. These guidelines are as follows:

- *Debt service coverage (operating cash flow to fixed charges):* This is an examination of the borrower's operating cash flow to cover debt service requirements. The effect of any new debt is included in the calculation.

- *Leverage (total liabilities to tangible net worth):* Leverage ratios are used to help determine a practice's level of debt relative to equity. Goodwill, other intangibles and A/R from officers, owners and affiliates must be excluded from tangible net worth. Debt that is fully subordinated to the bank may be deducted from total liabilities and added to tangible net worth.

- *Profitability:* Profitability ratios reveal whether the practice has adequate earnings and how effectively the practice is being managed. The bank will want to see positive earnings before taxes for two of the three prior fiscal years, excluding extraordinary items, with the most recent year being profitable.

- *Liquidity (current assets divided by current liabilities):* Equivalent to the current ratio, liquidity is used to assess the availability of cash, or near cash resources, for meeting the practice's obligations. Other liquidity ratios include a quick ratio (quick assets divided by current liabilities) and A/R turnover ratio.

In addition, the bank may also consider other credit-granting guidelines such as collateral coverage guidelines and guarantor's financial strength.

Financial Covenants

Financial covenants are contracts attached to a formal debt agreement, promising certain activities will or will not be carried out. The purpose of a covenant is to give the lender more security. In general, covenants are required to control debt service coverage, liquidity and leverage for long-term credit facilities. Covenants will require the practice to keep these core factors within acceptable ranges. These ranges may vary slightly from bank to bank. Short-term working capital lines of credit do not typically have financial covenants. Term loans or leases for equipment, leaseholds or real estate acquisitions will, at a minimum, include the following covenants:

- Cash flow after shareholder distributions and physician bonuses to debt service with minimum 1.0 × coverage. This assures adequate cash flow is retained for debt service coverage.

- A certain amount of equity in the practice by establishing minimum tangible net worth and earnings retention requirements.

- No additional loans without approval from the bank. That is, the practice will not apply for or accept additional loans from other sources without approval from the bank.

Types of Loans and How They Are Used

Medical professional groups typically look for financing such as short-term working capital lines of credit, permanent working capital loans, term loans and mortgages for owner-occupied medical office buildings. It's a plus if the practice can show affiliation with a strong hospital, large medical groups or a managed care sponsor.

Short-term working capital financing is generally used for lump sum expenses such as bonuses, tax planning strategies or malpractice insurance premiums. Because the purpose of this type of debt is only for short-term needs, the bank will require a 30-day clearance of the balance during the fiscal year.

Permanent working capital financing is typically used to fund A/R when a practice is establishing a new location by adding physicians or merging with or acquiring another practice. These loans generally require personal guarantees. More rapid payout is encouraged when cash flow permits.

Term loans (or leases) are used to purchase medical and office equipment, make leasehold improvements to office space, purchase real estate or for practice buy-in or buy-out. The bank will be very cautious, as should the practice, when considering financing for magnetic resonance imaging (MRI), computed axial tomography (CAT) or other high-tech radiology equipment without alternative sources of repayment, collateral or guarantees. The loan amortization should not exceed the useful life of the asset.

Owner-occupied mortgage loans are granted for medical office buildings. Given the rapid and ongoing changes in the health care industry, the bank will prefer the practice have hospital alliances and be located close to a hospital.

Collateral When collateral is required, the bank generally places blanket liens on all types of collateral such as health care insurance receivables, inventory, equipment, software and general intangibles of the practice. A *blanket lien* is a security interest covering nearly all assets owned by the debtor. The bank will follow recommended guidelines for advance rates:

- *A/R advance rate of 70 percent of eligible A/R:* Eligible A/R are receivables net of bad debts and contractual allowances from third-party payers including Medicare, Medicaid, managed care and some commercial insurance. When Medicare/Medicaid receivables represent more than 50 percent of total receivables, expect the advance rate to drop below 70 percent; oftentimes it may drop to 60 percent or less. In general, the bank may require A/R aging monthly that provides a breakdown by payer and excludes or identifies anything more than 90 days past due for secured lines of credit.

- *Inventory advance rate of 50 percent.*

- *Equipment advance rate for new equipment of 80 percent of invoice or fair market value:* Recommended guidelines for used equipment are 50 percent of invoice or fair market value. Upward deviations are based on above-average quality, age and liquidation value of the specific collateral.

Guarantees In the case of loans to smaller medical practices, expect the bank to require all stockholders of the operating entity to guarantee the obligation. In larger groups, limited guarantees may be required. The bank will first conduct an overall financial evaluation of the practice and only then will it determine a requirement, if any, for full or limited guarantees. With a full guarantee, the guarantor is responsible for the full amount of the debt obligation to the lender, whereas with a limited guarantee, the guarantor is only responsible for a predetermined portion of the debtor obligations to the lender.

When the practice is a partnership or has an expense-sharing arrangement, the bank will require a copy of the agreement. This agreement should describe how assets and liabilities are allocated among the parties, particularly in the event the practice should dissolve.

As in most professional service organizations, the success of a medical practice depends on the principals. The bank will consider whether existing life and disability insurance policies would cover outstanding obligations if a principal were to die or become disabled.

Other Elements   The bank will also examine the following:

- *Subordination:* For term debt, shareholder notes or notes payable to physicians should be subordinated to the bank's lien. Subordination is the priority of interests in the ownership of property or placement of liens.

- *Trend analysis of total physician compensation:* Because most professional groups do not require capital to be maintained in the business, total physician compensation and dividends normally produce debt service coverage of 1:1. The bank will analyze trends in income streams of physicians to determine the success of the practice. A rapidly declining trend or income relative to the physician's personal leverage above 40 percent are warning signs. Debt service coverage is a ratio used in determining sufficient personal income to service personal debt. Ideally, this ratio should be below 45 percent. That would mean the individual is generating sufficient income to pay debt obligations.

- *Capitation:* The bank will determine the managed care position of the practice by completing an analysis of capitation contracts. This is of concern because, under managed care, financial risk is shifted from the patient and the payer to the practice. The bank will want to see the practice actively managing capitation and managed care pricing. Capitation is a fixed payment remitted at regular intervals to a medical provider by a managed care organization for an enrolled patient.

- *Employment contracts:* The bank will analyze all employment contracts and physician contracts. In general, physicians should not be allowed to exit the practice without one or all of the following penalties:

    - A/R stay with the practice;

    - Restrictions on practicing within a particular geographic area, to limit patient loss; and

    - Financial penalty.

These penalties should not be used if the physician is a guarantor, provided the guarantee is not released when the physician leaves.

- *Personal leverage:* The bank will perform an analysis and verification of all guarantors, owners or significant revenue generators by running credit checks and examining three years of federal income tax returns.

- *Malpractice insurance:* The bank will verify amounts with insurance carriers to determine if any material liabilities are outstanding.

- *Disability insurance:* The bank will verify amounts with insurance carriers to determine if the practice is adequately covered.

- *A/R:* The bank may require aging reports, certified by an officer of the practice, at least quarterly.

Conclusion   The types of intense financial scrutiny cited in this chapter can be daunting. However, the right banking partner will conduct it in such a way that the practice will gain a clear picture of its current health and, if needed, a prescription to help strengthen its condition. The bank wants to minimize risk to itself — and to the practice as it is in the bank's best interest, as well as the practice, for the practice to be successful. And finally, consider the bank's scrutiny a tool to use for long-term growth and success.

Chapter 6

Measuring Practice Operations

"Until you can measure something and express it in numbers, you have only the beginning of understanding."

—Lord Kelvin

Practice operations are as important to the practice as quality patient care; that is, without both activities, the practice would not exist. Therefore, this chapter will provide several techniques for measuring medical practice operations at the patient, provider and staffing levels.

Patient Demographics

Demographics are population characteristics and can be used to help understand and prepare for patient needs and expectations (Exhibit 6.1). Age and gender are the primary demographics most practices should measure to identify the distribution of established patients and predict the characteristics of new patients.

Charting patient ages and genders provides a method for describing the types of patients seen in a practice. Although, at the practice level, age and gender distributions provide some insight, at the provider level they may uncover significant differences between providers when sorted by new and established patients.

In most cases, the type (or specialty) of the practice will determine the "shape" of the patient age distribution (Exhibits 6.2 through 6.4). The most common is a histogram (Exhibit 6.2, or bar chart without spaces between bars). Each bar represents an age range of patients at the practice

Exhibit 6.1   Types of Demographics[1]

Age	Education
Gender	Family size
Race	Marital status
Socioeconomic status (SES)	Ownership (home, car, pet, etc.)
Religion	Language
Nationality	Mobility
Occupation	

Exhibit 6.2   Profile of Patient Ages for Practice 1

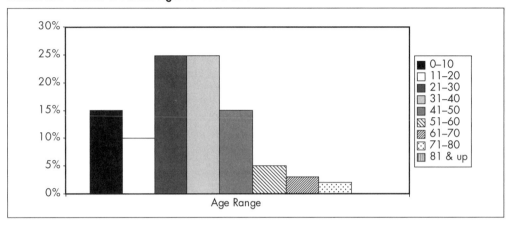

Exhibit 6.3   Profile of Patient Ages for Practice 2

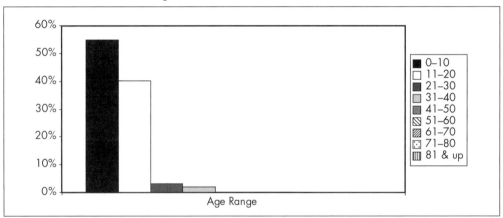

Exhibit 6.4   Profile of Patient Ages for Practice 3

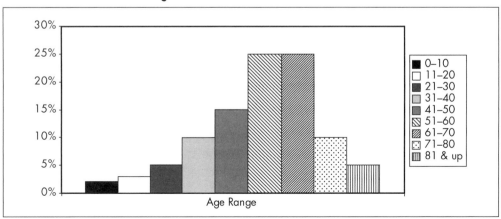

Exhibit 6.5   Profile of Patient Gender

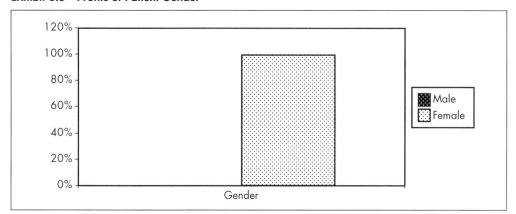

level starting at 0–10, 11–20 and so forth. The profile of patient ages in Practice 1 (Exhibit 6.2) could be from a family practice clinic because the greatest proportion of patients tends to be between 21 to 40 years of age (50 percent). Obviously, this distribution would not be expected from an internal medicine or cardiology practice because patients seen in these types of practices tend to be older. If this chart was representative of an internal medicine practice's patient population, it might suggest the need for further investigation.

The profile of patient ages in Practice 2 (Exhibit 6.3) is probably from a pediatric practice because the greatest proportion of its patients are under 20 years of age (95 percent).

The profile of patient ages in Practice 3 (Exhibit 6.4), however, is probably from an internal medicine practice because the greatest proportion of its patients are 51 years of age or older (65 percent).

Based on the distribution in Exhibit 6.5, what type of practice might this be? If you immediately thought obstetrics/gynecology, you'd probably be right. Because 100 percent of patients seen in this practice are female, the distribution certainly points to an entirely female-oriented practice type (specialty).

Patient Satisfaction

In general, the purpose of surveying patients is to uncover how patients feel about or perceive the practice. The importance of patient satisfaction was rated very high (mean of 4.61 on a scale with 5 being "extremely important") by practices identified as successful medical groups.[2] And patient satisfaction is typically assessed using some type of survey instrument. Survey questions should be simple and easy to understand — patients shouldn't have to "read into" the questions to understand what is being asked. That is, interpretation of questions should be consistent

Exhibit 6.6   Qualitative versus Quantitative Survey Questions

Qualitative	Quantitative
• How satisfied were you with the care you received today? • What could this practice do to improve the care you received today? • What brought you into the practice today? • How would you describe what you're feeling? • How satisfied were you with the care you received today? • What could this practice do to improve the care you received today?	Using the choices below, how would you rate the ease of making today's appointment by phone? (Circle "1" for poor, "2" for good or "3" for excellent.) Using the choices below, how many times did you or someone else try to schedule today's appointment? (Circle "1 "for one time, "2" for two or three times or "3" for four or more times.)

among patients, and there are statistical methods for determining consistency. However, there are many sources of survey questions that have been thoroughly tested for consistency so there's usually no reason to "create" new questions — no need to "re-invent the wheel."

A great deal of value can be found in using the same questions over time to uncover trends or changes. The same questions also provide value when used before, during and after a change in the practice to provide insights into the effect of a change. In addition, the types of questions used must be carefully selected because qualitative questions tend to provide greater opportunity and flexibility for patients to explain their feelings, whereas quantitative questions are better for focusing of specific topics (see Exhibit 6.6). The strength of qualitative (open-ended) questions lies in their ability to let patients elaborate in their own words because the questionnaire usually provides open white space for the answer. However, it's somewhat difficult to organize qualitative question responses, given their unstructured nature. The strength behind quantitative questions lies in the specific focus of the questions and numeric nature of the responses — this makes analysis much easier. These types of questions provide patients with a list of preset answers to choose from (for example, circle "1" for poor, "2" for good or "3" for excellent).

Provider Profiles   Profiles display data by provider for most any measure. They typically consist of information related to each provider matched to selected benchmarks. Profiling can be used for many purposes. For instance, some practices use profiles as part of their physician compensation methodology. But, in many cases, profiling is used to provide individual providers with a summary of their unique measures in relation to the overall practice.

Exhibit 6.7 Profiles of Dr. Smith's E&M Established Patients Vs. the Overall Practice

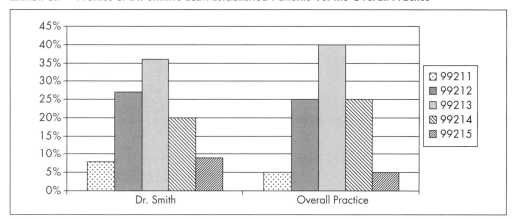

For example, a typical use of profiling is to portray the evaluation and management (E&M) coding distribution by provider for "new" and "established" patients compared to the overall practice distribution. Exhibit 6.7 illustrates a percent distribution of E&M codes for "established" patients seen by an individual provider (Dr. Smith) versus the distribution for the entire practice. These profiles may indicate Dr. Smith has a slightly different patient population than other providers in the practice; however, it might also suggest Dr. Smith may benefit from additional coding training.

Cost of Nonclinical Services

For the most part, practice revenue and physician compensation are directly related to the number of clinical services provided to patients. When physicians spend time at meetings, making phone calls, answering telephone consults and corresponding with patients, revenue is not being generated; however, overhead costs continue. Because every practice will engage in some nonclinical activities, it is possible to approximate the cost (or lost revenue) in response to the performance of these types of activities using an estimation of the physician's hourly rate. For instance, the following formula can be used to assess cost (or lost revenue): number of hours spent performing non-clinical activities multiplied by physician's estimated hourly rate.

Payer Mix

Payer mix typically consists of Medicare fee-for-service (FFS), Medicare managed care FFS, Medicare capitation, Medicaid FFS, Medicaid managed care FFS, Medicaid capitation, commercial FFS, commercial managed care FFS, commercial capitation, workers' compensation, charity care and professional courtesy, self-pay and other federal government payers.

Payer Mix Ratio[2,3]

Definition: Indicates the sources of payment as a percentage or the relative value of a specific health insurance plan to the bottom line.[3]

$$\text{Version 1:}^2 \quad \frac{\text{Gross charges by payer}}{\text{Total gross charges}}$$

$$\text{Version 2:}^3 \quad \frac{\text{Each payer's net charges}}{\text{Total net charges}}$$

Total Percentage Distribution of Payers

    % Medicare FFS
+ % Medicare managed care FFS
+ % Medicare capitation
+ % Medicaid FFS
+ % Medicaid managed care FFS
+ % Medicaid capitation
+ % commercial FFS
+ % commercial managed care FFS
+ % commercial capitation
+ % workers' compensation
+ % charity care and professional courtesy
+ % self-pay
+ % other federal government payers
= 100%

Providers, Physicians, and Staff FTEs

The following support staffing formulas are from the MGMA Cost Surveys (FTE support staff should be calculated to the nearest 10th FTE).

FTE Provider Staffing[2]

    FTE nonphysician providers
+ FTE physicians

Total FTE Physicians[2]

    FTE primary care physicians
+ FTE nonsurgical specialty physicians
+ FTE surgical specialty physicians

FTE Providers[2]

    Total FTE nonphysician providers
+ Total FTE physicians

Total Business Operations FTE Support Staff[4]

Number of general administration FTE support staff (administrator, CFO, medical director, human resources, marketing)

+ Number of patient accounting FTE support staff (billing, collection)

= Number of general accounting FTE support staff (controller, account manager, accounts payable and budget)

+ Number of managed care administration FTE support staff (contract administration and utilization review)

+ Number of information technology FTE support staff (data processing, programming, telecommunications)

+ Number of housekeeping, maintenance and security FTE support staff

Total Front Office FTE Support Staff[4]

Number of medical receptionist FTE support staff

+ Number of medical secretaries and transcriber FTE support staff

+ Number of medical records staff FTE support staff

+ Number of other administrative support staff FTE support staff

Total Clinical FTE Support Staff[4]

Number of registered nurse FTE support staff

+ Number of licensed practical nurse FTE support staff

+ Number of medical assistant and nurses aide FTE support staff

Total Ancillary FTE Support Staff[4]

Number of clinical laboratory FTE support staff

+ Number of radiology and imaging FTE support staff

+ Number of other ancillary medical support services FTE support staff

Total Employed FTE Support Staff[4]

Total number of business operations support FTE support staff

+ Total number of front office support FTE support staff

+ Total number of clinical support FTE support staff

+ Total number of ancillary support FTE support staff

Total FTE Support Staff[4]

Total employed FTE support staff

+ Total contracted and temporary FTE support staff

Staffing Ratio[3]

$$\frac{\text{Total number of FTE employees}}{\text{Total number of FTE providers or physicians}}$$

Total FTE Medical Support Staff per FTE Physician[5]

$$\frac{\text{Total FTE medical support staff}}{\text{Total FTE physicians}}$$

Total FTE Administrative Staff per FTE Physician[5]

$$\frac{\text{Total FTE administrative staff}}{\text{Total FTE physicians}}$$

Total FTE Laboratory Staff per FTE Physician[5]

$$\frac{\text{Total FTE laboratory staff}}{\text{Total FTE physicians}}$$

Total FTE Radiology (Imaging) Staff per FTE Physician[5]

$$\frac{\text{Total FTE radiology (imaging) staff}}{\text{Total FTE physicians}}$$

Relative Value Units

A relative value unit (RVU) is a measure of resources/work performed based on coding documentation of E&M and Current Procedural Terminology (CPT®) codes, and each code is associated with a specific number of RVUs. For example, in family practice, the average RVUs per patient will typically vary around one (1) RVU. The Centers for Medicare & Medicaid Services (CMS) publishes RVU tables every year in an itemized format consisting of malpractice, facility and professional components. These components can be added to arrive at a total RVU per E&M or CPT code and the professional component can be used to determine total physician work RVUs.

Physician Work RVUs per Visit (for a single visit)

Sum of RVUs by E&M codes
+ Sum of RVUs by CPT codes

Note: A more valuable measure is to calculate the mean (average) RVUs per visit across a user-defined time frame.

Average Physician Work RVUs per Visit

$$\frac{\text{(Sum of RVUs by all E\&M codes + Sum of RVUs by all CPT codes)}}{\text{Total number of visits}}$$

Note: An adjustment must be made when calculating this measure across multiple calendar years because CMS publishes new RVU values every year for E&M and CPT codes.

Other Operational Measures   Operational measures related to supply (physician availability), access to care and utilization of space also provide a basis for benchmarking standard operations of the practice.

Ambulatory Patient Encounters (Visits/Appointments) per FTE Physician[5]

$$\frac{\text{Physician ambulatory patient encounters}}{\text{Total FTE physicians}}$$

Hospital Admissions per FTE Physician[5]

$$\frac{\text{Hospital inpatient admissions}}{\text{Total FTE physicians}}$$

New Patient Registrations per FTE Physician[5]

$$\frac{\text{New patient registrations}}{\text{Total FTE physicians}}$$

Physician Weeks Worked per Year

Total number of weeks worked per year per physician

Clinical Service Hours Worked per Week

Total number of clinical service hours worked per week per physician

Appointment Duration (average) in Minutes

$$\frac{(\text{Total number of clinical service hours worked per week per physician} \times 60)}{\text{Number of total scheduled appointments per physician}}$$

Appointment Type Mix

$$\frac{\text{Number of each appointment type}}{\text{Number of total scheduled appointments}}$$

Note: Some practices use different types of appointments to ensure patients are allocated an appropriate amount of time with the physician.

Appointment Availability[2]

Number of days to next available "new" or "established" patient appointment

Exhibit 6.8   Other Operational Metrics[3]

• Amount of wait time per visit	• Accounts worked per billing clerk/collector FTE per day
• Wait time on the telephone	• Words or lines transcribed per day
• Access wait time by appointment type	• Authorization turnaround time
• Number of no-shows	• Return telephone call wait time
• Transcription turnaround time	

No-Show Rate[2]

$$\frac{\text{Number of appointment no-shows}}{\text{Number of total scheduled appointments}}$$

Cancellation Conversion Rate[2]

$$\frac{\text{Number of cancellations converted to appointments}}{\text{Total cancellations}}$$

New Patient Appointments as a Percentage of Total Appointments[2]

$$\frac{\text{Number of new patient appointments}}{\text{Number of total scheduled appointments}}$$

Productivity by Space (RVUs per square foot)[2]

$$\frac{\text{Total RVUs}}{\text{Total square footage}}$$

In addition to the previous formulas and ratios, there a several other operational metrics that, if possible, should be collected, monitored and communicated to all practice personnel (see Exhibit 6.8).[3]

Notes

1. Wikipedia, "Demographics," www.wikipedia.com (2006).

2. Elizabeth W. Woodcock, "Practice Benchmarking," Chapter 11 of *Physician Practice Management,* ed. Lawrence F. Wolper (Boston: Jones and Bartlett Publishers, 2005).

3. The Coker Group, *Physician Ancillary Services: Evaluation, Implementation, and Management of New Practice Opportunities* (Boston: Jones and Bartlett Publishers, 2006).

4. MGMA, Cost Survey Questionnaire Based on 2004 Data (Englewood, CO: MGMA, 2005).

5. E.J. Pavlock, *Financial Management for Medical Groups*, 2nd ed. (Englewood, CO: MGMA, 2000).

Chapter 7

Tools for Measuring Practice Finances

"Innovation has nothing to do with how many R&D dollars you have. When Apple came up with the Mac, IBM was spending at least 100 times more on R&D. It's not about the money. It's about the people you have, how you're led, and how much you get it."

— Steve Jobs

There are a handful of key financial performance indicators used by the majority of practices to manage financial operations. Many of these formulas are presented in this chapter as a comprehensive "starter set" of key performance indicators and financial metrics for benchmarking.

Key Financial Indicators

Benchmarks for many of the following formulas are available in the MGMA *Cost Survey and Performance and Practices of Successful Medical Groups* reports.

Total Net Collections[1]

Net fee-for-service (FFS) revenue
+ Capitation revenue
− Provision for bad debt

Gross (Unadjusted) Collection Ratio[1]

Definition: Indicates how much of what is being charged is actually collected.

Goal: Higher the better.

$$\frac{\text{Total net collections}}{\text{Total gross charges}}$$

Note: In general, the goal of this measure is "higher the better;" however, this metric will vary significantly depending on the fee schedule of the practice. For instance, a practice with a high fee schedule will have a lower gross collection ratio than a practice with a low fee schedule (setting a fee schedule too low can have a negative effect on net revenue). This metric is often used to measure billing office performance.

Gross Collection Ratio

Definition: Indicates a ratio of the amount of revenue "actually" collected over the amount charged.

Goal: Higher the better.

$$\frac{\text{Net FFS revenue or collections}}{\text{Gross FFS charges}}$$

Adjusted (Net) Collection Ratio[1]

Definition: Indicates how much of what is being charged (gross FFS charges) is actually collected after total adjustments to charges; does not include funds the practice should not receive (contractual allowances) and funds it will not receive (bad debt).

Goal: Higher the better.

$$\frac{\text{Net FFS collections}}{\text{Net FFS charges}}$$

Average Adjusted Revenue per Day[1]

Definition: Indicates the average amount of revenue generated per business day.

Goal: Higher the better.

$$\frac{\text{Adjusted charges for the last three months}}{\text{Number of business days for the same time period}}$$

Note: It isn't required that the time period be three months; rather, it should be a recent period of time.

Days Revenue Outstanding[2]

Definition: Indicates how long it takes before claims/charges are paid.

Goal: Lower the better.

Step 1: Calculate "days revenue"

$$\frac{\text{Total revenue for the last three months}}{\text{Number of business days in the last three months}}$$

Step 2: Calculate "days revenue outstanding"

$$\frac{\text{Outstanding net accounts receivable (A/R)}}{\text{Day's revenue}}$$

Days in A/R[3]

Definition: Indicates how long it takes before claims/charges are paid.

Goal: A net collection ratio (NCR) of 96 percent to 99 percent and 40 to 50 days in A/R (days in A/R of 45 or less is ideal) indicate your practice is functioning efficiently and doing very well. If NCR is 93 percent to 95 percent and 50 to 60 days in A/R, there is some (little) room for improvement. And if 92 percent or less and 70 or more days in A/R, there is significant room for improvement in billing operations.[2]

$$\frac{\text{Outstanding A/R}}{(\text{Average monthly charges} \times 30)}$$

Note: Include the last three months.

Days in A/R (alternate calculation)[4]

Definition: Indicates how long it takes before claims/charges are paid.

Goal: Lower the better.

$$\frac{\text{Outstanding net A/R}}{\text{Average adjusted revenue per day}}$$

Months Revenue in A/R

Definition: Indicates the average number of months charges are outstanding for collection.

Goal: Lower the better.

$$\frac{\text{Total A/R}}{(\text{Annual adjusted FFS charges} \times 1/12)}$$

Expense to Earnings[4]

Definition: Indicates the ratio of overhead (expenses) to revenue (collections).

Goal: Lower the better.

$$\frac{\text{Total operating expenses}}{\text{Total collections}}$$

Average Revenue per Patient [4]

Definition: Indicates the average amount of revenue generated per patient seen. In addition, it can be used to determine the number of patients that must be treated to receive a predetermined amount of revenue (collections).

Goal: Higher the better.

$$\frac{\text{Total monthly collections for last month}}{\text{Total patient visits last month}}$$

Average Cost per Patient[4]

Definition: Indicates the average cost of providing treatment per patient visit.

Goal: Lower the better.

$$\frac{\text{Total operating expenses}}{\text{Total patient visits}}$$

Departmental or Service Ratio[4]

Definition: Indicates the expenses to revenues ratio for a specific department or service.

Goal: Lower the better.

$$\frac{\text{Total expenses for ancillary service for the last three months}}{\text{Total net charges for all current procedural terminology (CPT\textregistered) codes related to ancillary service}}$$

Collections Rate by Payer[1]

Definition: Indicates different rates of reimbursement by payer.

Goal: Depends on many practice factors; should be proportional to the percentage of patients covered by each payer.

$$\frac{\text{Net collections by payer}}{\text{Total gross charges by payer}}$$

Note: Reimbursement received from a payer is based on the specific fee schedule established with a payer and is on a per procedure basis. Net collections is the sum of all reimbursement received from a payer, whereas gross charges is what the practice billed the payer.

Volume and Reimbursement by Service Line[1]

Definition: Indicates workload volume and revenue generated by service line; provides a method for identifying the relative contribution of each service line.

Goal: Depends on many practice factors; in most cases, volume should be directly related to revenue generated by service line.

Volume by service line:

$$\frac{\text{Volume measurement (encounters/visits, relative value units (RVUs), etc.) by service line}}{\text{Volume measurement for total practice}}$$

Reimbursement by service line:

$$\frac{\text{Revenue by service line}}{\text{Total practice revenue}}$$

Surgical Yield[1]

Definition: Indicates relative contribution of revenue generated from surgical or procedural workload to total practice revenue.

Goal: Depends on many practice factors; in most cases, volume should be directly related to revenue generated by service line.

$$\frac{\text{Revenue derived from surgeries or procedures}}{\text{Total practice revenue}}$$

Reimbursement per Procedure Code

Definition: Indicates average amount of revenue generated from procedures provided to patients.

Goal: Depends on many practice factors; in general, it will be higher if the procedures provided to patients are higher RVU procedures.

$$\frac{\text{Net collections}}{\text{Total number of procedures}}$$

Note: This metric can be adapted to show average reimbursement per procedure by payer using net collections by payer divided by total number of procedures charged to a payer.

FFS Activities   FFS activities consist of gross FFS charges (not including capitation charges), adjustments to FFS charges (value of services performed for which payment is not expected; that is, bad debts or noncontractual write-offs), adjusted FFS charges, bad debts due to FFS activity (accounts assigned to collection agencies), and net FFS collections/revenue.

Adjusted FFS Charges

Gross FFS charges (not including capitation charges)
− Adjustments to FFS charges (value of services performed for which payment is not expected)

Capitation Activity   Capitation activity consists of gross charges for patients covered by capitation contracts, gross capitation revenue (per member per month capitation payments and capitation patient copayments), purchased services for capitation patients, and net capitation revenue.

Net Capitation Revenue

Gross capitation revenue (per member per month capitation payments and capitation patient copayments)
− Purchased services for capitation patients

Other Medical Activities Other medical activities consists of other medical revenue (research contract revenue, honoraria and teaching income), revenue from the sale of medical goods and services, gross revenue from other medical activities, cost of sales and/or cost of other medical activities, and net other medical revenue.

Gross Revenue from Other Medical Activities

Other medical revenue (research contract revenue, honoraria and teaching income)
+ Revenue from the sale of medical goods and services

Net Other Medical Activities Revenue

Gross revenue from other medical activities
− Cost of sales and/or cost of other medical activities

Performance Indicators[3] The physician is typically the primary revenue-generating unit for a practice. Therefore, gross charges, net revenue, operating costs, medical revenue after operating costs and gross collections at the per FTE physician level provide much insight into the general performance of all FTE physicians in a practice. Also, "gross collection ratio" is an excellent performance indicator (see section on "Key Financial Indicators").

Total Gross Charges per FTE Physician[3]

Definition: The average gross charges per FTE physician; indicates financial productivity of all physicians in the practice.

Goal: Higher the better.

$$\frac{\text{(Gross FFS charges + Gross charges for patients covered by capitation contracts)}}{\text{Total FTE physicians}}$$

Total Net Revenue per FTE Physician[3]

Definition: The average medical revenue per FTE physician to include all revenues from medical activities. Indicates financial stability and can be used to compare productivity and profitability among practices.

Goal: Higher the better.

$$\frac{\text{Total net revenue}}{\text{Total FTE physicians}}$$

Total Operating Costs per FTE Physician

Definition: Indicates amount of operating costs used to provide patient care per FTE physician.

Goal: Lower the better.

$$\frac{\text{Total operating costs}}{\text{Total FTE physicians}}$$

Note: Rightsizing, treating a higher volume of patients and lowering costs can help to optimize and lower this measure.

Total Medical Revenue After Operating Costs per FTE Physician

Definition: Indicates the amount per FTE physician of remaining revenue available for physician compensation, as retained earnings, or for reinvestment (measure of profitability).

Goal: Higher the better.

$$\frac{(\text{Total medical revenue} - \text{Total operating costs})}{\text{Total FTE physicians}}$$

Operating Costs Indicators[3] Costs associated with operating the practice are also referred to as "overhead" and typically consist of employee salaries and benefits, equipment and supplies, professional insurance and facility expenses. However, the definition of overhead is dependent on its use. For instance, when computing profitability in a practice, physicians are typically not included, whereas, when calculating costs for contracting purposes, physician costs are included. This highlights the importance of understanding the definition of overhead, particularly when comparing with external benchmarks; that is, how does the external organization or external benchmark define overhead?

Total Operating Cost as a Percent of Total Medical Revenue

Definition: Indicates overhead in relation to total revenue.

Goal: Lower the better.

$$\frac{(\text{Total operating costs} \times 100)}{\text{Total medical revenue}}$$

Total Support Staff Salary Expenses per FTE Physician

Definition: Indicates average cost of support staff salary per FTE physician.

Goal: Depends on many practice factors; in general, lower the better. However, it has been found that too few staff (too low support staff expense) results in poor productivity; therefore, rightsizing is imperative.

$$\frac{\text{Total support staff salary expenses}}{\text{Total FTE physicians}}$$

Total Medical and Surgical Supply Expenses per FTE Physician

Definition: Indicates supply expenses per FTE physician.

Goal: Depends on many practice factors; in general, lower the better. However, because supply expenses are a variable cost, the more productive providers will have greater medical and surgical supply expenses due to their higher volume.

$$\frac{\text{Total medical and surgical supply expenses}}{\text{Total FTE physicians}}$$

Total General and Administrative Expenses per FTE Physicians

Definition: Indicates average cost of general and administrative costs per FTE physician.

Goal: Lower the better.

$$\frac{\text{Total general and administrative expenses}}{\text{Total FTE physicians}}$$

Note: Rightsizing and attention to productivity issues can help to optimize and lower this measure.

A/R Indicators[3] A/R consist of bills to patients, third-party payers and other sources of revenue. Several aspects of A/R can be monitored at per FTE physician, adjustments, bad debts, adjusted collections and months revenue in A/R levels. Typically, A/R aging categories include receivables that are current to 30 days, 31 to 60 days, 61 to 90 days, 91 to 120 days, and over 120 days. In addition, A/R that has been turned over to a collection agency should also be considered (that is, it can be included or excluded from A/R totals/categories). Also, "gross/net/adjusted collection ratio," "days in A/R," "adjustments as a percent of gross FFS charges" and "months revenue in A/R" are excellent performance indicators (see section on "Key Financial Indicators").

Total A/R

    Current to 30 days
  + Cost of sales and/or cost of other medical activities
  + 31 to 60 days
  + 61 to 90 days
  + 91 to 120 days + Over 120 days

Adjustment Ratio[3]

Definition: Indicates the percentage of gross FFS charges that will not be collected.

Goal: The adjustment ratio should be consistent over 12, 18, and 24 months. If your adjustment ratio doesn't show large fluctuations over time, it indicates a steady revenue cycle that is functioning properly.[2] In most cases, lower the better.

$$\frac{\text{Adjustments (write-offs)}}{\text{Gross FFS charges}}$$

A/R per FTE Physician

Definition: Indicates the average charges outstanding per FTE physician.

Goal: Depends on many practice factors; in general, higher the better. However, there are two main drivers associated with this metric: (1) higher charges result in higher A/R; and (2) slow collections.

$$\frac{\text{Total A/R}}{\text{Total FTE physicians}}$$

Bad Debts Due to FFS Activity as a Percent of Gross FFS Charges

Definition: Indicates the percentage of gross FFS charges that will not be collected.

Goal: Lower the better

$$\frac{(\text{Bad debts due to FFS activity} \times 100)}{\text{Gross FFS charges}}$$

Prepaid Services Indicators[3] Prepaid services are generally synonymous with capitation payments for members enrolled in a prepayment plan (HMO or PPO). In order to monitor increases or decreases in revenue and charges, there are several measures for identifying these charges.

Net Capitation Revenue as a Percent of Total Medical Revenue

Definition: Indicates the percentage of total revenue associated with capitation payments.

Goal: Depends on many practice factors; should be directly related to the proportion of average number of prepaid plan members to all charges.

$$\frac{\text{Net capitation revenue}}{\text{Total net medical revenue}}$$

Net Capitation Revenue per Member per Month

Definition: Indicates the average revenue collected per member per month.

Goal: Depends on many practice factors; should be directly related to the proportion of average number of prepaid plan members to all charges.

$$\frac{\text{Net capitation revenue for 12 months}}{\text{Average number of prepaid plan members for 12 months}}$$

FFS Equivalent Charges (for capitation plan patients) per Member per Month

Definition: Indicates the average monthly FFS equivalent charges per member per month.

Goal: Depends on many practice factors; should be directly related to the proportion of average number of prepaid plan members to all charges.

$$\frac{\text{FFS equivalent charges (for capitation plan patients) for 12 months}}{\text{Average number of prepaid plan members for 12 months}}$$

Net Capitation Revenue as a Percent of FFS Equivalent Charges

Definition: Indicates the ratio of capitation revenue over FFS equivalent charges

Goal: Depends on many practice factors; should be directly related to the proportion of average number of prepaid plan members to all charges

$$\frac{\text{Net capitation revenue}}{\text{FFS equivalent charges}}$$

Revenue and Cost Measures

Medical revenue and costs are the bottom-line drivers of practice success and longevity, because the difference between them is typically physician compensation. In general terms, profit is defined as revenue minus expenses. And, provided revenue surpasses expenses, the practice will continue to operate. The greater the difference, the more profitable the practice will be and the higher the income of the physicians. Therefore, management and oversight of revenue and expenses should be a top priority for all practices.

Total Medical Revenue After Operating Cost (Profitability)

Total medical revenue
− Total operating cost

Total Medical Revenue

Net FFS collections/revenue
+ Net capitation revenue (Gross capitation revenue minus purchased services for capitation patients)
+ Net other medical revenue (Gross revenue from other medical activities)
− Cost of sales and/or cost of other medical activities

Total General Operating Cost

Cost of information technology (data processing, computer, telecommunication services and telephone)

+ Cost of drug supply (chemotherapy/allergy drugs and vaccines)

+ Cost of medical and surgical supply (medical/surgical instruments and laundry)

+ Cost of building and occupancy (rental/lease, depreciation, interest on real estate loans, utilities, maintenance, and security)

+ Cost of furniture and equipment (exclude cost for furniture and equipment used in information technology, clinical laboratory, radiology and imaging, and other ancillary services)

+ Cost of administrative supplies and services (printing, postage, books, subscriptions, forms, stationary, purchased medical transcription services)

+ Cost of professional liability insurance premiums (malpractice and professional liability insurance for physicians and employees)

+ Cost of other insurance premiums (other policies such as fire, flood, theft, casualty, general liability, officers' and directors' liability, and reinsurance)

+ Cost of outside professional fees (infrequent services such as legal and accounting services and management, financial and actuarial consultants)

+ Cost of promotion and marketing (promotion, advertising and marketing activities, fliers, brochures and Yellow Page listings)

+ Cost of clinical laboratory (CPT code 36415, 36416, and 80048 to 89356)

+ Cost of radiology and imaging (ultrasound, nuclear medicine, echocardiography)

+ Cost of other ancillary services (all ancillary services except clinical laboratory and radiology and imaging)

+ Cost of billing and collections purchased services (claims clearinghouse)

+ Cost of management fees paid to an MSO or PPMC

+ Cost of miscellaneous operating costs (recruiting, health, business and property taxes, other interest, charitable contributions, entertainment, and business transportation)

+ Cost allocated to medical practice from parent organization (indirect cost allocations or shared services)

Total Operating Cost

Total cost of support staff

+ Total general operating cost

Nonmedical Revenue and Cost

Nonmedical revenue and cost consist of nonmedical revenue (investment and rental revenue), extraordinary nonmedical revenue, financial support for operating costs (from parent organization), goodwill amortization, nonmedical cost (income taxes), extraordinary nonmedical cost and net nonmedical revenue.

Net Nonmedical Revenue

$$\frac{[\text{Nonmedical revenue (investment and rental revenue)} + \text{Extraordinary nonmedical revenue} + \text{Financial support for operating costs (from parent organization)}]}{[\text{Goodwill amortization} + \text{Nonmedical cost (income taxes)} + \text{Extraordinary nonmedical cost}]}$$

Net Practice Income or Loss

    Total medical revenue after operation cost
-   Total provider cost
+   Net nonmedical revenue

Cost of Providers and Physicians

Nonphysician providers are typically treated as employed staff in most practices, whereas physicians function as owners. Therefore, the salaries and benefits of nonphysician providers should be a component of the total cost of staff. However, because physicians are generally owners, their compensation generally consists of remaining revenue after operating costs. And in some cases (benchmarks), nonphysician provider compensation is treated the same as physician–owner compensation so the importance of understanding how a benchmark is calculated and how the variables are defined is imperative for proper benchmarking.

Total Provider Cost

    Total nonphysician provider cost
+   Provider consultant cost
+   Total physician cost

Total Nonphysician Provider Cost

    Nonphysician provider compensation
+   Nonphysician provider benefit cost

Total Physician Cost

    Total physician compensation
+   Total physician benefit cost

Note: This is the amount received by all physician owners as compensation and benefits.

Cost of Staff

In many practices, the total cost of staff (salaries and benefits) consume a large percentage of total revenue. Therefore, it's imperative these costs receive attention as part of the practice's cost management program.

Total Cost of Business Operations Support Staff

Cost of general administration staff (administrator, CFO, medical director, human resources, marketing)
+ Cost of patient accounting staff (billing, collection)
+ Cost of general accounting staff (controller, account manager, accounts payable, and budget)
+ Cost of managed care administration staff (contract administration and utilization review)
+ Cost of information technology staff (data processing, programming, telecommunications)
+ Cost of housekeeping, maintenance, and security staff

Total Cost of Front Office Support Staff

Cost of medical receptionists
+ Cost of medical secretaries and transcribers
+ Cost of medical records staff
+ Cost of other administrative support staff

Total Cost of Clinical Support Staff

Cost of registered nurses
+ Cost of licensed practical nurses
+ Cost of medical assistants and nurse's aides

Total Cost of Ancillary Support Staff

Cost of clinical laboratory staff
+ Cost of radiology and imaging staff
+ Cost of other ancillary medical support services staff

Total Cost of Employed Support Staff

Total cost of business operations support staff
+ Total cost of front office support staff
+ Total cost of clinical support staff
+ Total cost of ancillary support staff

Return on Investment (ROI)[3]

Definition: A method of evaluating an investment's expected gains compared to its cost. In addition, this calculation has been used as a measure of profitability, efficiency and financial control.

Goal: Higher the better.

$$\frac{(\text{Total revenue} - \text{Total costs})}{\text{Total costs}}$$

Note: There are many methods for calculating ROI, and care should be taken when comparing ROIs.

Compensation Measures

There are other measures that can be benchmarked against in a practice that don't require calculation. In general, these measures are either easily extracted from the practice's information system or hardcopy documents.

Physician Compensation and Benefits

Physician compensation is generally determined by subtracting practice overhead or total expenses from revenue. In most cases, the physicians, through their compensation method, share the remaining revenue after all expenses have been paid. And in many practices, physician benefits (for example, health insurance, retirement plan, licenses) are treated as a practice expense.

Staff Compensation and Benefits

In many practices, the administrator or human resources department can produce staff compensation and benefit amounts.

Other Financial Measures

In addition to the previous formulas and ratios, there a several other financial measures that, if possible, should be collected, monitored and communicated to physician leadership (Exhibit 7.1).

Total Assets

Definition: Includes current assets (short-term assets that can be liquefied quickly) and noncurrent and all other assets (long-term assets that cannot

Exhibit 7.1   Other Financial Metrics[4]

- Gross charges per visit
- Net charges per visit
- Staff payroll and benefits or total personnel costs to net charges
- Provider compensation as a percentage of revenue and number of visits

be liquefied quickly). Noncurrent and all other assets typically consist of investments and long-term receivables; property, furniture, fixtures and equipment; and intangibles and other assets.

Current assets
+ Noncurrent and all other assets

Total Liabilities

Definition: Includes current liabilities (obligations from past transactions that must be paid within one year) and long-term liabilities (obligations from past transactions that don't have to be paid within one year). Current liabilities consist of accounts payable; claims payable; notes and loans payable; long-term debt (current portion); payroll withholdings; accrued payroll liabilities; accrued vacation, holiday and sick pay; accrued liabilities (nonpayroll); patient deposits; and claims payable (incurred but not reported).[3] And long-term liabilities consist of long-term notes payable, mortgage payable, construction loans payable, capital lease obligation (long-term portion) and deferred income taxes (long-term portion).[3]

Current liabilities
+ Noncurrent and all other liabilities

Total Net Worth

Total assets
− Total liabilities

Notes

1. E.W. Woodcock, "Practice Benchmarking," in *Physician Practice Management: Essential Operations and Financial Knowledge* (Sudbury, MA: Jones and Bartlett Publishers, 2005).

2. DecisionHealth, "A/R Benchmarks," Part B News 20, no. 40 (October 16, 2006).

3. E.J. Pavlock, *Financial Management for Medical Groups*, 2nd ed. (Englewood, CO: MGMA, 2000).

4. The Coker Group, *Physician Ancillary Services: Evaluation, Implementation, and Management of New Practice Opportunities* (Sudbury, MA: Jones and Bartlett Publishers, 2006).

Chapter 8

Hospital and Inpatient Metrics

"Never compare your inside with somebody else's outside."
— *Hugh Macleod*

As with other performance measurements, hospital and inpatient metrics should identify common goals, provide clear definitions and focus on cause and effect relationships that impact an organization's strategies, goals and mission. Metrics should allow comparison against historical trends and industry standards, and, ideally, they should help managers address issues proactively before they become serious problems.

Generally, metrics are categorized under broader areas of performance that are considered contributors to the organization's mission. These measures may include quality of care and patient satisfaction, as well as financial and productivity/efficiency measurements (Exhibit 8.1).

Standardizing metrics across departments and locations allows meaningful comparison and analysis of common processes to identify best practices and areas for improvement. Preferably, metrics should be used not just to monitor but also to improve performance over time. However, sustained improvements often require changes in organization behavior, such as standardizing supplies to reduce costs or adopting clinical protocols to improve outcomes. Metrics are used to measure different aspects of the hospital environment, such as:

- *Provider profiling:* Analyzing individual physician practice patterns by looking at clinical, quality, satisfaction and economic indicators.
- *Clinical decision support:* Analyzing clinical performance to optimize resource utilization, cost effectiveness and evidence-based decision-making.
- *Disease management:* Using metrics to identify high-risk patients in order to proactively manage conditions and optimize care.
- *Benchmarking/quality measurement:* Data analysis to support comparisons to internal and external benchmarks and to meet industry reporting requirements.
- *Error reduction/safety:* Analysis to track and trend clinical errors and safety incidents.

Exhibit 8.1   Sources for Metrics and External Benchmarks

- National Committee for Quality Assurance (NCQA)—www.ncqa.org
- Agency for Healthcare Research and Quality (AHRQ)—www.ahrq.gov
- Joint Commission for Accreditation of Healthcare Organizations (JCAHO)—www.jcaho.org
- Centers for Medicare & Medicaid Services (CMS)—www.cms.hhs.gov
- National Quality Forum—www.qualityforum.org
- The Leapfrog Group—www.leapfroggroup.org

Wherever possible, managers should identify external benchmarks to evaluate internal metrics. Such comparison may help identify reasonable metric thresholds, as well as identify competitive opportunities and weaknesses among organizations. External benchmarks are available from numerous sources, including federal and state programs, industry organizations and vendors. However, managers should be mindful of the limitations that metrics present. Historical data represents the results of past decisions and does not predict future results. Variations in operations and data quality among benchmark facilities may cloud comparisons.

The following exhibits list common metrics in the areas of quality of care, productivity and efficiency, financial performance, operations and maintenance, and patient demographics. The measures are not all-inclusive, and managers should identify metrics applicable to their organizations according to their goals, objectives, regulatory requirements and other pertinent factors.

Quality   Quality of care is a measure of perceived and evaluated need and consumer satisfaction (see Exhibit 8.2). That is, the patient perceives a need for a level of care based on his/her health status. And the patient becomes a satisfied consumer (feels the quality of care is high) when the care provided meets or exceeds his/her perceived need. From the patient's first impression of the building and reception area, to the greeting and check-in procedures by front-desk staff, to the time spent and friendliness of provider, to other environmental, process and people factors, the practice is being measured by the patient for quality of care. Benchmarks for assessing patient perceived quality of care consist of surveys, mystery patient programs, patient longevity as a customer, and other factors.

More often, however, medical staff evaluate (determine) need and quality of care using professionally assigned triage categories, accepted protocols, evidence-based diagnosis, treatment, and outcomes, and other common metrics.

Exhibit 8.2 Common Quality Metrics

Metrics	Notes
Average length of stay (LOS) = Total patient days / Total discharges	Utilization measure that estimates the average length of inpatient stay. Lower LOS is generally preferred.
Patient satisfaction • Outpatient • Inpatient • Emergency department • Ambulatory surgery	Requires survey mechanism. May include indicators for:[1] • Communication with doctors • Communication with nurses • Responsiveness of hospital staff • Cleanliness and quietness of hospital • Pain control • Communication about medicines • Discharge information • Overall rating of care • Overall recommendation
Physician satisfaction	Requires survey mechanism for providers Example: Percent of referring physicians that "recommend to others"[2]
Medication error rate = (Total number of medication errors / Total number of doses administered) × 10,000	The rate of total medication errors that occurred per 10,000 doses administered.
Patient fall rate = (Total number of falls / Total patient days) × 1,000	Ratio of number of patient falls per 1,000 patient days.
Mortality rates for medical conditions • Acute myocardial infarction (AMI) (IQI* 15) • AMI, without transfer cases (IQI 32) • Congestive heart failure (IQI 16) • Stroke (IQI 17) • Gastrointestinal hemorrhage (IQI 18) • Hip fracture (IQI 19) • Pneumonia (IQI 20)	
Mortality rates for surgical procedures • Esophageal resection (IQI 8) • Pancreatic resection (IQI 9) • Abdominal aortic aneurysm repair (IQI 11) • Coronary artery bypass graft (IQI 12) • Percutaneous transluminal coronary angioplasty (IQI 30) • Carotid endarterectomy (IQI 31) • Craniotomy (IQI 13) • Hip replacement (IQI 14)	

Exhibit continued on next page

Exhibit 8.2   Common Quality Metrics (continued)

Metrics	Notes
Hospital-level procedure utilization rates	
• Cesarean section delivery (IQI 21)	
• Primary Cesarean delivery (IQI 33)	
• Vaginal Birth After Cesarean (VBAC), Uncomplicated (IQI 22)	
• VBAC, All (IQI 34)	
• Laparoscopic cholecystectomy (IQI 23)	
• Incidental appendectomy in elderly (IQI 24)	
• Bi-lateral cardiac catheterization (IQI 25)	
Area-level utilization rates	
• Coronary artery bypass graft (IQI 26)	
• Percutaneous transluminal coronary angioplasty (IQI 27)	
• Hysterectomy (IQI 28)	
• Laminectomy or spinal fusion (IQI 29)	
Volume of procedures	
• Esophageal resection (IQI 1)	
• Pancreatic resection (IQI 2)	
• Abdominal aortic aneurysm repair (IQI 4)	
• Coronary artery bypass graft (IQI 5)	
• Percutaneous transluminal coronary angioplasty (IQI 6)	
• Carotid endarterectomy (IQI 7)	

* IQI = Inpatient quality indicators, as defined by the Agency for Healthcare Research and Quality[3]

Productivity and Efficiency

Beyond quality of care measures, health care managers also use metrics to help monitor and trend productivity and efficiency, as well as identify areas for improvement. In addition, Exhibit 8.3 identifies common management metrics used to identify and improve organizational performance.

Financial Performance

Financial metrics analyze an organization's revenue cycle, operating expenses, profitability and balance sheet and other financial statements to assess financial performance and uncover opportunities to improve overall fiscal health and profitability (Exhibit 8.4). Key performance indicators should be monitored on a regular basis (for example, weekly, monthly, etc.) and trended over time. In addition, when using a trend, the importance of knowing the context (historical events) is vital to ensure appropriate conclusions are taken from the data. For example, if an

Exhibit 8.3   Common Productivity and Efficiency Metrics

Metric	Notes
Maintained bed occupancy rate = Occupied bed days / Maximum possible occupied bed days	Higher rate indicates more efficient use of available resources.
FTEs per adjusted occupied bed = (FTE × IP %) / Average occupied bed days	Cost indicator estimates the number of employees assignable to inpatient beds.
Case mix index (CMI) The average diagnostic related group (DRG) weight for a hospital's patient volume.	Though not itself an actionable metric, CMI indicates an average complexity of care and is used to compare measurements (costs, bed days, etc.) across disparate organizations. Example: A hospital reports an average cost per patient of $1,000 in a given year and its CMI is .85. Its CMI-adjusted cost per patient = $1,000/.85 = $1,176.
Number of CMI-weighted adjusted discharges = Total discharges / CMI	Measures inpatient workload volume.
Monthly surgical cases	Measures workload volume; should be broken out by outpatient and inpatient.
Surgical cases percentage = Total Medicare inpatient surgical cases / Total Medicare inpatient cases × 100	Measures proportion of inpatient care driven by surgical cases.
Inpatient admissions error ratio	Monitors admitting process performance. • Typical goal: <3% error
Outpatient registration error ratio	Monitors registration process performance. • Typical goal: <3% error

administrator were to trend a practice's current ratio over time on a month-by-month basis for the past two years, there would be instances showing highs and lows. The highs and lows may indicate capital expenses, such as the purchase of an MRI unit or the receipt of funds from a loan. Without knowing the practice's activities (historical events) at the high and low points, it would be impossible to attribute the changes to anything specific — making this trend useless for evaluating the current state or predicting the future.

In addition to organizational financial measures, managers often monitor financial performance at the department level in order to pinpoint areas needing improvement. Exhibit 8.5 shows common metrics used to measure the financial well-being of specific departments or cost centers.

Operations and Maintenance

Another category of metrics evaluates cost and efficiency of operating and maintaining the health care facility (Exhibit 8.6).

Patient Demographics

A discussion of health care measures would be incomplete without considering how beneficiary populations are measured. Differences in demographics and patient complexity make "apples to apples" comparisons

Exhibit 8.4 Common Financial Metrics[4]

Metric	Notes
Gross revenue per patient day = Gross revenue / (Discharges × Average LOS)	Measured over a specific time frame (quarter, fiscal year, etc). Higher rate and upward trend is preferred.
Net income per patient day = Net income / (Discharges × Average LOS)	Measured over a specific time frame (quarter, fiscal year, etc). Higher rate and upward trend is preferred.
Operating expense per inpatient day = Operating expense per day = (Total operating expense × IP %) / Total patient days	Cost indicator that estimates the level of resources used to treat a patient during an inpatient day. Lower rate and downward trend is preferred.
Expense per CMI–weighted adjusted discharge = Expense / (CMI × Total discharges)	Usually broken out by: • Labor • Other direct expenses • Medical supply • Other supply • Total expenses
Operating margin (%) = (Total operating revenues – Total operating expenses) / Operating revenue × 100	Identifies relative profitability based on hospital operations.
Long-term debt-to-capitalization (%) = Long-term debt / (Long-term debt + Fund balance) × 100	Percentage of assets funded by long-term debt. Indicates the organization's current leverage and ability to assume additional debt.
Debt-service coverage = (Net income + Interest expense + Depreciation) / (Interest expense + Debt principal)	Measures ability to meet debt service payments from cash flow. Indicates the organization's ability to safely assume additional debt. A higher ratio and upward trend is preferred.
Days cash on hand (liquidity ratio) = (Cash + Cash equivalents + Limited-use assets) / [(Total operating expenses – Depreciation – Amortization) / 365]	Higher ratio indicates a greater ability to meet liabilities.
Debt financing percentage = Total assets – Net assets / Total assets × 100	Indicates what percentage of assets are financed by debt.
Overall charge index = (Average charge per Medicare discharge [case mix adjusted] /U.S. Median × Inpatient revenue %) + (Average charge per APC [risk weight adjusted] / U.S. median × Outpatient revenue %)	Compares charges to U.S. median.
Cost per adjusted patient day	Efficiency measure; should be calculated separately for inpatient and outpatient services.

Exhibit continued on next page

Exhibit 8.4 Common Financial Metrics[4] (continued)

Metric	Notes
Market share percentage = Net patient revenue / Sum of net patient revenues in county × 100	Measures market penetration; can be broken out by product line for more granular view.
Non-government payers percentage	Percent of revenue from sources other than Medicare or Medicaid.
Net operating income (NOI) per FTE = NOI / Total FTEs	Measures how effectively staff time is utilized.
Days in accounts receivable days = Net patient A/R / (Net annual patient revenue / 365)	Measures liquidity, as well as how efficient the organization manages its revenue cycle; lower value and downward trend is desirable.
Current ratio = Current assets / Current liabilities	Liquidity measure of an organization's ability to meet short-term debt obligations.
Quick ratio = Quick assets / Current liabilities	Liquidity measure of an organization's ability to use its "near cash" assets to immediately eliminate its current liabilities. Quick assets include current assets that can be quickly converted to cash at near-book values (e.g., stocks).
Fixed asset turnover ratio = Revenue / Value of fixed assets	Indicates how effectively an organization uses its fixed assets to generate revenue.
Return on assets = Earnings before interest and taxes / Total assets	Measures how effectively assets are used to generate income.
Charge capture quality[5]	Measures charge accuracy; requires audit mechanism; typical benchmark: 98% compliance.
Accounts receivable[5]	Liquidity measure; Percent over 90 days (typical benchmark: <20%); percent over 120 days (typical benchmark: <10%); percent over 1 year (typical benchmark: <2%).
Clean claims submission[5]	Percentage of claims accepted on first submission; higher rate shortens revenue cycle; typical benchmark: 97%.
Payer turnaround time[5]	Typical benchmark: 7 to 10 days (electronic), <45 days (paper).
Denial overturn ratio[5]	Percentage of denied claims eventually accepted; typical benchmark: 95%.
Underpayments overturn ratio[5]	Percentage of underpaid claims paid at full amount upon resubmission; typical benchmark: 95%.
Bad debt expense[5]	Percentage of accounts receivable written off as uncollectible; typical benchmark: <4% of gross revenue, <2% of net revenue.

Exhibit 8.5   Common Departmental Financial Metrics[6]

Department	Metrics
Medical/Surgical ICU	• Average LOS (days) • Hours worked per discharge • Labor expense per patient discharge
Emergency Room (ER)	• Percentage of ER patients admitted to total ER visits • Percentage of ER patients admitted to total discharges • Hours worked per patient visit • Total expense per patient visit
Family Practice	• Hours worked per patient visit • Labor expense per patient visit
Home Health	• Client visits • Client visits per day • Hours worked per client visit • Labor expense per client visit • Total expense per client visit
Operating Room (OR)	• Inpatient OR cases per 100 general acute discharges • Percentage of ambulatory surgery cases to all OR cases • Operating minutes per OR case • OR cases per OR day • Hours worked per OR case • Labor expense per OR case • Total expenses per OR case
Laboratory Services	• Inpatient billed tests per CMI-weighted discharge • Percentage of outreach billed tests to total billed tests • Total expense per 100 billed tests
Imaging Services	• Procedures per room per day • Percentage of inpatient procedures to total procedures • Percentage of portable procedures to total procedures • Inpatient procedures per 100 CMI-weighted discharges • Hours worked per 100 procedures • Total expense per 100 procedures
Pharmacy Services	• Doses billed per CMI-weighted discharge • Drug expense per 100 CMI-weighted discharges • Total expense per 100 CMI-weighted discharges
Materials Management	• Hours worked per 100 adjusted discharges • Percentage of all division expenses to hospital expenses

Exhibit 8.6   Common Health Facilities Metrics[7]

Management Area	Metrics
Facilities Operations/Maintenance	• Hours worked per 100 adjusted discharges • Labor expense per 100 adjusted discharges • Labor expense per 1,000 gross square feet maintained • Total expense per 1,000 gross square feet maintained • Percentage of division expenses to total hospital expenses
Plant/Ground Maintenance	• Hours worked per 100 adjusted discharges • Labor expense per 100 adjusted discharges • Labor expense per 1,000 gross square feet maintained • Total expense per 1,000 gross square feet maintained
Clinical Engineering	• Hours worked per beds served • Labor expense per beds served • Hours worked per 100 devices serviced • Labor expense per 100 devices serviced • Hours worked per 100 work requests • Labor expense per 100 work requests
Housekeeping /Environmental Services	• Hours worked per adjusted discharge • Labor expense per adjusted discharge • Hours worked per 1,000 net square feet cleaned • Labor expense per 1,000 net square feet cleaned • Percentage of division expenses to total hospital expenses
Security	• Hours worked per adjusted discharge • Labor expense per adjusted discharge • Hours worked per 1,000 gross square patrolled • Labor expense per 1,000 gross square feet patrolled
Dietary/Food Service	• Hours worked per adjusted discharge • Labor expense per adjusted discharge • Hours worked per 100 meals served • Labor expense per 100 meals served • Percentage of division expenses to total hospital expenses
Materials Management	• Hours worked per 100 adjusted discharges • Labor expense per 100 adjusted discharges • Stock inventory turns • Percentage of division expenses to total hospital expenses

Exhibit 8.7   Risk-Adjustment Models[8]

Model	Source	Notes
Adjusted Clinical Groups	Johns Hopkins University	Clusters beneficiaries with similar comorbidities into groups with similar clinical characteristics, resource intensity.
Burden of Illness Score	MEDecision, Inc.	Groups care into episodes that share services, medications and acuity.
Clinical Complexity Index	Solucient, Inc.	Categorizes patients according to age, acuity, comorbidity, admissions and diagnostic category.
Diagnostic Cost Groups	DxCG, Inc.	Provides multiple linear regression models that use patient demographics and diagnoses to explain health care expenditures.
Episode Risk Groups	Symmetry Health Systems	Provides risk scores for patients based on age, gender and history of care.
General Diagnostic Groups (GDGs)	Allegiance, LLC	Predicts health care costs based on diagnostic categories and claims histories.

among different populations difficult. However, several proprietary models have been developed that classify patients according to risk-adjusted categories in order to normalize data (Exhibit 8.7). By compensating for population differences, these data models allow for meaningful comparisons across populations and health care organizations. Risk-adjustment models have two main functions:

1. To predict the costs of caring for different population groups. Such analysis is especially valuable for capitation-based systems, such as HMOs.

2. To facilitate efficiency comparisons (also known as economic profiling) across disparate organizations by normalizing patient data according to demographics and complexity.

Other Key Hospital Ratios

There are many hospital metrics and ratios derived from internal reports and financial statements; however, in most hospitals, there is a short list of "key" ratios used to monitor the financial condition of the organization.

Excess Margin

Definition: Profit margin related to overall revenues.

Goal: Higher the better.

$$\frac{(\text{Total operating revenue} + \text{Non-operating revenues} - \text{Total operating expenses})}{(\text{Total operating revenues} + \text{Non-operating revenues}) \times 100}$$

Cushion Ratio

Definition: Available cash and total debt service relationship.

Goal: Higher the better.

$$\frac{(\text{Cash} + \text{Short-term investments} + \text{Unrestricted long-term investments})}{(\text{Principal} + \text{Interest payments})}$$

Average Payment Period in Days

Definition: The length of time, in days, it takes to pay the bills.

Goal: Lower the better.

$$\frac{\text{Current liabilities}}{(\text{Total expenses} - \text{Depreciation}) / 365}$$

Average Age of Plant in Years

Definition: Relative age of the facility and capital equipment.

Goal: Lower the better.

$$\frac{\text{Accumulated depreciation}}{\text{Depreciation expense}}$$

Debt-to-Capitalization

Definition: Percentage of debt compared to net assets.

Goal: Lower the better.

$$\frac{\text{Long-term debt}}{(\text{Long-term debt} + \text{Net assets}) \times 100}$$

Capital Expense

Definition: Percentage of the purchase of fixed assets to total expenses

Goal: Downward trend is better; depends on many practice factors.

$$\frac{(\text{Interest expense} + \text{Depreciation expense})}{(\text{Total expenses} \times 100)}$$

Personnel Costs as a Percentage of Total Operating Revenues (also known as labor compensation ratio)

$$\frac{(\text{Total cost of salaries/wages} + \text{Total cost of benefits} + \text{Total cost of professional fees})}{\text{Total operating revenues}}$$

Bad Debt Expense as a Percentage of Total Operating Revenues

$$\frac{\text{Bad debt expense}}{\text{Total operating revenues}}$$

It's important to keep in mind that no two health care organizations are alike, and no two will need to monitor the same metrics in the same way. Likewise, many measures will only need to be monitored temporarily, until a process is fixed and performance improves. Monitoring a few metrics at a time will yield better results than trying to measure every process at once. Managers should strive to focus their efforts on those key performance indicators that truly impact their organization's mission.

Notes

1. Centers for Medicare & Medicaid Services, Hospital CAHPS 2007 Survey.

2. John R. Griffith and Kenneth R. White, *The Well-Managed Healthcare Organization* (Chicago: Health Administration Press, 2002).

3. Agency for Healthcare Research and Quality, www.ahrq.gov (Accessed April 30, 2007).

4. Marian C. Jennings, ed., *Health Care Strategy for Uncertain Times* (San Francisco: Jossey-Bass, 2000), pp. 155–179.

5. Jim Quist and Brian Robertson, "Key Revenue Cycle Metrics," *Healthcare Financial Management* (September 2004).

6. Jennings, *Health Care Strategy for Uncertain Times.*

7. Health Facilities Management 16:5 (May 2003).

8. HSR: Health Services Research 39:4, part I (August 2004): 987–988.

Chapter 9

Talking Numbers to Physicians

"The most important thing in communication is to hear what isn't being said."

— Peter Drucker

The value of memos, executive summaries, general correspondence, e-mail, graphs, charts, exhibits, presentations and dashboards cannot be understated. In particular, physician decisions, the physician–administrator relationship, and staff behavior determine practice success; therefore, it's imperative the administrator communicate efficiently and effectively to all members of the practice. Communication builds trust, improves decision-making, encourages an open and honest interaction and develops buy-in.

Focus on the purpose, scope and audience are necessary first steps. Ultimately, the purpose of presenting numbers to physicians is to efficiently relay important information. Physicians are most productive when treating patients; therefore, time reading lengthy explanations or deciphering busy graphs and charts is time wasted. Concise, brief and clear communication should be your goal. The scope of your topic should be specific and related. Trying to present multiple, unrelated items on a single chart would only frustrate and potentially confuse a reader — thereby wasting the reader's time and teaching him or her to disregard future presentations. The information-rich environment we live in makes us all susceptible to information overload (that is, when there is too much information to process, associate and commit to memory, information loses its value).

The educational and experiential background and your relationship with the audience must be considered when determining how and what to present. In addition, recognizing the differences in how people process information is necessary for effective communication (that is, some people process information via listening, reading and/or visual aids). When preparing written documents, the following characteristics will help ensure your message is delivered efficiently: (1) readability; (2) accuracy; (3) interesting writing; and (4) professional look, feel and style.[1]

Readability refers to the flow, organization, word choice and sentence length, whereas accuracy is the precision, attention to detail, and exactness of the content.[1] Interesting writing will keep your audience's attention,

Exhibit 9.1   Methods for Emphasizing Data[2]

• Bold	• Line width (thick)
• Underline	• Word orientation (slanting)
• Italics	• Size (large)
• Hue (darker text)	• Enclosure (lines/shapes)
• Color intensity (bright)	

increase the chances of your document being read from start to finish and will entertain.[1] After all, if you're going to take the time to write a report, its value is increased if your audience retains highlights. And a professional look, feel and style provide you and your report with credibility (if the report is sloppy, how much do you think your audience will trust the findings and recommendations?).[1]

Communication of data requires prioritization and emphasis (see Exhibit 9.1). Data should be ranked according to importance, and the most important data should be emphasized. The Pareto Principle can be used as a guide to select data for emphasis — 80 percent of practice variation is caused by 20 percent of practice activities.[3]

For example, if staff turnover is higher than the median found in MGMA's *Performance and Practices of Successful Medical Groups*, it may be possible to identify a list of potential causes. From this list and the context/dynamics in the practice, it is also possible to identify the "most likely" causes — this is the Pareto Principle at work. That is, only a few causes are truly affecting the bulk of staff turnover. In addition, if the data is numeric, it is possible to graph in a Pareto chart (a bar chart with values ranked from highest to lowest). Oftentimes, however, the item for emphasis is not simply based on the numbers; rather, it's a judgment call based on the situation, the numbers and the message the presenter wants to portray. Many methods are available to draw attention to specific data.

Memos and Executive Summaries

Memos and executive summaries are one or two pages in length and include all the sections of a typical document in short form. Memos tend to be less formal and loosely formatted, whereas executive summaries should adhere to the structure of a formal report (Exhibit 9.2).

General Correspondence and E-mails

These formats should follow the KISS principle — keep it short and simple (Exhibit 9.3). For example, if there were multiple important issues that needed to be addressed by the physician staff, in keeping with the KISS principle, only one topic should be addressed in detail per e-mail or correspondence. That is, they should be one page in length and cover one topic. General correspondence and e-mails should be used to relay a single

Exhibit 9.2   Example Structures of Memos and Executive Summaries[1]

From	Introduction	Statement of purpose and rationale
To	Background	Theoretical framework
Subject	Definitions	Research questions
Body	Problem statement	Key terms and variables
Salutation	Procedure	Definition of population of interest
Signature	Results	Description of research design
	Examples	Assumptions and limitations
	Discussion	Implications of findings
		Dissemination of findings

Exhibit 9.3   Guidelines for Correspondence and E-mails

- Keep it short and simple (KISS)
- Professional style
- Limit acronyms/symbols
- Discretion and patience
- One page, one topic
- Proper grammar, punctuation, and spelling

thought, piece of information or topic using the least number of words with few graphs/charts. In addition, the writing should be professional and adhere to accepted methods of grammar, punctuation and spelling. In particular, the style of writing in e-mails has evolved into a unique use of acronyms and symbols (e.g., LOL = laugh out loud or smiley faces using a combination of keys). E-mail acronyms and symbols should be used sparingly for emphasis. Because e-mails are easily shared (forwarded), the importance of maintaining professionalism cannot be understated — how you are perceived will be decided by your e-mail style. A poor first impression can easily result from a poorly crafted e-mail message. Furthermore, the use of e-mail requires discretion and patience due to its capabilities and speed of delivery. Because most e-mail is short, sending a lengthy narrative with multiple attachments will quickly prompt a receiver to hit "delete." And an e-mail sent in haste or in the heat of the moment can easily snowball into a serious problem you might regret (for example, sending an emotional e-mail with excessive exclamation marks and four-letter words to your boss). Also, unlike any other method of communication, aside from verbal, once the e-mail has been sent, the opportunity to proofread or edit has passed.

Graphs, Charts and Tables   Graphs, charts and tables (visual aids) are excellent tools for supporting a message but when used poorly, can slow decision-making. That is, they can help, hinder, clarify or confuse.[4] Each visual aid should be used with a clear purpose in mind (Exhibit 9.4). For instance, aids can be used to persuade, highlight, explain or orient.[5]

Exhibit 9.4   Chart Selection[4]

Chart Type	Percent of Time	Practicality Rating
Bar chart	25%	High
Column chart (histogram)	25%	High
Line chart/graph	25%	High
Dot chart (scatter plot)	10%	High
Pie chart	5%	Low
Combination chart	10%	Varies

Exhibit 9.5   Key Principles of Using Visual Aids

- Fewer is better.[4]
- What should the audience get out of it?[4]
- What should the audience "take away"?
- Bigger is better.[5]
- Keep it short and simple.[5]
- Make it memorable.[5]

Visual aids are ideally suited to display benchmarking results such as percentage of total, ranking, changes over time, frequency distribution and correlation (relationship between factors).[4] Exhibit 9.4 recommends the percentage of time a particular type of chart should be used based on its practicality.[4]

Several key principles should be followed to effectively use visual aids (Exhibit 9.5). First, "fewer is better" because the more visual aids used, the less people will retain.[4] Second, concern should be placed on "what the audience should get out of it" versus "what is put into it."[4] Third, "bigger is better" — this should help to ensure the visual aid is easy to see and read.[5] Fourth, the KISS principle applies again — keep it short and simple so it's easy for the audience to understand. Fifth, "make it memorable." And sixth, visuals should "stand on their own" — that is, the purpose, title, timeframe and scope should be easy to find and understand (if possible, a short narrative should be included to describe and explain).

Depending on what you want to show, certain visual aid formats are more appropriate (Exhibit 9.6). For instance, graphs should be used when the message in the information is clearly represented by the shape of the data or to demonstrate relationships between multiple types of data.[2] Tables are best for presenting specific numbers, comparing numbers or to show

Exhibit 9.6   Recommended Methods for Presenting Data[1]

If you want to present:	Use a:
Frequencies (discrete data)	Bar chart
Frequencies (continuous data)	Histogram
Percentages (relative frequencies)	Pie chart
Trends (continuous data)	Line graph
Relationships (between two variables)	Scatter plot

Exhibit 9.7   Benchmarking Illustration

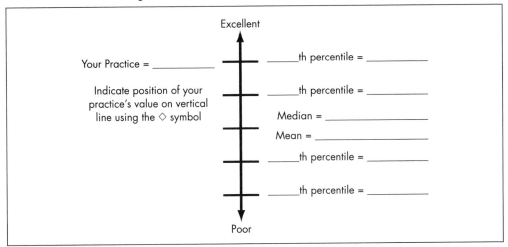

different types of numbers (for example, relative value units [RVUs] and relative weighted products [RWPs] by inpatient work center).[2]

In addition, a visual aid that presents detailed information in an intuitive format is ideal for presenting meaningful information that can stand on its own. That is, the visual aid doesn't require significant explanation or a lengthy description, and the chances of misinterpretation are minimal. Exhibit 9.7 is a template for illustrating a practice measure and associated benchmarks.

Presentations   Nowadays, presentations are usually constructed using software applications such as Microsoft PowerPoint. When developing a presentation, care should be taken to consider the length of time available/desired, audience and intended message. In addition, the intended purpose should be determined prior to the start of writing the presentation because this will help when selecting and organizing content. For instance, a presenta-

Exhibit 9.8   Presentation Considerations

- Limit to less than 1 hour (provide at least 10 minutes for questions and answers); if you tell your audience the presentation will be 50 minutes, stick to your 50 minutes.

- Identify audience and design around audience (what are your audience's expectations, background, education, etc.?).

- Determine purpose of presentation.

- Ensure that font of text is:

  — Consistent throughout.

  — Large enough to be seen from a distance.

- Limit number of characters per slide (too much text is distracting and difficult to see).

- Special effects should be used sparingly (using animation, action settings and sound can be distracting).

- Images should be used in moderation but can be used to consume white space (real-life pictures are preferable to clip art).

- Limit the total number of slides based on other considerations (how much time do you have and how long does it take to present a slide?).

- Structure presentation logically (title, outline/agenda, content, summary, Q&A).

- Maintain professionalism, dress properly and don't use slang or technical jargon.

- Move around (try not to stand in one place like a statue).

- Use hands to talk in a mature manner, but remember this is not a karate demonstration so don't get carried away.

- Plan, prepare and take a break from your presentation, then reread and reproof.

- Arrive early to the presentation room (walk around room to get comfortable with it and check to make sure equipment works and presentation can be read from the back of the room).

- Don't read from presentation; use it to supplement, illustrate and organize.

tion is an excellent tool for: introducing a new process, explaining the need for change or a decision, reinforcing an idea or position, highlighting a problem, presenting a sequence of events or recommending a new course of action or process.[2] Additionally, several considerations should be addressed to maximize the value, credibility and overall readability of a presentation (Exhibit 9.8).

How many slides should be in a presentation? This is a common question and is dependent on many factors; however, a good rule of thumb is 2 to 3 minutes per slide.[5] Other factors that can affect this formula are related to technique, for instance, talking too fast or reading from the slides.

Giving a good presentation that is memorable and valuable can be an elusive goal. Exhibit 9.9 identifies the top 10 presentation killers; therefore,

Exhibit 9.9 Presentation Killers (Things to Avoid)[6]

- Monotone voice
- Reading
- Being boring, uninteresting
- The "and-uh" syndrome (uh, um, you know…)
- Lack of preparation: being unorganized, rambling, becoming sidetracked
- Nervous habits: fidgeting, swaying, annoying body language
- Speaking too long, going overtime
- Repeating, repeating, repeating
- Not making eye contact
- Not relating to the audience; no audience involvement, not tuned in to the audience's needs

they should be avoided at all costs. To counter these pitfalls, practice, practice, practice. This doesn't mean practice a single presentation until it's memorized — this can be dangerous if something unexpected happens during the presentation. What this means is take every opportunity to give presentations — the old adage, "practice makes perfect" definitely applies.

Dashboards   Dashboards are typically visual representations of metrics, benchmarks, practice activities and process status in a single (or few) display screens (see Exhibit 9.10). For example, an RVU dashboard might show physician work RVUs by physician in a line graph with an exhibit populated by the attached number of RVUs. In addition, the line graph might contain a line representing the practice average and a line depicting the MGMA average for the practice's specialty. The dashboard example in Exhibit 9.10 is from the MGMA Medical Practice Simulation online course. It shows five metrics from the "Revenue by Payer" menu option that comply with the tenets of an effective report: accurate, brief, clear and timely.[7]

In addition, this dashboard has multiple layers (see menu in lower left of exhibit) for displaying different practice metrics; when the cursor is placed over chart areas, additional information is automatically displayed.

Ultimately, a dashboard functions as a "one-stop-shop" for quickly monitoring, comparing and identifying current status and potential problems — a dashboard is an excellent "early warning" tool. Nowadays, many practices have automated dashboards that use Web (Internet, intranet and extranet) and database technologies. This enables users to access the dashboard from any PC with Internet connectivity. In addition, the benefits of Web-enabling a dashboard permits custom calculations, flexibility and

Exhibit 9.10   Example Dashboard from the MGMA Virtual Medical Practice Course

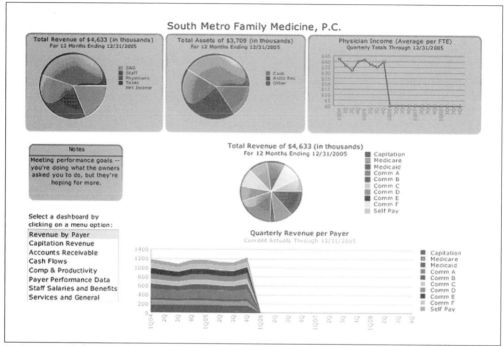

Regis Learning Solutions. Used with permission.

real-time availability of practice measures. Dashboards improve management capabilities by automating data collection, display and analysis. That is, they eliminate tedious hours of number crunching and analysis and speed decision response time driven by readily available, real-time practice information.

Notes

1. D.L. Kelley, *Measurement Made Accessible: A Research Approach Using Qualitative, Quantitative, and Quality Improvement Methods* (Thousand Oaks, CA: SAGE Publications, 1999); and S. Plichta, Old Dominion University (Norfolk, VA), personal communications (2001 to 2005).

2. S. Few, *Show Me the Numbers: Designing Exhibits and Graphs to Enlighten* (Oakland, CA: Analytics Press, 2004).

3. D. Balestracci and J. Barlow, *Quality Improvement, Practical Applications for Medical Group Practice*, 2nd ed. (Englewood, CO: Center for Research in Ambulatory Health Care Administration, 1998).

4. G. Zelanzny, *Say It with Charts*, 4th ed. (New York: McGraw-Hill, 2001.

5. P. Reimold and C. Reimold, *The Short Road to Great Presentations* (Piscataway, NJ: IEEE Press, 2003).

6. S. Gaulke, *101 Ways to Captivate a Business Audience* (New York: American Management Association, 1997).

7. E.J. Pavlock, *Financial Management for Medical Groups*, 2nd ed. (Englewood, CO: MGMA, 2000).

Chapter 10

Performance and Practices of Successful Medical Groups

"The price is what you pay; the value is what you receive."
— *Unknown*

Better-performing practices are selected from the domains of profitability and operating costs; productivity, capacity and staffing; accounts receivable and collections; and managed care. Selection criteria for a better performer in the profitability and operating costs category are (1) greater than the median for total medical revenue after operating costs per FTE physician and (2) less than the median for operating cost, not including nonphysician providers, per medical procedure, inside the practice. Criteria for productivity, capacity and staffing in "nonsurgical" specialties are (1) greater than the median for in-house medical procedures per square foot and (2) greater than the median for total gross charges per FTE physician. Criteria for productivity, capacity and staffing in "surgical" specialties are (1) greater than the median for total medical procedures per FTE physician; (2) greater than the median for total gross charges per FTE physician; and (3) anesthesia practices, greater than the median for American Society of Anesthesiology units per FTE physician. And the criteria for accounts receivable and collections are (1) less than the median for percent of total accounts receivable (A/R) over 120 days; (2) greater than the median for adjusted fee-for-service (FFS) collection percentage; and (3) less than the median for months gross FFFS charges in A/R.

Traits of Successful Medical Groups[1]

Patient satisfaction and quality orientation are based on the premise that patients are the first reason why medical groups exist. Therefore, organizational systems must be designed to meet patient needs by treating the patient–practice relationship as most important while maintaining all other business relationships (Exhibit 10.1). Ultimately, dedication to patients requires quality of care coupled with excellent service. Excellent service, however, is determined by the perception of the patient — not the practice, physicians or staff.

Exhibit 10.1   Patient Satisfaction and Quality Orientation of Successful Medical Groups[1]

Behaviors
• Formal patient satisfaction survey program
• Established protocol for resolving patient complaints
• Internal peer review program/observance of evidence-based clinical methods
• Regular coding and documentation reviews to ensure compliance
• Participation in disease registries
• Continuing education requirements for physicians and staff
• Essential practice information is made available to patients in paper and Web formats
• Extended hours for patient convenience
• In-house diagnostic services for patient convenience
• Customer service/communication training for physicians and staff
Metrics
• Patient satisfaction assessment for providers, staff and facilities
• Board certification for physicians
• Coding profiles for physicians
• Documentation standards
• Conformance with clinical care guidelines/protocols

Operational and business discipline is based on sound financial management to ensure profitability. Continuous improvement should focus on operational methods that promote efficiency and cost effectiveness, eliminate waste and reduce error, and involve physicians and staff in financial and cost management (see Exhibit 10.2).

The purpose of focusing on provider productivity is to ensure provider activities drive revenue (Exhibit 10.3). This also includes creating a system to leverage physician effort while monitoring productivity.

The purpose of innovation and improvement is to identify more advanced methods of doing business. This also includes evaluating operational activities for efficiency and quality, assessing organizational and provider performance to uncover improvement opportunities, promote provider and staff buy-in and reduce resistance to change (Exhibit 10.4).

The purpose of entrepreneurialism and growth perspective is to strive to expand the revenue base. This also includes being competitive and leading the market by taking risks as a group (see Exhibit 10.5).

The purpose of aligned incentives is to create individual and collective incentives to promote achievement of organizational goals. This also

Exhibit 10.2 Operational and Business Discipline of Successful Medical Groups[1]

Behaviors	
• Perform annual budget and business planning	• Monitor A/R and cash flow performance
• Incorporate financial goals into strategic plan	• Treat health plans as business partners, not enemies
• Monitor performance against budget	• Negotiate assertively/hold health plans accountable
• Set financial objectives to exceed peers	• Scrutinize all expenses, regularly bid vendor contracts, and participate in group purchasing organizations
• Document all policies and procedures	
• Implement performance management plans for employees	• Reward physicians and staff for cost savings
	• Maximize use of information systems and office automation technologies
• Reward employees for organizational contributions and eliminate poor performers	
	• Develop formal marketing programs

Metrics	
• Revenue and collections	• Staff turnover rates
• Total operating expense, support staff expenses and general operating expenses	• A/R aging
	• Adjusted collection percent
• Expenses as a percent of revenue	• Denial rates
• Revenue after operating expenses	• Payer mix
• Physician/provider compensation	• Revenue and expense per relative value unit
• Staff per FTE physician	

Exhibit 10.3 Focus on Provider Productivity of Successful Medical Groups[1]

Behaviors	
• Utilize productivity-based compensation programs for providers and staff	• Develop practice cultural values that promote work ethic
• Set productivity expectations for providers and staff	• Implement a hiring process that ensures new physicians will embrace productivity expectations
• Use nonphysician providers to leverage physician skills	• Design operational system and facilities, such as scheduling methods, office automation and extended hours, to facilitate productivity
• Maintain optimal staffing level to maximize efficiency	
• Develop mentoring program for new physicians	• Evaluate physicians for optimal coding patterns to minimize lost revenue due to inappropriate under coding
• Ensure new physicians are credentialed before beginning billable work	

Metrics	
• RVUs per physician	• Billable days per month per physician
• Encounters or procedures per physician	• No-show rates
• Revenue per physician	• Referral patterns and trends
• Staff per physician	

Exhibit 10.4   Innovation and Improvement in Successful Medical Groups[1]

Behaviors	
• Benchmark internally against past performance and externally against peers • Develop formal business and project plans to ensure efficient management and implementation of change initiatives	• Invest in technology and office automation prudently • Seek mutually beneficial collaborations when independent action is not possible • Test operational changes before full implementation
Metrics	
• Advances in process efficiency • Status of technology adoption compared to peers, such as use and integration of electronic health records	• Status of facility updates, such as the time since the last remodel or expansion

Exhibit 10.5   Entrepreneurialism and Growth Perspective of Successful Medical Groups[1]

Behaviors	
• Maintain and expand relationships with referral sources • Anticipate community needs, such as developing new facilities in population growth areas • Exploit advantages offered by new technologies • Maximize profitability of ancillary services • Nurture relationships with potential business partners including hospitals, other groups, professional service providers and bankers	• Perform thorough and complete business planning in connection with new business endeavors • Participate in community health programs and charitable events along with professional associations • Maintain a managed marketing program • Adapt successful behaviors of other medical groups
Metrics	
• Revenue increase per year • New patients per month • Additions to new service offerings and addition of new physicians	• Revenue and expense per ancillary service line • Return on investment per marketing program • Referral physician satisfaction

includes ensuring key operating systems support organizational objectives while seeking goal alignment among physicians and staff (see Exhibit 10.6).

The purpose of having a clear vision and cohesive culture is to define the direction of the organization.[1] This also includes instilling a common value system among physicians and staff, working as a team to achieve organizational objectives and confronting issues that cause dissatisfaction (see Exhibit 10.7).

Exhibit 10.6   Aligned Incentives of Successful Medical Groups[1]

Behaviors	
• Provide market-based compensation for staff with incentives for achievement of individual and organizational goals • Develop staff bonus programs that reward at the time goals are achieved rather than just at the end of the year • Disclose organizational performance information to staff, such as financial statements and patient satisfaction survey results	• Involve staff in operational planning to enlist their support in achieving goals and improving performance • Acknowledge (show visible appreciation) individual staff contributions to organizational success • Involve physicians in operational and business improvement initiatives • Design policies and procedures to ensure consistency with organizational goals and values
Metrics	
• Support staff costs per physician • Physician compensation to production ratios such as compensation per RVU • Physician satisfaction	• Employee/staff satisfaction • Operating efficiencies such as claims processed per billing staff

Exhibit 10.7   Clear Vision and Cohesive Culture of Successful Medical Groups[1]

Behaviors	
• Conduct comprehensive, formal strategic planning exercises regularly and establish explicit group values and articulate the vision • Remind physicians and staff of goals and vision • Conduct regular stakeholder needs assessments of patients, physicians and staff • Assess alignment of expectations among physicians and staff	• Ensure practice leadership connects with and establishes and nurtures relationships with staff • Conduct formal teambuilding exercises • Create opportunities for physicians and staff to interact socially • Identify a cultural profile • Recruit physicians and staff for cultural fit
Metrics	
• Cultural profile • Strategic planning updates	• Physician and staff satisfaction • Physician and staff voluntary turnover rates

The environment most practices must contend with are, in general, very similar: declining reimbursement, rising costs, lack of qualified staff and complicated and ever changing regulatory and payer issues.[2] However, better-performing practices typically have more satisfied patients, more fulfilling work environments for physicians and staff and better economic outcomes.[2] Among better-performing practices, operational and business discipline was identified as most the important overall factor in determining practice success, and, in particular, superior management was considered the most influential.[2]

Profitability and Operating Costs

Many practices identified as better performers have provided tips for maximizing revenue and accurately allocating, analyzing, understanding and controlling costs.[2] In general, several steps are associated with better-performing practices (see Exhibit 10.8).

Practices selected by MGMA as better performing in the profitability and operating costs category provided several of their keys to success (see Exhibits 10.9 and 10.10). These keys were used by real practices and resulted in success through best practices. The use of these keys does not guarantee success, but they will increase a practice's potential.

Total Gross Charges per FTE Physician

Goal: Higher the better.

$$\frac{\text{Total gross charges}}{\text{Total FTE physicians}}$$

Gross Charges per Medical Procedure Inside the Practice

Goal: Higher the better.

$$\frac{\text{Total gross charges (generated from inside the practice)}}{\text{Total number of medical procedures (provided from inside the practice)}}$$

Total Employed Support Staff Cost per FTE Physician

Goal: Depends on the practice; however, according to the research, a balance between practice productivity and number of support staff is necessary.

$$\frac{\text{Total employed support staff cost}}{\text{Total FTE physicians}}$$

Total General Operating Cost per FTE Physician

Goal: Lower the better.

$$\frac{\text{Total general operating cost}}{\text{Total FTE physicians}}$$

Total Operating Cost per FTE Physician

Goal: Lower the better.

$$\frac{\text{Total operating cost}}{\text{Total FTE physicians}}$$

Total Medical Revenue After Operation Cost per FTE Physician

Goal: Higher the better.

$$\frac{(\text{Total medical revenue} - \text{Operating cost})}{\text{Total FTE physicians}}$$

Exhibit 10.8   Seven Steps to Better Profitability and Operating Costs Performance[3]

1. Detailed cost accounting	5. Effective managed care contracting
2. Transaction costing	6. Effective coding
3. Zero-based budgeting	7. Improved service delivery
4. Physician incentives	

Exhibit 10.9   Keys to Profitability and Operating Costs Success[2]

- Physicians who see their patients in the hospital
- Growing community
- Unique approaches to billing and staff retention
- Long-time employees
- Entrepreneurial culture
- Staffing mix that allows for greater productivity
- Physician who are involved in practice operations
- Strong positive presence in the community
- Billing staff responsible for a physician site

- Visionary leader
- Team approach to practice operations
- Strong emphasis placed on efficiencies
- Working smarter, not harder
- World-wide fellowship program
- Shift in culture
- Established physicians mentoring others
- Change in staff recruitment procedures

Exhibit 10.10   Other Profitability and Operating Costs Measures[4]

- Medical procedures inside the practice to total gross charges
- Surgical procedures inside the practice to total gross charges
- Laboratory procedures to total gross charges
- Radiology procedures to total gross charges
- Total gross charges per total procedures
- Total gross charges per surgical/anesthesia procedure inside the practice
- Total gross charges per clinical lab and pathology procedure inside the practice
- Total gross charges per diagnostic radiology/imaging procedure inside the practice
- Net FFS revenue per FTE physician
- Net capitation revenue per FTE physician

- Other medical revenue per FTE physician
- Nonmedical revenue per FTE physician
- Total medical revenue after operating cost as a percent of total medical revenue
- Total nonphysician provider cost per FTE physician
- Total support staff cost as a percentage of total medical revenue
- Total nonphysician provider cost as a percentage of total medical revenue
- Total provider cost per medical procedure inside the practice
- Total provider cost per surgical/anesthesia procedure inside the practice
- Total provider cost per clinical laboratory and pathology procedure inside the practice
- Total provider cost per diagnostic radiology/imaging procedure inside the practice

Note: There are several other measures involving procedures conducted outside the practice that should also be considered, particularly when analyzing revenue generating centers/activities

Total Operating Cost as a Percentage of Total Medical Revenue

Goal: Lower the better.

$$\frac{\text{Total operating cost} \times 100}{\text{Total medical revenue}}$$

Productivity, Capacity and Staffing

Many practices identified as better performers have provided tips for maximizing physician productivity, optimizing capacity and investing time and energy into their support staff.[2] Physician productivity is the primary revenue-generating activity of a practice that consists of patient visits/encounters and procedures.[2] Better-performing practices focus on capacity by investing in the proper resources and optimizing the efficient use of those resources.[2] The common characteristics of better-performing practices are related to infrastructure, policies and procedures, staffing numbers and mix, hiring, training, physician compensation methods, information systems and patient satisfaction.[2] In general, there are several steps that are associated with better-performing practices (see Exhibit 10.11).

Practices selected by MGMA as better performing in the productivity, capacity and staffing category provided several of their keys to success (see Exhibits 10.12 and 10.13). These keys were used by real practices and resulted in success through best practices. The use of these keys does not guarantee success, but they will increase a practice's potential.

Total Gross Charges per FTE Physician

Goal: Higher the better.

$$\frac{\text{Total gross charges}}{\text{Total FTE physicians}}$$

Total Medical Revenue per FTE Physician

Goal: Higher the better.

$$\frac{\text{Total medical revenue}}{\text{Total FTE physicians}}$$

Physician Work RVUs per FTE Physician

Goal: Higher the better.

$$\frac{\text{Total physician work RVUs}}{\text{Total FTE physicians}}$$

Exhibit 10.11   Five Steps to Better Productivity, Capacity and Staffing Performance[3]

1. Build capacity	4. Patient satisfaction
2. Compensation formula	5. Scheduling system
3. Appropriate staffing	

Exhibit 10.12   Keys to Productivity, Capacity and Staffing Success[2]

- Educate staff on procedures and treatments
- Have pharmacist and technicians onsite
- Have well-trained nurses
- Have dedicated, hardworking and involved physicians
- Involve staff in decision-making
- Provide staff incentive plans
- As a group, focus on improving operational efficiencies
- Provide relaxed and comfortable atmosphere for patients

- Have good working relationship with local hospital(s)
- Have experienced staff
- Provide state-of-the-art care
- Hire the right team
- Benchmark for continued improvement
- Implement technology to improve service and productivity
- Use information technology

Exhibit 10.13   Other Productivity, Capacity and Staffing Measures[2,4]

- Total RVUs per FTE physician
- Patient per FTE physician
- Total nonphysician providers per FTE physician
- General administrative staff per FTE physician
- Managed care administrative staff per FTE physician
- Medical records staff per FTE physician
- Clinical support staff per FTE physician
- Clinical laboratory staff per FTE physician
- Radiology and imaging staff per FTE physician

- Inside medical/surgical procedures per FTE clinical support staff
- Medical procedures inside the practice per FTE physician
- Surgical procedures inside the practice per FTE physician
- All laboratory procedures per FTE physician
- All radiology/imaging procedures per FTE physician
- Total square feet per FTE physician

Patient Encounters per FTE Physician

Goal: Depends on the practice, specialty and patient mix; typically, the higher the better.

$$\frac{\text{Total number of patient encounters}}{\text{Total FTE physicians}}$$

In-house Professional Procedures per Square Foot

Goal: Higher the better.

$$\frac{\text{Total number of professional (physician/provider) procedures}}{\text{Total square footage of entire practice}}$$

Total Procedures per Square Foot

Goal: Higher the better.

$$\frac{\text{Total number of all types of procedures}}{\text{Total square footage of entire practice}}$$

Total Procedures per FTE Physician

Goal: Higher the better.

$$\frac{\text{Total number of all types of procedures}}{\text{Total FTE physicians}}$$

Total Procedures per Patient

Goal: Higher the better.

$$\frac{\text{Total number of all types of procedures}}{\text{Total number of unique patients}}$$

Total Employed Support Staff per FTE Physician

Goal: Depends on the practice; however, according to the research, a balance between practice productivity and number of support staff is necessary.

$$\frac{\text{Total number of employed support staff}}{\text{Total FTE physicians}}$$

Total Employed Support Staff Cost per FTE Physician

Goal: Depends on the practice; however, according to the research, a balance between practice productivity and number of support staff is necessary.

$$\frac{\text{Total employed support staff cost}}{\text{Total FTE physicians}}$$

Total Employed Support Staff Cost as a Percentage of Total Medical Revenue

Goal: Depends on the practice; however, according to the research, a balance between practice productivity and number of support staff is necessary.

$$\frac{(\text{Total employed support staff cost} \times 100)}{\text{Total medical revenue}}$$

Exhibit 10.14   Five Steps to Better A/R and Collections Performance[3]

- Consider billing to be everyone's responsibility
- Push billing "to the front" of the cycle
- Enter charges into the system immediately and with accuracy
- Ensure billing for all services
- Analyze A/R by various components

Exhibit 10.15   Keys to A/R and Collections Success[2]

- Use of information technology
- Involved physicians
- Close watch on trends in the health care market
- Outsourced billing functions
- Looking at data from different angles
- Use of an electronic health record system
- In-house billing and collections procedures
- Volunteer efforts in the community
- Aggressive incentive plan for employees
- Coding audits
- Physicians engaged in billing processes
- Physicians dedicated to their patients
- An internal report card for benchmarking
- Dedicated staff working as a team
- Staff with a vested interest in making the practice successful

A/R and Collections

Because A/R is usually the single largest balance sheet item, most practices identified as better performers generally invest significant time and energy managing this asset.[3] In particular, better-performing practices treat A/R and collections as a practice-wide endeavor; that is, every department, staff member, and physician are involved in the process.[3] Therefore, better-performing practices have provided tips for actively managing A/R and collections to increase cash flow and improve working capital position (see Exhibit 10.14).[3]

Practices selected by MGMA as better performing in the A/R and collections category provided several of their keys to success (see Exhibit 10.15 and 10.16). These keys were used by real practices and resulted in success through best practices. The use of these keys does not guarantee success but they will increase a practice's potential.

Total A/R per FTE Physician

Goal: Higher the better.

$$\frac{\text{Total A/R}}{\text{Total FTE physicians}}$$

Gross FFS Collection Percentage

Goal: Higher the better.

$$\frac{\text{Gross FFS charges}}{\text{Gross FFS collections}}$$

Exhibit 10.16   Other Methods/Measures for Improving A/R and Collections[4]

- Total A/R
- Days in A/R (aging reports)
- Aged accounts by payer
- Adjusted collections percent
- Adjustments to FFS charges
- Bad debts due to FFS activity per FTE physician
- Payer mix as a percent of charges
- Payer mix as a percent of collections
- Time to generate a claim (including ambulatory and hospital encounters)
- Claim turnaround

- Explanation of benefits (EOB) review (used to determine denial rates, audit payers and assess fee schedule)
- Percent of total A/R 0–30 days, 31–60 days, 61–90 days, 91–120 days, and 120+ days
- Days and months gross FFS charges in A/R
- Total number of patient accounting support staff per FTE physician
- Patient accounting support staff cost per FTE physician
- Total number of general accounting support staff per FTE physician
- General accounting support staff cost per FTE physician

Gross FFS Charges per FTE Physician

Goal: Higher the better.

$$\frac{\text{Gross FFS charges}}{\text{Total FTE physicians}}$$

Adjustments to FFS Charges per FTE Physician

Goal: Lower the better.

$$\frac{\text{Gross FFS charges} - \text{Adjusted FFS charges}}{\text{Total FTE physicians}}$$

Number of Business Office Support Staff per FTE Physician

Goal: Depends on the practice; however, according to the research, a balance between practice productivity and number of support staff is necessary.

$$\frac{\text{Total number of business office support staff}}{\text{Total FTE physicians}}$$

Business Office Support Staff Cost per FTE Physician

Goal: Depends on the practice; however, according to the research, a balance between practice productivity and number of support staff is necessary.

$$\frac{\text{Total cost of business office support staff}}{\text{Total FTE physicians}}$$

Exhibit 10.17 Five Steps to Better Patient Satisfaction and the Costs of Poor Patient Satisfaction[4]

Five Steps to Better Patient Satisfaction	Costs of Poor Patient Satisfaction
• Ensure physicians and staff understand the practice's philosophies in delivering care	• Costs of handling irate customers often take multiple levels of personnel
• Define the feedback process	• Cost of negative publicity
• Link service delivery with performance plan	• Lost revenue from the inability to accept new patients in a timely manner
• Communicate practice values regularly	• Lost revenue due to staff who do not focus on patient satisfaction
• Define and explain how physicians and staff will be measured	• Cost of damaged marketing efforts
	• Loss of referral relationships

Exhibit 10.18 Keys to Patient Satisfaction Success[2]

• Keep a small-practice perspective	• Low management overhead
• Surveying patients on many satisfaction measures	• Strong, decisive physician owners
• Retaining employees	• Commitment to an established vision and core values
• Focusing on one patient for one physician for life	• Respect for all patients and staff
• High patient satisfaction feedback from surveys	• Philosophy that encourages staff involvement in decision-making
• Staff focus and dedication to quality care and valued services	• Continual process improvement and streamlining patient care
• Benchmarking with key indicator reports	• Physicians who create a good working environment
• Adding open-access scheduling	

Patient Satisfaction

The health care environment has increasingly become more competitive and consumer driven; therefore, most practices have recognized the key role patient satisfaction plays as patient loyalty and word-of-mouth advertising determine practice success and longevity.[4] Many practices identified as better performers have provided tips for maximizing patient satisfaction and reducing the costs associated with poor patient satisfaction (see Exhibit 10.17).

Practices selected by MGMA as better performing in the patient satisfaction category provided several of their keys to success (see Exhibit 10.18). These keys were used by real practices and resulted in success through best practices. The use of these keys does not guarantee success but they will increase a practice's potential.

Better-performing practices have identified the following key patient satisfaction measures: access, staff performance, practice and patient communication, physician performance, overall patient satisfaction, willingness to refer other patients to the practice and facilities (see Exhibit 10.19).[4] In addition, many practices seeking improved patient satisfaction measured

Exhibit 10.19   Other Methods for Improving Patient Satisfaction[4]

- Use of surveys:
  - Patient satisfaction
  - Physician satisfaction
  - Employee/staff satisfaction
  - Referral physician satisfaction
- Existence of a patient safety program
- Physicians formally meet to discuss clinical issues
- Practice has a Web site
- Practice considers the following important areas for extra attention:
  - A/R
  - Information technology

- Human resource management
- Governance
- Physician–administrator team
- Physician compensation program
- Patient satisfaction
- Practice relationships with hospitals and payers
- Practice response to environmental changes
- Development of new revenue sources
- Balancing physician autonomy
- Containing costs

Exhibit 10.20   Behaviors for Improving Managed Care Operations Performance[4]

- Support managed care objectives by providing preventative and qualitative patient care
- Improve patient outcomes through a variety of chronic disease management programs

- Review and manage contracts
- Address operational problems that delay timely access to care
- Establish and monitor performance goals

their progress using metrics related to ease of making an appointment, facility access, waiting time, staff courtesy, physician treatment of patients and quality of medical care.[5]

Managed Care Operations   Practices identified as better performers seek to optimize their managed care operations, to include, negotiating contracts, managing charges and collections, utilization reviews, and credentialing.[4] Ultimately, improved managed care operations result in increased quality of care and profits and decreased costs.[4] Better-performing practices have provided several behaviors for improving managed care operations performance (see Exhibit 10.20).

Practices selected by MGMA as better performing in the managed care operations category provided several of their keys to success (see Exhibits 10.21 and 10.22). These keys were used by real practices and resulted in success through best practices. The use of these keys does not guarantee success but they will increase a practice's potential.

Net Capitation Revenue as a Percent of Gross Capitation Charges

Goal: Higher the better.

$$\frac{\text{Net capitation revenue} \times 100}{\text{Gross capitation charges}}$$

Exhibit 10.21   Keys to Managed Care Success[4,5]

- Provide physicians with mobile technology to increase efficiency
- Coordinate EHR, laboratory, and computer systems to communicate with one another
- Stay informed of advances in technology and changes in your community
- Use state laws to look for innovative ways to structure operations
- Offer extensive provider networks to keep referrals in-house
- Be creative in the referral authorization process
- Have specialist in-service programs for primary care physicians
- Provide multiple site locations close to work and home for patients
- Provide alternate work schedule for staff with extended practice hours
- Treat physicians who are employees as owners
- Institute a single formulary that incorporates all insurance plan formularies
- Invest in new technology that provides patients with substantial results
- Incorporate new positions into the practice that increase care and cost containment
- Partner with local area hospitals to expand products and services
- Create programs that help the physician be more efficient
- Use technology to foster cross-communication between primary and specialty care physicians
- Collaborate and innovate
- Have bilingual staff
- Mix on-site and ancillary services

Exhibit 10.22   Other Managed Care Operations Measures

- Net capitation revenue as a percent of total revenue
- Total medical revenue per FTE physician
- Medical revenue after operating cost per FTE physician
- Net capitation revenue per FTE physician
- Capitation revenue per FTE physician
- Gross capitation charges per FTE physician
- Total gross charges per FTE physician
- Patients per FTE physician
- Total procedures per FTE physician
- Square feet per FTE physician
- Purchased services for capitation patients per FTE physician
- Total nonphysician providers per FTE physician
- Total employed support staff per FTE physician

Number of Visits per Member per Month

Goal: Depends on the proportion of total revenue derived from capitation payments; if capitation payments account for the majority share of total revenue, then the higher the better (direct relationship).

$$\frac{\text{Total number of visits by capitation patients}}{\text{Total number of unique capitation patients seen}}$$

Number of Referrals per 1,000 Members

Goal: Depends on many practice factors; should be balanced between physician and practice productivity expectations and needs of the patients.

$$\text{Step 1:} \quad \frac{\text{Total number of unique patients seen}}{1{,}000}$$

$$\text{Step 2:} \quad \frac{\text{Number of referrals}}{\text{Result from Step 1}}$$

Number of Bed Days per 1,000 Members

Goal: Depends on many practice factors; should be balanced between physician and practice productivity expectations and needs of the patients.

$$\text{Step 1:} \quad \frac{\text{Total number of unique patients seen}}{1{,}000}$$

$$\text{Step 2:} \quad \frac{\text{Number of bed days}}{\text{Result from Step 1}}$$

Total Physician Work (RVUs per physician)

Goal: Depends on many practice factors; should be balanced between physician and practice productivity expectations and needs of the patients.

$$\text{Total physician work RVUs per physician}$$

Total RVUs per Physician

Goal: Depends on many practice factors; should be balanced between physician and practice productivity expectations and needs of the patients.

$$\text{Total RVUs per physician}$$

Cost per Visit per Case

Goal: Depends on many practice factors; should be balanced between physician and practice productivity expectations and needs of the patients.

$$\frac{\text{Total cost}}{\text{Total number of capitation patient encounters/visits}}$$

Cost per Visit per Covered Life

Goal: Depends on many practice factors; should be balanced between physician and practice productivity expectations and needs of the patients.

$$\frac{\text{Total cost}}{\text{Total number of unique capitation patients seen}}$$

Patient Panel Size per Physician

Goal: Depends on many practice factors; should be balanced between physician and practice productivity expectations.

Total number of unique capitation patients seen per physician

Charges by Payer Type

Goal: Depends on many practice factors; should be directly related to the type of coverage by patient seen.

Sum of charges organized by payer type

Revenue by Payer Type

Goal: Depends on many practice factors; should be directly related to the type of coverage by patient seen and contracted rates.

Revenue organized by payer type

Other Formulas   The following formulas were also used to evaluate practices in the categories presented earlier (for example, profitability and cost management, etc.). In addition to formulas presented earlier in this chapter, the following calculations can be used to gain additional insight into the operational and business discipline activities of a practice.

Adjusted FFS Charges

Goal: Higher the better.

Gross FFS charges
− Adjustments to FFS charges

Adjusted FFS Collection Percentage

Goal: Higher the better.

$$\frac{(\text{Net FFS revenue} \times 100)}{\text{Adjusted FFS charges}}$$

Days of Gross FFS Charges in A/R

Goal: Lower the better.

$$\frac{\text{Total A/R}}{\text{Gross FFS charges}}$$

Months of Gross FFS Charges in A/R

Goal: Lower the better.

$$\frac{\text{Total A/R}}{\text{Gross FFS charges}}$$

Gross FFS Collection Percentage

Goal: Higher the better.

$$\frac{(\text{Net FFS revenue} \times 100)}{\text{Gross FFS charges}}$$

Net Capitation Revenue to Gross Capitation Charges Ratio

Goal: Higher the better.

$$\frac{(\text{Net capitation revenue} \times 100)}{\text{Gross capitation charges}}$$

Notes

1. "The Traits of Successful Medical Groups." *Performance and Practices of Successful Medical Groups, 2005 Report Based on 2004 Data* (Englewood, CO: MGMA, 2005).

2. MGMA, *Performance and Practices of Successful Medical Groups: 2005 Report Based on 2004 Data* (Englewood, CO: MGMA, 2003).

3. MGMA, *Performance and Practices of Successful Medical Groups: 1998 Report Based on 1997 Data* (Englewood, CO: MGMA, 1998).

4. MGMA, *Performance and Practices of Successful Medical Groups: 2003 Report Based on 2002 Data* (Englewood, CO: MGMA, 2003).

5. MGMA, *Performance and Practices of Successful Medical Groups: 2004 Report Based on 2003 Data* (Englewood, CO: MGMA, 2003).

Chapter 11

Conclusion and Future Implications

"Leadership is lifting a person's vision to higher sights, the raising of a person's performance to a higher standard."

— *Peter Drucker*

Benchmarking will continue to be an invaluable tool for comparison and practice improvement as challenges and changes continue to emerge. Legislation, costs, compensation plans, managed care, health savings accounts, advances in technology and emphasis on outcomes and patient satisfaction, to name a few, all contribute to the need for measurement, benchmarking and practice improvement. In addition, and more than likely, the methods, formulas and ratios presented in this book will not change significantly. However, the focus on particular benchmarks may change depending on the particular needs of a given practice, changes in the regulatory environment or changes in payment/reimbursement methods or physician compensation (for example, pay-for-performance, or P4P) programs.

There are several frameworks that can be used to design and focus benchmarking activities; for instance, the "three-legged stool" of medical practice objectives: (1) good financial performance; (2) high patient satisfaction; and (3) good clinical outcomes can guide an organization in a benchmarking endeavor. Other frameworks for designing and focusing benchmarking activities consist of (1) cost, quality and access; and (2) people, environment, and process affect the 3 Ps of success (profitability, productivity and performance).[1]

Historically, benchmarking and operational improvement have been focused on the financial performance area, and although this area remains very important to the success and longevity of a practice, greater emphasis is being placed on patient satisfaction and clinical quality/outcomes. With this shift to add greater attention to nonfinancial measures, the development and widespread use of new patient satisfaction and clinical metrics will start to appear. In particular, high patient satisfaction results in high "perceived" quality of care, fewer no-shows and cancellations, and greater patient loyalty. And clinical metrics are being used to establish reimbursement and physician P4P programs and to monitor population health initiatives.

"The health care industry is the only service industry that doesn't act like one." This was a profound statement made at the 2006 MGMA Conference during a session that presented a case study of a practice that used techniques proven to be successful by nonhealth care companies (for example, customer service methods used by Disney and supply chain management by Wal-Mart). Best practices and lessons learned can be found and adapted from any industry, and the methods, measures and data used to benchmark will continue to evolve. The ability of the health care industry to adapt and remain flexible will ensure its long-term success and value.

Therefore, the techniques presented in this book will serve as a foundation and guide to benchmarking, but their limitations should not be overlooked: use the right tool for the right job — don't use a hammer to put in a screw. And finally, when benchmarks and benchmarking are used properly, they can uncover hidden treasures, open people's eyes, create buy-in, improve financial performance, and increase patient (and staff) satisfaction and clinical quality/outcomes.

Notes   1. SmHart Triad, www.SmHart.net (Accessed May 1, 2007).

Example Practice: Description, Reports and Financial Statements

As stated in the Preface, the items in this appendix are meant to help organize the benchmarking tools presented in this book. Most variables for the formulas and ratios are associated with the following "example" accounts receivable (A/R) aging report, operational report, balance sheet and income statement.[*]

Description:

- Single-specialty family practice without obstetric (OB) services.
- 12 FTE physicians (no nonphysician providers).
- Physician compensation based partly on collections for professional charges (incentive/bonus based on service quality).
- Accounting method: income tax basis; Internal Revenue Code Section 446(a) requires that taxable income be computed on the same basis of accounting that the taxpayer uses in keeping its books.
- Legal organization: professional corporation (physicians as majority owner).
- Centralized administrative department.
- Local area: metropolitan (population of 250,001 to 1,000,000).

Patient Net A/R Aging Report (as of Dec. 31, 2006)

0–30 days	$ 399,338	58%
31–60 days	96,392	14%
61–90 days	55,081	8%
91–120 days	27,541	4%
>120 days	110,162	16%
Total	**$ 688,514**	**100%**

---

[*] Balance sheet and income statement adapted from *Physician Practice Management: Essential Operational and Financial Knowledge*, L.F. Wolper, editor, 2005, Jones and Bartlett Publishers, Sudbury, MA. www.jbpub.com. Adapted with permission.

Operations Report (for the year ended Dec. 31, 2006)

Total FTE physicians	12	
Total FTE business operations support staff	12.36	22%
Total FTE front-office support staff	18.84	34%
Total FTE clinical support staff	18.84	34%
Total FTE ancillary support staff	5.28	10%
Total FTE support staff	54.96	100%
Payers		
Medicare: fee-for-service (FFS)		14.0%
Medicare: managed care FFS		2.0%
Medicare: capitated		0.4%
Medicaid: FFS		4.0%
Medicaid: managed care FFS		0.7%
Medicaid: capitated		0.3%
Commercial: FFS		43.0%
Commercial payer #1		40.0%
Commercial payer #2		31.0%
Commercial payer #3		17.0%
Commercial payer #4		12.0%
Commercial: managed care FFS		24.0%
Commercial: capitated		2.5%
Workers' compensation		1.1%
Charity care and professional courtesy		1.6%
Self-pay		6.0%
Other government payers		0.1%
Total gross charges		100.0%
Total square footage	22,800	
Total physician work RVUs	61,476	
Total RVUs	123,576	
Total unique patients seen	29,352	
New patients	3,229	11%
Established patients	26,123	89%
Total procedures	121,452	
Total encounters	70,692	
Clinical services hours worked per week	Average = 36.74	Median = 36
Weeks worked per year	Average = 46.99	Median = 47

Balance Sheet (as of Dec. 31, 2006)*

		2006
Assets		
Current assets:		
Cash		$ 25,000
Marketable securities		25,000
A/R — other		1,300
Total current assets		$ 51,300
Investments:		
Investment in securities		$ —
Property held for future use		50,000
Total investments		$ 50,000
Long-term receivables:		
Notes receivable — physicians		$ 10,000
Property and equipment, at cost:		
Leasehold improvements		$ 68,200
Equipment		688,100
		$ 756,300
Less accumulated depreciation:		$ 429,400
Property and equipment, net		$ 326,900
Other assets:		
Goodwill, net of accumulated amortization of $200,000		$ 40,000
Total assets		$ 478,200
Liabilities and stockholders' equity		
Current liabilities:		
Notes and loans payable		$ 23,500
Current maturities of long-term debt		102,000
Accrued benefits and payroll taxes		45,000
Total current liabilities		$ 170,500
Long-term notes payable		
Long-term debt, less current maturities		$ 285,000
Total liabilities		$ 455,500
Stockholders' equity:		
Common stock, $1 par, authorized 200,000 shares; issued and outstanding 100,000 shares		$ 10,000
Capital contributed in excess of par		140,000
Retained earnings (deficit)		(127,300)
Total stockholders' equity		$ 22,700
Total liabilities and stockholders' equity		$ 478,200

* Balance sheet and income statement adapted from *Physician Practice Management: Essential Operational and Financial Knowledge*, L.F. Wolper, editor, 2005, Jones and Bartlett Publishers, Sudbury, MA. www.jbpub.com. Adapted with permission.

Income Statement (for the year ended Dec. 31, 2006)*

	2006
Revenues:	
Net FFS revenue	$4,180,700
Capitation revenue	551,100
Other revenue	133,500
Net revenue	$4,865,300
Operating expenses:	
Salary and fringe benefits:	
Business operations support staff salaries	$ 405,280
Front office support staff salaries	357,600
Clinical support staff salaries	429,120
Ancillary support staff salaries	178,100
Payroll taxes	108,400
Employee benefits	129,100
Total salaries and benefits	$1,607,600
Service and general expenses:	
Professional liability insurance (malpractice insurance)	$ 85,900
Medical supplies and drugs (clinical and other)	201,300
Depreciation	190,200
Amortization	4,000
Rent	186,000
Other general and administrative	474,600
Total services and general expenses	$1,142,000
Purchased services:	
Purchased outside professional services	$ 294,000
Purchased data processing services	—
Total purchased services	$ 294,000
Provider-related expenses:	
Physician salaries and benefits	$1,828,800
Total operating expenses	$4,872,400
Income (loss) from operations	$ (7,100)
Other income (expenses):	
Interest expense (net)	$ (34,100)
Income from long-term investments	$ 3,500
Other income (expense), net	$ (30,600)
Income before provision for income taxes	$ (37,700)
Provision for income taxes	$ 0
Net income (loss)	$ (37,700)
Retained earnings (deficit), beginning of year	$ (89,600)
Retained earnings (deficit), end of year	$ (127,300)

* Balance sheet and income statement adapted from *Physician Practice Management: Essential Operational and Financial Knowledge*, L.F. Wolper, editor, 2005, Jones and Bartlett Publishers, Sudbury, MA. www.jbpub.com. Adapted with permission.

Group Practice Measures in Military Health Care

This appendix describes unique measures used throughout the military health care environment and provides examples of civilian metrics for unique comparisons. Benchmarking metrics in military health care have been evolving for many years and continue to be refined. Currently, agreement on a set of standardized metrics among the different military branches is a primary goal for the military health care system to achieve. Two types of benchmarks are presented in this section. First, examples are presented of what the military currently uses, and, second, metrics the military can adapt from civilian practices. Therefore, metrics specific to military health care followed by nonmilitary (civilian) metrics that can be used in the military health care environment are discussed.

Military Health Care Metrics Metrics used in military health care have been developed as a result of unique environment, organization and managed care system factors. The environmental and organizational factors consist of readiness requirements (e.g., military training, deployments, temporary duty at other locations), layers of leadership, rotation and selection of personnel, and supply and demand issues, to name a few. Managed care system factors are related to private sector care, referral management and managing demand for services — the system has minimal controls (copays) for military retirees and their family members to limit overuse/abuse and to balance the supply–demand equation. Controls are virtually nonexistent for active-duty members and their families, because their medical care is free.

Access to Care In the Military Health System (MHS), appointments are categorized by type based on appointment standardization rules (see Exhibit B.1). This takes into consideration the needs of the patient including appointment duration and the purpose of visit. Typically, templates are constructed for most providers with a mix of appointment types determined by historical demand. Several of the appointment types have a required-by-law period in which the patient can expect to be seen for care — this is referred to as access to care standards. For example, the 1-7-28 rule is used by all military medical facilities to schedule acute, routine and wellness care.

Exhibit B.1　MHS Appointment Types

• ACUT (acute need within 24 hours)	• PROC (procedure)
• OPAC (same day access/care)	• TCON (telephone consult)
• ROUT (routine need within 7 days)	• GRP (group appointment)
• WELL (preventive care within 28 days)	• PCM (first routine appointment with primary care manager/provider)
• SPEC (specialty care within 28 days)	

Exhibit B.2　Access to Routine Care[1]

Calculation: The proportion of routine appointment searches that resulted in the selection of any appointment type that met the routine access-to-care standard of seven days for routine appointments

Formula:

　Routine appointment searches meeting the routine access-to-care standard

　All routine appointment searches

Performance thresholds:

　• Substandard (less than 85%)

　• Marginal (85% to less than 90%)

　• Above standard (90% or more)

Notes:

　Excludes walk-in and sick call visits

　There are other notes and special criteria not included here

Access measures are meant to assess how well military health care meets the routine and same-day needs of patients enrolled to a specific hospital and/or clinic. The following were defined and are used by the Air Force Medical Service (AFMS).[1]

First, access to routine care (see Exhibit B.2) is measured to answer the business question, "How well do we meet our enrollee's need for routine services in primary care elements and primary care clinics?" The desired outcome is for 90 percent or more of patient requests for routine care to be met within the next seven days.

Second, access to same-day care (see Exhibit B.3) is measured to answer the business question, "How well do we meet our patient's need for same-day services in primary care open access clinics?" The desired outcome for the same-day access metric is at or above 60 percent but not to exceed 80 percent. Seeking to remain at or under 80 percent creates an opportunity for those patients requesting appointments outside of the same day to obtain a visit at a future date (good backlog).

Exhibit B.3   Access to Same-Day Care[1]

Calculation: The proportion of primary care appointments scheduled for a given month that are requested and scheduled on the same day

Formula:

Number of appointments scheduled during the report month where the request date is the same date as the final scheduled appointment

All appointments requested and scheduled with the appointment date in the report month

Performance thresholds:

- Substandard (54% or less)

- Marginal (greater than 55% to less than or equal to 59%)

- Above standard (60% or more)

Note:

There are several notes and special criteria not included here

There are inherent systemic limitations in the value of the routine and same-day access to care metrics. In particular, the metric is focused more on capturing the method used to schedule (search for) an appointment rather than whether the appointment occurs within an appropriate period of time following the day and time the patient calls.

HEDIS Some of the clinical benchmarks used in the AFMS are based on Health Plan Employer Data and Information Set (HEDIS) measures of asthma, breast cancer screening, cervical cancer screening, childhood immunizations, diabetic care by A1C screening, diabetic care by A1C control and colorectal cancer screening (see Exhibit B.4).[1] According to the National Committee for Quality Assurance (NCQA), HEDIS are a standardized set of clinical performance measures related to several public health issues. For more information, visit the NCQA HEDIS website at www.ncqa.org/Programs/HEDIS/index.htm.

Coding Because coding is the first step in getting credit for providing health care services to patients, the military goes to great lengths to ensure coding is accurate and timely. Benchmarking for accuracy of coding is accomplished for Current Procedural Terminology (CPT®), evaluation & management (E&M), and international classification of diseases (ICD) codes. In addition, metrics are categorized based on code type and whether the code is for an ambulatory procedure visit (APV; outpatient surgery) or a non-ambulatory surgery visit (typical outpatient care).

The metrics for E&M accuracy for non-APV and APV (see Exhibit B.5) were designed to answer the question, "What percentage of E&M codes is accurately being accomplished for non-APV and APV?"

Exhibit B.4   Clinical Question and Performance Thresholds for HEDIS Measures[1]

Asthma: What percentage of beneficiaries 5 to 56 years of age with persistent asthma are prescribed medications acceptable as primary therapy for the long-term control of asthma in accordance with HEDIS?
- Substandard (54% or less)
- Marginal (greater than 55% to less than or equal to 59%)
- Above standard (60% or more)

Breast cancer screening: What percentage of women 52 to 69 years of age continuously enrolled have completed breast cancer screening in accordance with HEDIS and the minimum screening recommendations from the American Academy of Family Physicians and the US Preventive Services Task Force?
- Substandard (73% or less)
- Marginal (greater than 73% to less than 81%)
- Above standard (81% or more)

Cervical cancer screening: What percentage of women 21 to 64 years of age continuously enrolled have completed cervical cancer screening in accordance with HEDIS and the minimum screening recommendations from the American Academy of Family Physicians and the U.S. Preventive Services Task Force?
- Substandard (less than 81%)
- Marginal (81% to less than 87%)
- Above standard (87% or more)

Childhood immunizations: What percentage of children 24 to 35 months of age continuously enrolled to Air Force medical treatment facilities (hospitals) completed four DPT/DTaP, three IPV/OPV, one MMR, three Hepatitis B, three Hib, one VZV, and four PCV vaccinations in accordance with HEDIS and the Centers for Disease Control and Prevention, the American Academy of Pediatrics, American Academy of Family Physicians and the Advisory Committee on Immunization Practices?
- Substandard (less than 30%)
- Marginal (30% to less than 55%)
- Above standard (55% or more)

Diabetic care by A1C screening: What percentage of enrollees with diabetes (Type 1 or 2) aged 18 to 75 years of age continuously enrolled who have had an A1C test in the past 12 months in accordance with HEDIS and the minimum screening recommendations from the Diabetes Quality Improvement Project (DQIP) and the U.S. Preventive Services Task Force?
- Substandard (less than 86%)
- Marginal (86% to less than 92%)
- Above standard (92% or more)

Diabetic care by A1C control: What percentage of enrollees with diabetes (Type 1 or 2) aged 18 to 75 years of age continuously enrolled whose most recent A1C test during the past 12 months was less than or equal to 9.0 in accordance with HEDIS?
- Substandard (less than 70%)
- Marginal (70% to less than 79%)
- Above standard (79% or more)

Colorectal cancer screening: What percentage of men and women 51 to 80 years of age continuously enrolled who have at received at least one colon cancer screening procedure in accordance with HEDIS and the minimum screening recommendations from the US Preventive Services Task Force?
- Substandard (less than 49%)
- Marginal (49% to less than 61%)
- Above standard (61% or more)

Note:
   There are several notes and special criteria not included here

Exhibit B.5 E&M Accuracy for Non-APV and APV[1]

Non-APV formula:

Number of encounters with correctly coded non-APV E&M

Number of non-APV E&M audits completed during the measurement period

APV formula:

Number of encounters with correctly coded APV E&M

Number of APV E&M audits completed during the measurement period

Performance thresholds:

- Substandard (71% or less)
- Marginal (71% to 96%)
- Above standard (97% or more)

Notes:

Encounters selected for audit are at random

There are other notes and special criteria not included here

Exhibit B.6 CPT Accuracy for Non-APV and APV[1]

Non-APV formula:

Number of encounters with correctly coded non-APV CPT

Number of non-APV CPT audits completed during the measurement period

APV formula:

Number of encounters with correctly coded APV CPT

Number of APV CPT audits completed during the measurement period

Performance thresholds:

- Substandard (71% or less)
- Marginal (71% to 96%)
- Above standard (97% or more)

Notes:

Encounters selected for audit are at random

There are other notes and special criteria not included here

The metrics for CPT accuracy for non-APV and APV (see Exhibit B.6) were designed to answer the question, "What percentage of CPT codes is accurately being accomplished for non-APV and APV?"

The metrics for ICD accuracy for non-APV and APV (see Exhibit B.7) were designed to answer the question, "What percentage of ICD codes is accurately being accomplished for non-APV and APV?"

Exhibit B.7   ICD Accuracy for Non-APV and APV[1]

Non-APV formula:

Number of encounters with correctly coded non-APV ICD

Number of non-APV ICD audits completed during the measurement period

APV formula:

Number of encounters with correctly coded APV ICD

Number of APV ICD audits completed during the measurement period

Performance thresholds:

- Substandard (71% or less)

- Marginal (71% to 96%)

- Above standard (97% or more)

Notes:

Encounters selected for audit are at random

There are other notes and special criteria not included here

High Utilizers   Capturing the number of high utilizers is an elusive measure without a standard. The Centers for Medicare and Medicaid Services (CMS) has defined high utilizers as patients with 10 or more visits to different providers and 20 or more different prescriptions over the course of 12 months. On the other hand, the AFMS Population Health Support Office defines high utilizers as patients with 10 or more primary care visits over the past 12 months. However, many case managers, health care integrators and practice administrators select a population-specific (user-defined) number of primary care visits over the past 12 months as a definition for high utilizers.

These differences suggest the criteria used to define high utilizers should be based on the objective or purpose associated with identifying this group. For instance, if case/disease managers want to focus on patients with multiple medical issues and chronic conditions, they might select more restrictive criteria such as the CMS definition. However, if practice administrators want to reduce unnecessary use of access, they might select more inclusive criteria such as the Population Health Support Office's definition.

Individual Medical Readiness   A unique composite metric used in the military health care environment is the measurement of medical mobility status of personnel (see Exhibit B.8). That is, "what percentage of military personnel have met all medical mobility requirements?"

Exhibit B.8 Individual Medical Readiness (IMR)[1]

Formula:

Number of personnel meeting all IMR requirements

Adjusted population minus students, personnel that have permanently changed station and those on terminal leave

Performance thresholds:

- Substandard (less than 65%)

- Marginal (65% to less than 75%)

- Above standard (75% or more)

Note:

There are several notes and special criteria not included here

Exhibit B.9 Common Civilian Benchmarks for Use in the Military[2]

Per Clinical FTE Physician/Provider	Other Benchmarks
• Physician work RVUs	• Physician weeks worked per year
• Patients	• Physician clinical service hours worked per week
• Encounters	• Ambulatory encounters
• Total procedures	• Hospital encounters
• Square feet	• Surgical/anesthesia cases
• Total support staff	
• Total front office support staff	
• Total clinical support staff	

Using Civilian Measures in the Military

Applying civilian benchmarks in the military environment can be a valuable exercise that provides new insights into the performance of a clinic or military treatment facility (hospital). However, caution must be taken when using any type of benchmark because the background characteristics behind the benchmark and the practice being compared may be very different; ensure differences and caveats are explored and understood before decisions are made. For example, there may be regional, population, organizational dynamics, and/or physician differences. Therefore, it is recommended that when using a benchmark for comparison more than one benchmark be used to thoroughly diagnose performance. In addition, the formula and data behind a benchmark from the civilian sector must be matched as closely as possible to those in the military environment — keeping in mind that a perfect match is rarely possible even when in the same sector or environment (see Exhibit B.9).

Exhibit B.10   Civilian Benchmarks for Use in the Military[2]

- Unique patient seen
- Total work RVUs
- Encounters (visits)
- Work RVUs per encounter
- Procedures
- Square feet

- Total support staff FTE
- Total front office support staff FTE
- Total clinical support staff FTE
- Weeks worked per year
- Clinical service hours worked per week

Standardization data permits comparison of data and the use of benchmarks from different sizes and types of organizations. Examples of standardized data are: per FTE physician, per FTE provider, per square foot, per patient, per resource-based relative value scale (RBRVS) and per procedure. Some of the issues associated with using civilian benchmarks in the military environment consist of how to define a standard FTE in the military, demographic differences, demand limitations (copay versus no copay) and data quality. Examples of data quality concerns in the military are related to expense and staff availability reporting, arbitrary appointment durations, misuse of appointment types, inconsistent coding, and poor supply/demand forecasting. Once standardization is applied, however, it is possible to use civilian benchmarks in the military environment (see Exhibit B.10).

The following formulas were used to establish civilian benchmarks and adjust military measures to maximize comparability. In addition, the sources for civilian benchmarking data are also identified but other sources may also be available.

Unique Patients Seen

Civilian benchmarking measure:
> Patients per physician
> Data source: MGMA Cost Survey

Military benchmarking measure:
> Unique patients seen per primary care manager (PCM)
> Note: The measure should ensure that all unique patients include empanelled and all others

Total Work RVUs

Civilian benchmarking measure:
> Physician work RVUs per physician
> Data source: CMS RBRVS Exhibits, MGMA Cost Survey

Military benchmarking measure:

Provider RVUs per PCM

Note: Facility and malpractice RVU components not included in either measure

Encounters (Visits)

Civilian benchmarking measure:

Encounters per provider

Data source: MGMA Cost Survey

Military benchmarking measure:

KEPT, WALK-IN, and S-CALL visits per PCM

Note: The measure should include only "count" visits and exclude TCONS

Definitions: KEPT are scheduled visits in which patients arrive and are seen (that is, the patient "keeps" the appointment); WALK-IN are visits by unscheduled patients at times that are unplanned; and S-CALL are visits by unscheduled patients during planned times.

Work RVUs per Encounter

Civilian benchmarking measure:

Physician work RVUs per patient per provider

Data source: CMS RBRVS Exhibits, MGMA Cost Survey

Military benchmarking measure:

Provider work RVUs per unique patient seen per PCM procedures

Note: Facility and malpractice RVU components not included in either measure

Procedures

Civilian benchmarking measure:

Total procedures per provider

Data source: MGMA Cost Survey

Military benchmarking measure:

Total E&Ms and CPTs per PCM

Square Feet

Civilian benchmarking measure:

Square feet per provider

Data source: MGMA Cost Survey

Military benchmarking measure:
>   Square feet per PCM

Total Support Staff FTE

Civilian benchmarking measure:
>   Total support staff FTE per provider
>   Data source: MGMA Cost Survey
Military benchmarking measure:
>   Total support staff FTE per PCM

Total Front Office Support Staff FTE

Civilian benchmarking measure:
>   Total front office support staff FTE per provider
>   Data source: MGMA Cost Survey
Military benchmarking measure:
>   Total front office support staff FTE per PCM

Total Clinical Support Staff FTE

Civilian benchmarking measure:
>   Total clinical support staff FTE per provider
>   Data source: MGMA Cost Survey
Military benchmarking measure:
>   Total clinical support staff FTE per PCM

Weeks Worked per Year

Civilian benchmarking measure:
>   Physician weeks worked per year per physician
>   Data source: MGMA Physician Compensation and Production Survey
Military benchmarking measure:
>   PCM weeks worked per year per PCM

Clinical Service Hours Worked per Week

Civilian benchmarking measure:
>   Physician clinical service hours worked per week per physician
>   Data source: MGMA Physician Compensation and Production Survey
Military benchmarking measure:
>   PCM clinical service hours worked per week per PCM

As mentioned previously, adjustments must be made to increase the degree of comparability when using civilian benchmarks with military measures. For instance, many civilian benchmarks use the standard of "per physician" or "per provider," whereas military measures should be adjusted to "per PCM" when in the primary care environment or "per physician" when comparing a specialty.

Caveats and limiting factors must also be considered when using civilian benchmarks in the military environment. Typically, the impact of these caveats and limiting factors cannot be controlled for or eliminated; therefore, caution should be taken when using a single benchmark. Multiple benchmarks should be used when possible, and recognition of the caveats and limiting factors will ensure decisions resulting from benchmarking are based on a more thorough understanding of the patient factors.

Notes

1. SG Executive Global Look (SG EGL; N.D.). Retrieved August 2, 2007, from https://sgegl.afmoa.af.mil, "Define" link.

2. MGMA, *Cost Survey for Single-Specialty Practices and Physician Compensation and Production Survey: 2005 Reports Based on 2004 Data* (Englewood, CO: MGMA, 2005).

Four Methodologies to Improve Healthcare Demand Forecasting

This appendix contains an article from *Healthcare Financial Management* on methodologies to improve heathcare demand forecasting:

- Four Methodologies to Improve Healthcare Demand Forecasting (from *Healthcare Financial Management*, May 2001, pages 54–58)

Four Methodologies to Improve Healthcare Demand Forecasting

Forecasting methods based upon recent data can help healthcare organizations more accurately project demand for their services in a dynamic marketplace.

BY MURRAY J. CÔTÉ, PhD, AND STEPHEN L. TUCKER, DBA

Forecasting demand for health services is an important step in managerial decision making for all healthcare organizations. This task, which often is assumed by financial managers, first requires the compilation and examination of historical information. Although many quantitative forecasting methods exist, four common methods of forecasting are percent adjustment, 12-month moving average, trendline, and seasonalized forecast. These four methods are all based upon the organization's recent historical demand. Healthcare financial managers who want to project demand for healthcare services in their facility should understand the advantages and disadvantages of each method and then select the method that will best meet the organization's needs.

Forecasting demand for services represents the essential first step in setting a healthcare organization's future direction. As such, healthcare organizations need the best possible projections of the demand for their services.

Many quantitative forecasting methods exist. Whatever method is used, it should satisfy the following concerns:

- The necessary data should be readily available. Financial records typically represent the best source of historical data regarding utilization. The forecasting method should be able to use these data.
- Existing staff members equipped with readily available tools, such as spreadsheet software, should be able to perform the forecasting in-house.
- The forecasting method and its results should be understandable not only to financial management staff but also to those who use the results for decision making.

In addition to these concerns, a critical aspect of the forecasting process is recognizing that forecasts based on historical data represent only the starting point for demand forecasting. While in the short term, historical data provide for the best forecast, healthcare managers realize that the demand for healthcare services is dynamic. Therefore, managerial judgment must be used in terms of both internal variables (eg, changes in productivity and

capacity) and external variables (eg, changes in demographics, healthcare demand patterns, technology, payment mechanisms, and competition).

Many healthcare organizations routinely make forecasts using very simple techniques, such as the percent-adjustment forecasting method. However, three other forecasting methods—12-month moving average, trendline, and seasonalized forecast—can project demand on the basis of historical utilization with increasing accuracy and usefulness. Each of these techniques meets the tests of reasonableness outlined above: they use readily available data, they can be done in-house, and they are easy to understand.

Four Forecasting Methods

The four forecasting methods can be illustrated by projecting patients' demand for visits to a hypothetical primary care group practice. Exhibit 1 contains two years of historical data for monthly visits to the practice. The objective is to provide a reasonable forecast of monthly visits for the third year. Columns A through C establish the time periods used in this example. Column D gives the historic number of visits per month to the primary care practice for the past two years. Columns E, F, and G present forecast results for the percent-adjustment, 12-month moving-average, and trendline forecasting methods.

Percent adjustment. The percent-adjustment method is based upon a simple percentage adjustment of the past 12 months of historic demand. The percentage increase (or decrease) is essentially a best guess of what is expected to happen in the next year. There were 20,265 visits in year 2, a decrease of 7 percent from year 1. Therefore, assuming that year 3 will behave similarly, the total number of visits for year 3 should be 7 percent less than year 2. This implies that the group practice should expect 18,846 visits for the year, an average of 1,571 visits per month (see Exhibit 1, column E, rows 26 to 37).

Although this method is commonly used, it can give

(Continued on next page)

inaccurate results because it ignores a considerable amount of historical data and fails to recognize any seasonal effects.

12-month moving average. The 12-month moving-average forecasting method averages the number of patient visits for the previous 12 months to forecast the number of visits for the next month. For example, the forecast of 1,689 for January in year 3 is the average of the 12 months of year 2 (ie, the average of cells D14 to D25 in Exhibit 1). Similarly, the forecast of 1,657 for February in year 3 is the average of February in year 2 to January in year 3 (ie, the average of cells D15 to D25 and F26).

The moving-average forecasting method more accurately predicts demand for each month in the 12-month period and works well for short-term forecasting, but this method tends to yield results that lag behind any changes in the data and does not account for trends or seasonal effects. For instance, if patient visits show a steep decline over the most recent seven months, the method dampens this trend, averaging in the higher visits in the preceding five months as well.

Trendline. Using a trendline determined from the recent demand for the service is more accurate than the percent adjustment and 12-month moving average methods. This method provides the best-fitting straight line, in terms of a regression analysis, between the past months (the x variable) and the actual utilization experienced during those months (the y variable). The steps for determining and using the trendline to forecast demand for future periods are explained in Exhibit 2, page 56, and the forecast results are displayed in cells G26 to G37 of Exhibit 1. This forecasting method explicitly determines the general direction of demand, increasing or decreasing over time. (As shown in Exhibit 1, the trendline's slope, –12.0, indicates decreasing demand.)

Although the trendline obtained is not as easy to calculate or explain as the two previous methods, it can be computed using the statistical functions included in any standard spreadsheet program. While the trendline forecasting method recognizes historical demand, it assumes that the trend of the recent past will continue into the near future, and seasonal effects have not been considered.

Seasonalized forecast. The seasonalized forecast method recognizes the seasonal variations in demand during the year and provides projections of demand that include seasonal variation. Exhibit 3, page 57, displays the

EXHIBIT 1: ILLUSTRATION OF THE PERCENT-ADJUSTMENT, 12-MONTH MOVING-AVERAGE, AND TRENDLINE FORECASTING METHODS

	A	B	C	D	E	F	G
	Year	Month	Numbered Month	Visits	Percent Adjustment	12-Month Moving Average	Trendline*
2	1	January	1	1,557			
3	1	February	2	1,741			
4	1	March	3	1,776			
5	1	April	4	1,864			
6	1	May	5	1,858			
7	1	June	6	1,875			
8	1	July	7	2,168			
9	1	August	8	1,976			
10	1	September	9	1,915			
11	1	October	10	1,855			
12	1	November	11	1,720			
13	1	December	12	1,568			
14	2	January	13	1,736			
15	2	February	14	1,933			
16	2	March	15	1,826			
17	2	April	16	1,808			
18	2	May	17	1,568			
19	2	June	18	1,751			
20	2	July	19	1,761			
21	2	August	20	1,800			
22	2	September	21	1,640			
23	2	October	22	1,551			
24	2	November	23	1,520			
25	2	December	24	1,371			
26	3	January	25		1,571	1,689	1,606
27	3	February	26		1,571	1,685	1,594
28	3	March	27		1,571	1,664	1,582
29	3	April	28		1,571	1,651	1,570
30	3	May	29		1,571	1,638	1,558
31	3	June	30		1,571	1,643	1,546
32	3	July	31		1,571	1,634	1,534
33	3	August	32		1,571	1,624	1,522
34	3	September	33		1,571	1,609	1,510
35	3	October	34		1,571	1,607	1,498
36	3	November	35		1,571	1,611	1,486
37	3	December	36		1,571	1,618	1,474

* The calculation for the trendline method is based on an intercept of 1,906.3 and a slope of –12.0.

(Continued on next page)

results (cells F27 to F37) and the necessary intermediate calculations for the primary care practice data used in Exhibit 1 (columns A through D). Of the four forecasting methods, this is the one that requires the most computa-

tions. Three processes, with a total of five steps, are involved (see Exhibit 4, below).

First, the effects of seasonal variation in demand are determined (see steps 1 and 2 of Exhibit 4). Second, the

EXHIBIT 2: CALCULATING A TRENDLINE

Step	Forecast Input or Output	Spreadsheet Location	Description
1	Input historical months	Cells containing the numbered months (ie, cells C2 to C25)	x-variable component of the trendline
2	Input historical demand	Cells containing demand by month corresponding to the numbered months (ie, cells D2 to D25)	y-variable component of the trendline
3	Calculate coefficients for the trendline	Cells where the coefficients are calculated by functions in the spreadsheet	Regression analysis is performed to obtain the trendline coefficients (ie, intercept = 1,906.3 and slope = −12.0)
4	Calculate a forecast	Cells where the trendline is used to forecast future demand using the equation: Intercept + [Slope × Numbered Month of Forecast]; for example, cell G26 = Intercept + [Slope × cell C26], cell G27 = Intercept + [Slope × cell C27], etc.	The forecasts are obtained for year 3; for example, January's forecast value is 1,906.3 − (12 × 25) = 1,606; February's forecast value is 1,906.3 − (12 × 26) = 1,594, etc.

EXHIBIT 4: CALCULATING A SEASONALIZED FORECAST

Step	Forecast Input or Output	Spreadsheet Location	Description
1.	24-month average	Cell containing the 24-month average (ie, cell H16)	Average of past 24 months of historical visits
2.	Seasonal indexes	Cells containing the monthly seasonal indexes (ie, cells H2 to H13)	Indexes are calculated as the monthly average divided by the 24-month average (eg, January's average = 1,646.5; therefore January's seasonal index = 1,646.5/1,756 = 0.9376)
3.	Deseasonalized historical data	Cells containing the deseasonalized visits (ie, cells E2 to E25)	Deseasonalized visits are calculated by dividing each month's visits by its corresponding seasonal index (eg, January, year 1's deseasonalized visits = 1,557/0.9376 = 1,661; February, year 1's deseasonalized visits = 1,741/1.0463 = 1,664, etc.)
4.	Calculate a trendline based on the deseasonalized data		
	• Input historical months	Cells containing the numbered months (ie, cells C2 to C25)	x-variable component of the trendline
	• Input historical demand	Cells containing deseasonalized demand by month corresponding to the numbered months (ie, cells E2 to E25)	y-variable component of the trendline
	• Calculate coefficients for the trendline	Cells where the coefficients are calculated by functions in the spreadsheet	Regression analysis is performed to obtain the trendline coefficients (ie, intercept = 1,861.3 and slope = −8.4)
5.	Calculating a forecast	Cells where the trendline is used to forecast future demand using the equation: (Intercept + [Slope × Numbered Month of Forecast]) × Seasonal Index, eg, cell F26 = (Intercept + [Slope × cell C27]) × cell H3, etc.	The forecasts are obtained for year 3; eg, January's forecast value is (1,861.3 −[8.4 × 25]) × 0.9378 = 1,549; February's forecast value is (1,861.3 −[8.4 × 26]) × 1.0463 = 1,719, etc.

(Continued on next page)

EXHIBIT 3: ILLUSTRATION OF THE SEASONALIZED FORECAST

	A Year	B Month	C Numbered Month	D Visits	E Deseasonalized Visits	F Seasonalized Forecast	G Seasonal Indexes*	H
2	1	January	1	1,557	1,661		January	0.9376
3	1	February	2	1,741	1,664		February	1.0463
4	1	March	3	1,776	1,731		March	1.0258
5	1	April	4	1,864	1,783		April	1.0457
6	1	May	5	1,858	1,904		May	0.9757
7	1	June	6	1,875	1,816		June	1.0326
8	1	July	7	2,168	1,938		July	1.1189
9	1	August	8	1,976	1,838		August	1.0753
10	1	September	9	1,915	1,892		September	1.0124
11	1	October	10	1,855	1,912		October	0.9700
12	1	November	11	1,720	1,864		November	0.9227
13	1	December	12	1,568	1,873		December	0.8370
14	2	January	13	1,736	1,852			
15	2	February	14	1,933	1,848		24-month	
16	2	March	15	1,826	1,781		average =	1,756
17	2	April	16	1,808	1,729			
18	2	May	17	1,568	1,608			
19	2	June	18	1,751	1,696			
20	2	July	19	1,761	1,574			
21	2	August	20	1,800	1,674			
22	2	September	21	1,640	1,620			
23	2	October	22	1,551	1,600			
24	2	November	23	1,520	1,648			
25	2	December	24	1,371	1,639			
26	3	January	25			1,548		
27	3	February	26			1,719		
28	3	March	27			1,677		
29	3	April	28			1,701		
30	3	May	29			1,578		
31	3	June	30			1,662		
32	3	July	31			1,791		
33	3	August	32			1,712		
34	3	September	33			1,604		
35	3	October	34			1,528		
36	3	November	35			1,446		
37	3	December	36			1,305		

* The seasonal indexes calculation is based on an intercept of 1,861.3 and a slope of −8.4.

trendline of historical demand for the service is determined with the seasonal variations removed from the data (see steps 3 and 4 of Exhibit 4). (Note that the deseasonalized trendline is calculated using the same method described in Exhibit 2.) Last, in step 5 of Exhibit 4, forecasts are calculated by using the trendline, and each month's forecast is adjusted to account for the seasonality of the demand for services during the historical period upon which the forecast is based. Here again, computations are facilitated by the capabilities of standard spreadsheet programs. The formulas described in the Description column in Exhibit 4 are entered once and then copied into relevant cells to determine seasonalized indexes, deseasonalized historical data, and forecasted demand for the service.

Again, although the process and results of this forecasting method are somewhat more difficult to explain, this method offers a significant gain over the other forecasting methods: it recognizes both the overall trend in demand for the service and the inherent seasonality of the demand for many healthcare services.

Exhibit 5, page 58, displays the historical monthly visits and the forecasts from each of the methods described. The seasonal forecasting method here differs from traditional seasonal forecasting methods in one significant respect: it is based on two years of historical data. This difference recognizes the dynamic nature of the healthcare environment. For many healthcare organizations, so many significant changes, particularly in the external environment, have occurred recently that historical data older than two years not only may yield little relevant information, but also may distort the forecasting results. Although the use of data from a shorter time period lowers the degree of mathematical certainty of the results obtained from using this model, it increases its market relevance.

Managerial Implications

Forecasts based on historical demand provide baseline data for making final forecasts of demand for the organization's services. But such forecasts assume that other factors will be unchanged. Healthcare financial managers know that change is perhaps the only constant for the future. Therefore, knowledge of both the internal and external environments must be factored into final forecasts.

For instance, at the primary care practice in the example, the financial manager may need to consider

(Continued on next page)

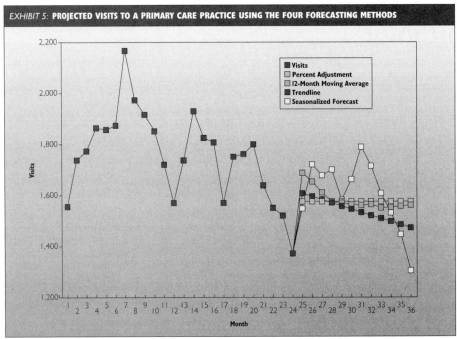

EXHIBIT 5: **PROJECTED VISITS TO A PRIMARY CARE PRACTICE USING THE FOUR FORECASTING METHODS**

whether new physicians in the practice have growing patient lists, or a senior physician who brings in a large number of new patients is likely to leave in the forthcoming budget year. Further, the financial manager needs to determine whether the summer dips in utilization illustrate a real lessening in demand or are simply the result of the unavailability of vacationing physicians. Regarding the external environment, the financial manager will need to consider whether blocks of patients will be added or subtracted from the practice because of changes to managed care contracts. Another consideration is whether competitors' moves in the market readily alter the demands for this practice's services.

Financial managers will draw upon their experience and knowledge of the healthcare organization and its environment in analyzing environmental factors that affect demand. This information needs to be considered in selecting the most appropriate forecasting method to project demand for the organization's services in a dynamic market. ■

ABOUT THE AUTHORS

Murray J. Côté, PhD, is an assistant professor, Department of Health Services Administration, University of Florida, Gainesville, Florida.

Stephen L. Tucker, DBA, is a professor, Department of Health Care Administration, Trinity University, San Antonio, Texas.

Questions or comments regarding this article may be sent to Murray J. Côté, PhD, at mjcote@hp.ufl.edu.

M.J. Côté and S.L. Tucker, "Four methodologies to improve healthcare demand forecasting," *Healthcare Financial Management*, May 2001, pp. 54–58. Reprinted with permission.

Benchmarking Guidance

This appendix contains an article from MGMA's *Performance and Practices of Successful Medical Groups* report on general benchmarking topics:

- Life Moves Pretty Fast…Some Thoughts on Benchmarking (from *Performance and Practices of Successful Medical Groups: 2002 Report Based on 2001 Data*, pages 18–20)

Life Moves Pretty Fast . . . Some Thoughts on Benchmarking

By W. David Holloway, MD, and Lisa Holloway, MS

Last year I wrote about my adventures with organizational learning and explained that my all time favorite movie is *2001: A Space Odyssey.* This year I've decided to continue the movie theme and tell you that my next favorite movie is *Ferris Bueller's Day Off.* In fact, it's quite a perennial family hit. My son created a screensaver with the movie line, "A man with priorities that are messed up does not deserve such a fine automobile as this." My wife particularly likes the statement, "Life moves pretty fast. Sometimes you have to stop and look around or you might miss it." And me, well, I just want to be like Ferris. You're probably wondering, though, how Ferris Bueller relates to the topic of benchmarking and its role in organizational learning.

Ferris is my hero. He is an authentic learner who knows that school isn't necessarily relevant to the core processes of life that he wants to learn. One fine spring day he plays hooky to do some enriching field research. Would I hire Ferris to be a part of my organization? You bet! He's got the adventurous, inventive, never-settle-for-mediocre kind of spirit that we need to deliver quality care.

Picture Ferris sitting in a classroom where the teacher is droning, "A benchmark is the point of reference from which measurements may be made. Benchmarking is the process of . . . *Anyone? Anyone?*" It's doubtful that Ferris would be the MBA scholar enthusiastically waving his hand with the answer. However, if called on, he'd probably say that

benchmarking is the process of stopping and looking around.

So, in the spirit of Ferris, as I offer some ideas on benchmarking, let me begin by admitting that I do not find the word "benchmarking" jazzy or sexy. In fact, it sounds like a dry, academic "ism." However, words like *curiosity*, *learning* and *exploration* are definitely exciting to me, and those are the very things that make benchmarking a great idea when an organization wants to improve a key process or solve a vexing problem. What follows here is a works-for-me, practical approach to benchmarking as a method for process improvement.

Change management expert Daryl Conner cautions that there is simply not enough time or capacity in organizations to implement everyone's good ideas. Nor is there time, I would suggest, to study and improve all of our processes. How do we know which ones to benchmark? Look around. Ask yourself what key activities make or break your bottom line. Pay attention to your data. What are your patients saying? What is your staff collectively frustrated with? If you're already the victor in market share, what sets you apart? Once an area of study has been identified, the research fun begins.

Get the Question Right

"The question that you ask determines the results that you will get." I don't know who said this, but it is wisdom to remember in this first phase of benchmarking. In trying to focus research topic questions, I've found it helpful to use an exercise called The Five Why's. To enrich the

perspective, gather together interested stakeholders and begin with your preliminary problem or question. Then simply ask, "Why?" As you get an answer, ask "Why?" again. Do this five times. You might find that an initial statement like "We need to hire more nurses" will evolve into "We need to free up nurses to spend more time at the bedside." Or maybe, "How do we reduce medication errors?" will become, "How do we get the right treatment to the right patient at the right time?"

Sketch Your Current Process

Take a "before" snapshot of the process that you're wanting to improve. Ask your stakeholders to help you sketch the general progression of actions that constitute the current process. Don't get bogged down in every procedural detail at this point. You're looking for the subtitles. For example, medication administration in a hospital might have three general steps: ordering, processing and delivery.

Discover Who Does This Best and How Do They Do It

Now it's time to go exploring. Reviewing any measurement data you have related to the process you're trying to improve is important. Otherwise, how can you determine if someone else's process results are better than yours? A quick search on the Web will turn up some outstanding benchmarking software products and benchmarking companies and consultants. I must

(Continued on next page)

admit, though, that with the exception of Medical Group Management Associate (MGMA), I've not used them. Lower tech, less costly methods such as conferences and workshops, Web searches, networking, interviewing, business books and articles have met my needs for information and analysis so far.

In general, I explore three areas: our organization, other organizations within our industry and other kinds of businesses. And, in all cases I find out as much detail as possible through interviews, written material, site observation or whatever else the person or company being benchmarked is willing to share about the best practice being researched.

First, I look within. Often employees or departments have different approaches to accomplishing the same process. When people are free to accomplish the task in different ways, chances are that someone has found a best way of doing it. Does one workgroup or person consistently score better than others? If so, they may have discovered a best practice worth sharing with others in your organization. Here are two examples of benchmarking within:

(1) There is always one physician in the group who is far busier than seems possible. We found that by making productivity reports available each month and by including names instead of disguises, physicians take note of the busiest. The physicians need no prompting to analyze the data and benchmark the best. Curt Coggins, MD, is consistently the busiest physician in the OMNI Medical Group, *and* his patients love him. He practices excellent medicine. In addition to the numbers displayed in the productivity reports, surveys told us that his patients think he spends far more time in the exam room with them than he actually does. Many of our physicians, without prompting, have asked

Coggins for his secrets. He freely shares and allows others to shadow him. This is a simple and extremely powerful form of internal benchmarking. Other doctors have changed their workflow and behaviors based on these observations.

(2) Information, combined with a team, leads to even more powerful learning. We organized our physicians into teams, meeting once a week over breakfast or lunch, and reviewed each other's utilization reports. We created the conditions for learning. During one meeting, Jill Wenger, MD, asked the five other doctors in her peer learning team why they referred women with urinary incontinence to urologists. "Aren't urologists surgeons? And isn't incontinence usually a nonsurgical problem?" She sketched on a napkin how she handled this condition, and the others converted the napkin into a protocol they follow to this day. Five benchmarked the one.

Another way to benchmark is to look within the industry. When the 80 physicians in the OMNI group needed to improve the bottom line, we asked MGMA's consulting area to work with us on staffing standards. They designed a staffing matrix that reflected various levels of productivity. The optimal level was so low that many doctors and staff were skeptical. We visited a clinic of similar size in Dallas running quite well with the new matrix, and in a matter of a few hours learned several new processes and approaches for becoming more efficient.

The third area I explore is other kinds of businesses. Part of the key to innovation seems to be learning about fields outside of one's expertise. When I want to make a major leap, my best success often comes from looking outside the medical field. As a quick example, let's return to that process sketch of administering medication mentioned earlier. Dell Computers,

Amazon.com and my favorite local florist all do order, process and delivery pretty well. By researching these three seemingly diverse industries, I might discover similarities in their processes related to order, process and delivery that I could adapt for my organization's use.

A process borrowed from Toyota was the key to the successful reorganization of OMNI's entire central business office. The goal was to create business processes with fewer errors. We studied various industries and saw that Toyota's manufacturing approach of cross-trained small teams might make sense for us. The key to Toyota's approach: teams, information and accountability. We converted our functionally organized (customer service, billing, posting, etc.) office into workgroups. A workgroup has three or four team members who handle all aspects of a business office for an assigned small group of physicians. The operation is now very modular, like an efficient manufacturer. As new physicians come on board, new workgroups can be created. The payoff: business office staff are more accountable for accuracy; communication between patients and business office staff has improved; and the system redesign has created better working relationships between physicians, clinical and business office staff.

Adapt and Adopt

At some time the exciting exploration period ends, and the last, most important step arrives. It may be tempting to grab onto a benchmarked process and implement it by saying, "Okay here's how Best Company A does it, and they get magnificent results, so that's how we're going to do it too." Resist the urge because that would be missing the point of benchmarking. Take the time to evaluate if and how someone else's best practice can be adapted into your

(Continued on next page)

organization in order to make it *your* best practice.

Perhaps the most exciting thing about benchmarking is the learning that takes place about the process being studied. Remember that example about Coggins? When other physicians benchmarked him, they did not *become* him. They molded his practices to fit their personality and abilities.

Here are just a few evaluation points to consider in the adapt/adopt phase:

- The cost of the new process;
- The effect on interaction with other processes and people in the organization;
- The implementation timetable; and
- Compatibility with the organization's culture.

Life moves pretty fast. So does a group practice. By stopping to look around you can learn from others. The three steps: (1) get the question right; (2) sketch your current process, discover who does this best and how do they do it; and (3) adapt and adopt to provide a workable approach to real world benchmarking and process improvement.

Profitability and Operating Costs

This appendix contains articles and data from MGMA's *Performance and Practices of Successful Medical Groups* on profitability and operating costs:

- The Practices of Successful Medical Groups (from *Performance and Practices of Successful Medical Groups: 2003 Report Based on 2002 Data*, pages 82–84)
- MGMA Benchmarks: Better Performing Practices Comparison Exhibits (from *Performance and Practices of Successful Medical Groups: 2005 Report Based on 2004 Data*, pages 142–160)

The Practices of Successful Medical Groups

" Today's better performing medical groups rely on systems to track cost information with the ability to access, on a real time basis, performance and revenue data needed to support various business and clinical decisions. "

Susan E. Davis and
Ernest J. Pavlock, PhD, CPA

Of the better performer categories, the Profitability and Cost Management selection criteria include the greatest number of Cost Survey variables (for example, medical charges and revenue, support staff and operating costs, general operating costs and output measures).

Due to the all-encompassing nature of this category, superior performance speaks directly to a practice's financial health as well as its cost consciousness. Specifically, the criteria used to select better performers in this category are:

■ Greater than the median for revenue after operating costs per full-time equivalent (FTE) physician; and

■ Less than the median for operating cost per medical procedure inside the practice.

An article published in the *Performance and Practices of Successful Medical Groups: 1999 Report Based on 1998 Data* outlined six performance areas in which better performers in this category have excelled:

• Strategic and profit planning;

• Cost management;

• Capital structure and instruments;

• Tax policy and management;

• Internal controls; and

• Financial reporting and performance evaluation.

The MGMA-conducted five-year qualitative analysis (see Executive Summary) based on MGMA better-performing data confirms the original article's findings and suggests additional information on the underlying characteristics contributing to maintaining profitability. For example, strategic and profit planning are more

effective when a formalized process for planning was employed and the process was conducted annually. For financial reporting and performance evaluation, the analysis shows that open sharing of performance information with physicians and staff enhances the information's usefulness. Other key ingredients to profitability include: maintaining a high degree of physician involvement in the planning process and management of the organization; ongoing monitoring of key organizational performance measures; diligent cost management; and the alignment of incentives among physicians and staff.

The qualitative analysis also highlighted the critical importance of the relationships between physicians and administrators. Trust, respect and open communication were commonly identified as success factors from practices. Interestingly, this finding was statistically validated by responses to the MGMA Performance and Practices of Successful Medical Groups Supplemental Survey. Practices identified as better performers rated the overall effectiveness of the physician-administrator team and the communication between physician-administrator team significantly higher than other performers.

As better-performing practices continue to be studied both quantitatively and qualitatively, common success factors have emerged. Although countless organizational behaviors contribute to practice profitability, the following information will provide a glimpse into the many strategies used by successful medical groups.

(Continued on next page)

Management and Culture

Culture

☐ Foster and develop strong physician leaders who can positively influence and guide other physicians and the broader organization

☐ Create an entrepreneurial spirit with physicians and administrators to control costs and encourage the identification of new business opportunities. Make physicians responsible (and give them control) over practice site profitability

☐ Establish practice financial performance as a cultural tenet of the practice and set expectations above industry standards

☐ Reward physicians for cost management. Pure productivity compensation systems, for example, relative value unit (RVU) based systems, may not adequately sensitize physicians to costs

☐ Involve and educate physicians on practice management through presentation and discussion of performance data

Management

☐ Regularly compare practice financial performance (key indicators) to external benchmarks to gain insights about improvement opportunities

☐ Continually monitor and track financial performance and prepare dashboard reports for physicians and staff

☐ Incorporate financial goals in the practice's strategic planning process and build accountability (for example, assign responsibility to physician committees) into the plan

☐ Involve an element of data analysis (such as evidence-based management) into management decision-making

☐ Incorporate quality improvement standards from other business disciplines

Profitability

☐ Maximize physician time with patients by employing adequate staffing

☐ Employ nonphysician providers such as nurse practitioners (NPs), and physician assistants (PAs), to perform lower complexity services

☐ Review physician coding and charting to ensure that patient encounters are optimally reimbursed. There may be a tendency among some physicians to undercode for fear of audits. Educate physicians on proper coding and chart documentation

☐ Minimize low-reimbursement payers, patients and procedures

☐ Compare coding profiles of physicians internally and externally to identify revenue improvement opportunities as well as compliance concerns

☐ Aggressively negotiate with payers to obtain best reimbursement. Establish rapport with payers, monitor claims reimbursement and hold payers accountable

☐ Offer a diverse array of services and ancillaries to provide stable sources of revenue

Increasing Revenue

☐ Evaluate opportunities to expand products and services. Find niches that provide benefits to patients and the practice

☐ Monitor ancillary services that are being referred out of the practice to determine if there is a lost revenue opportunity. Be sure to perform appropriate business planning and cost-benefit analyses to determine if adding a particular service really makes sense

☐ Employ aggressive marketing and public relation techniques. Establish programs to recognize and show appreciation to referring physicians

☐ Involve physicians in community and charity programs (for example, serving on board of directors, participating in free clinics, serving as media experts and sponsoring community wellness programs)

☐ Continually seek to add new patients to the practice. New patients reflect practice growth while churning established patients reflects stagnation

☐ Identify and implement viable expansion opportunities (such as mobile technologies and equipment, new practice locations and extended and weekend hours)

Cost Management

☐ Implement a formal profit and budget planning process that holds the organization accountable for adherence

☐ Utilize the MGMA Chart of Accounts for greater accuracy in financial management. The MGMA Chart of Accounts is an industry accounting standard that will facilitate more precise benchmarking and assist in cost allocation analysis

☐ Establish a detailed expense budget and compare actual expenses to the budget on a monthly basis; prepare and disseminate reports as appropriate

☐ Institute a competitive bidding process for service vendors, and annually conduct a contract/ price review to identify lower cost suppliers

☐ Participate in group-purchasing arrangements to achieve greater cost savings in medical, surgical and administrative supplies

☐ Educate physicians and staff on the need for and impact of cost management in patient care; track RVUs and measure efficiency on an RVU cost-allocated basis

(Continued on next page)

☐ Evaluate physicians in terms of clinical costs, to reduce variability and identify higher cost physicians — this tactic is critically important in heavily capitated environments

☐ Require managers to focus on cost savings by incorporating financial goals into individual annual performance plans; reward them accordingly

☐ Empower supervisor and department heads to be decision makers; hold them accountable

Other Ideas

• Encourage established physicians to mentor new and underperforming physicians on effective care management and patient interaction techniques

• Develop new patient communication packet with personalized letter from physician

• Conduct monthly meetings of multidisciplinary (department) teams to identify wasteful and inefficient processes and develop improvement plans

• Evaluate outsourcing certain areas of operating expense (for example, billing and collections) to determine if savings may be realized

• Base employee salaries on market standards

• Consider open access scheduling to reinforce patient focus and attract new patients

• Embrace new technologies such as EMR and computerized physician order entry to create process efficiencies and eliminate unnecessary costs

Key Profitability and Cost Management Measurements

• Total gross charges per FTE physician

• Gross charges per medical procedure inside the practice

• Total support staff cost per FTE physician

• Total general operating cost per FTE physician

• Total operating cost per FTE physician

• Total medical revenue after operating cost per FTE physician

• Total operating cost as a percentage of total medical revenue

What to Avoid

☐ Skimping on staff resources

☐ Not answering phones during the lunch hour. Schedule staff for complete phone coverage during business hours to ensure patient access and satisfaction. Unsatisfied patients go elsewhere for care and the lunch hour is often their only time to take care of personal business

☐ Not aligning incentives for physicians and staff

Other Standards

☐ _____

☐ _____

☐ _____

Notes

Figure V.A.1

Profitability and cost management demographic profile

	Anesthesiology			Cardiology			Family practice			Gastroenterology			Internal medicine			OB/GYN		
	Better Performers	Others	All	Better Performers	Others	All	Better Performers	Others	All	Better Performers	Others	All	Better Performers	Others	All	Better Performers	Others	All
Practice description																		
Number of practices	4	111	115	21	68	89	9	40	49	4	17	21	2	16	18	7	48	55
Total provider FTE	27.32	25.00	25.00	21.42	14.75	17.00	7.65	6.73	6.78	15.05	10.80	11.50	12.40	8.85	8.85	10.69	7.88	8.00
Total physician FTE	9.17	18.20	18.00	14.70	11.00	11.50	5.00	5.00	5.00	11.98	8.50	8.60	10.25	6.50	6.50	7.50	5.00	5.00
Total NPP FTE	12.28	10.00	10.00	4.00	3.00	3.10	2.90	1.75	1.80	2.00	2.20	2.10	2.15	1.00	1.15	3.75	2.68	2.75
Total support staff FTE	9.88	4.10	4.20	87.44	60.76	66.40	30.65	24.75	26.65	65.75	33.00	35.00	49.18	29.50	30.50	36.54	28.30	29.00
Number of branch clinics	3	1	1	6	4	4	1	3	2	*	2	2	*	3	3	3	2	2
Square footage of all facilities	6,224	2,500	2,500	29,288	19,000	21,638	10,800	9,524	10,000	12,208	10,063	10,563	18,607	13,604	13,604	17,533	10,900	11,202
Net capitation revenue as a percent of total revenue	*	11.66%	11.66%	17.58%	1.38%	5.55%	*	5.09%	5.09%	*	*	*	0.29%	4.88%	0.41%	*	19.40%	19.40%
Breakout of charges by payer																		
Medicare: fee-for-service	29.90%	27.00%	27.00%	48.50%	48.00%	48.00%	15.30%	14.00%	14.00%	30.20%	30.69%	30.69%	36.47%	51.51%	51.51%	3.10%	3.39%	3.24%
Medicare: managed care FFS	0.00%	0.00%	0.00%	0.00%	0.00%	0.00%	0.00%	0.00%	0.00%	0.00%	0.00%	0.00%	0.00%	0.00%	0.00%	0.00%	0.00%	0.00%
Medicare: capitated	0.00%	0.00%	0.00%	0.00%	0.00%	0.00%	0.00%	0.00%	0.00%	0.00%	0.00%	0.00%	0.00%	0.00%	0.00%	0.00%	0.00%	0.00%
Medicaid: fee-for-service	7.30%	6.00%	6.00%	2.76%	2.61%	2.61%	4.69%	3.00%	4.00%	1.35%	2.95%	2.55%	1.02%	1.00%	1.00%	5.80%	6.05%	6.05%
Medicaid: managed care FFS	0.00%	0.00%	0.00%	0.00%	0.00%	0.00%	0.00%	0.00%	0.00%	0.00%	0.00%	0.00%	0.00%	0.00%	0.00%	0.00%	0.00%	0.00%
Medicaid: capitated	0.00%	0.00%	0.00%	0.00%	0.00%	0.00%	0.00%	0.00%	0.00%	0.00%	0.00%	0.00%	0.00%	0.00%	0.00%	0.00%	0.00%	0.00%
Commercial: fee-for-service	7.20%	12.00%	11.60%	27.07%	23.90%	25.00%	9.00%	37.85%	37.69%	34.00%	41.35%	41.35%	15.88%	8.13%	8.13%	27.43%	39.55%	39.55%
Commercial: managed care FFS	39.20%	37.50%	38.00%	10.99%	15.00%	11.63%	3.36%	14.40%	14.30%	23.00%	10.00%	10.00%	42.67%	12.90%	12.90%	45.00%	25.00%	30.00%
Commercial: capitated	0.00%	0.00%	0.00%	0.01%	0.00%	0.00%	0.00%	0.00%	0.00%	0.00%	0.00%	0.00%	0.00%	0.00%	0.00%	0.00%	0.00%	0.00%
Workers' compensation	3.30%	2.39%	2.40%	0.00%	0.00%	0.00%	0.05%	0.58%	0.47%	0.05%	0.11%	0.11%	0.51%	0.00%	0.00%	0.00%	0.00%	0.00%
Charity care and prof courtesy	0.00%	0.00%	0.00%	0.00%	0.00%	0.00%	0.21%	0.05%	0.10%	0.25%	0.11%	0.11%	0.51%	0.00%	0.00%	0.00%	0.40%	0.25%
Self-pay	2.45%	3.16%	3.16%	2.90%	3.00%	2.92%	2.10%	4.40%	4.30%	3.00%	2.00%	2.00%	2.21%	1.70%	1.70%	3.00%	4.00%	3.95%
Other government payers	0.00%	0.20%	0.20%	0.00%	0.00%	0.00%	0.00%	0.00%	0.00%	1.00%	0.00%	0.00%	0.75%	0.00%	0.00%	0.00%	0.00%	0.00%
Geographic section																		
Eastern section	0.87%	20.00%	20.87%	3.37%	14.61%	17.98%	*	14.29%	14.29%	4.76%	14.29%	19.05%	5.56%	11.11%	16.67%	3.64%	18.18%	21.82%
Midwest section	0.87%	25.22%	26.09%	1.12%	24.72%	25.84%	8.16%	26.53%	34.69%	4.76%	14.29%	19.05%	*	22.22%	22.22%	7.27%	9.09%	16.36%
Southern section	1.74%	30.43%	32.17%	13.48%	23.60%	37.08%	6.12%	12.24%	18.37%	9.52%	33.33%	42.86%	5.56%	44.44%	50.00%	1.82%	29.09%	30.91%
Western section	*	20.87%	20.87%	5.62%	13.48%	19.10%	4.08%	28.57%	32.65%	*	19.05%	19.05%	*	11.11%	11.11%	*	30.91%	30.91%
Population designation																		
Nonmetropolitan (50,000 or less)	*	4.50%	4.50%	*	4.55%	4.55%	8.70%	34.78%	43.48%	*	*	*	*	5.56%	5.56%	1.82%	16.36%	18.18%
Metropolitan (50,000 to 250,000)	1.80%	35.14%	36.94%	6.82%	23.86%	30.68%	6.52%	26.09%	32.61%	5.00%	25.00%	30.00%	5.56%	44.44%	50.00%	7.27%	25.45%	32.73%
Metropolitan (250,001 to 1,000,000)	1.80%	36.04%	37.84%	7.95%	28.41%	36.36%	4.35%	8.70%	13.04%	5.00%	30.00%	35.00%	*	22.22%	22.22%	1.82%	30.91%	32.73%
Metropolitan (1,000,001 or more)	*	20.72%	20.72%	9.09%	19.32%	28.41%	*	10.87%	10.87%	10.00%	25.00%	35.00%	5.56%	16.67%	22.22%	1.82%	14.55%	16.36%

(Continued on next page)

Figure V.A.1 — Profitability and cost management demographic profile

	Orthopedic surgery			Pediatrics			Urology			Multispecialty, primary and specialty care, not hospital-owned			Multispecialty, primary care only, not hospital-owned			Primary care single specialties		
	Better Performers	Others	All	Better Performers	Others	All	Better Performers	Others	All	Better Performers	Others	All	Better Performers	Others	All	Better Performers	Others	All
Practice description																		
Number of practices	21	93	114	13	58	71	10	59	69	23	151	174	10	38	48	41	189	230
Total provider FTE	15.60	14.13	14.25	9.00	8.00	8.64	6.50	7.22	7.00	69.52	47.30	51.00	10.30	13.20	12.50	8.45	6.80	7.27
Total physician FTE	9.50	8.37	8.53	7.20	5.84	6.00	5.67	5.10	5.33	49.60	36.75	38.15	8.01	8.45	8.45	6.25	5.00	5.09
Total NPP FTE	6.00	4.23	4.75	2.63	1.70	2.00	1.50	1.15	1.30	17.20	8.00	8.60	2.91	3.00	3.00	2.45	1.35	1.50
Total support staff FTE	58.10	44.90	48.40	30.00	23.38	25.15	40.20	23.77	24.50	278.00	185.66	192.35	45.04	41.36	41.36	28.25	21.95	22.56
Number of branch clinics	5	2	2	2	2	2	4	2	3	7	6	6	3	4	4	2	2	2
Square footage of all facilities	24,925	16,794	18,656	14,447	10,058	10,700	11,669	10,106	10,389	103,000	71,743	76,326	19,024	17,325	17,525	11,500	9,524	10,000
Net capitation revenue as a percent of total revenue	*	9.29%	9.29%	9.82%	10.37%	10.37%	*	3.71%	3.71%	12.12%	8.92%	9.80%	14.71%	6.98%	7.16%	4.96%	10.61%	9.37%
Breakout of charges by payer																		
Medicare: fee-for-service	24.00%	22.29%	22.32%	0.00%	0.00%	0.00%	52.00%	42.00%	42.00%	27.15%	26.00%	26.00%	28.31%	22.57%	23.00%	0.00%	11.60%	10.42%
Medicare: managed care FFS	0.00%	0.00%	0.00%	0.00%	0.00%	0.00%	0.00%	0.00%	0.00%	0.00%	0.00%	0.00%	0.00%	0.00%	0.00%	0.00%	0.00%	0.00%
Medicare: capitated	0.00%	0.00%	0.00%	0.00%	0.00%	0.00%	0.00%	0.00%	0.00%	0.00%	0.00%	0.00%	0.00%	0.00%	0.00%	0.00%	0.00%	0.00%
Medicaid: fee-for-service	2.90%	2.00%	2.00%	3.75%	2.75%	2.75%	2.19%	2.00%	2.10%	4.00%	3.00%	3.09%	1.00%	4.80%	4.00%	4.00%	2.93%	3.00%
Medicaid: managed care FFS	0.00%	0.00%	0.00%	0.00%	0.00%	0.00%	0.00%	0.00%	0.00%	0.00%	0.00%	0.00%	0.00%	0.00%	0.00%	0.00%	0.00%	0.00%
Medicaid: capitated	0.00%	0.00%	0.00%	0.00%	0.00%	0.00%	0.00%	0.00%	0.00%	0.00%	0.00%	0.00%	0.00%	0.00%	0.00%	0.00%	0.00%	0.00%
Commercial: fee-for-service	23.00%	24.31%	23.72%	33.32%	35.00%	34.50%	26.66%	20.00%	20.00%	37.88%	40.55%	40.46%	42.40%	34.00%	34.80%	34.00%	30.70%	32.00%
Commercial: managed care FFS	27.00%	21.16%	22.00%	32.05%	20.00%	22.20%	14.32%	16.00%	15.00%	2.50%	0.00%	0.00%	6.64%	1.00%	2.28%	31.00%	17.50%	18.40%
Commercial: capitated	0.00%	0.00%	0.00%	0.00%	0.00%	0.00%	0.00%	0.00%	0.00%	1.00%	0.90%	1.00%	0.00%	0.55%	0.00%	0.00%	0.00%	0.00%
Workers' compensation	11.80%	10.00%	10.00%	0.00%	0.00%	0.00%	0.25%	0.08%	0.10%	0.00%	0.00%	0.00%	1.00%	1.00%	1.00%	0.00%	0.00%	0.00%
Charity care and prof courtesy	0.00%	0.20%	0.19%	0.00%	0.00%	0.00%	0.25%	0.26%	0.26%	0.00%	0.00%	0.00%	0.25%	0.49%	0.49%	0.05%	0.00%	0.00%
Self-pay	3.00%	2.60%	2.70%	2.00%	4.20%	4.00%	2.00%	2.00%	2.00%	3.50%	3.04%	3.15%	3.58%	6.00%	5.00%	3.00%	3.00%	3.00%
Other government payers	0.00%	0.00%	0.00%	0.00%	0.00%	0.00%	0.00%	0.00%	0.00%	0.00%	0.00%	0.00%	0.00%	0.00%	0.00%	0.00%	0.00%	0.00%
Geographic section																		
Eastern section	4.39%	14.91%	19.30%	4.23%	28.17%	32.39%	2.90%	23.19%	26.09%	2.87%	16.09%	18.97%	8.33%	20.83%	29.17%	3.91%	26.52%	30.43%
Midwest section	5.26%	21.93%	27.19%	1.41%	9.86%	11.27%	4.35%	14.49%	18.84%	6.90%	22.99%	29.89%	4.17%	18.75%	22.92%	3.91%	13.48%	17.39%
Southern section	4.39%	19.30%	23.68%	8.45%	18.31%	26.76%	4.35%	28.99%	33.33%	2.87%	24.14%	27.01%	4.17%	14.58%	18.75%	6.52%	23.04%	29.57%
Western section	4.39%	25.44%	29.82%	4.23%	25.35%	29.58%	2.90%	18.84%	21.74%	0.57%	23.56%	24.14%	4.17%	25.00%	29.17%	3.48%	19.13%	22.61%
Population designation																		
Nonmetropolitan (50,000 or less)	0.93%	15.74%	16.67%	2.90%	10.14%	13.04%	*	4.48%	4.48%	3.45%	27.59%	31.03%	11.11%	33.33%	44.44%	4.02%	18.75%	22.77%
Metropolitan (50,000 to 250,000)	5.56%	27.78%	33.33%	5.80%	28.99%	34.78%	8.96%	34.33%	43.28%	7.47%	32.76%	40.23%	4.44%	24.44%	28.89%	5.80%	27.23%	33.04%
Metropolitan (250,001 to 1,000,000)	6.48%	25.00%	31.48%	1.45%	23.19%	24.64%	2.99%	28.36%	31.34%	1.72%	18.97%	20.69%	4.44%	15.56%	20.00%	3.13%	27.23%	30.36%
Metropolitan (1,000,001 or more)	4.63%	13.89%	18.52%	8.70%	18.84%	27.54%	2.99%	17.91%	20.90%	0.57%	7.47%	8.05%	*	6.67%	6.67%	4.91%	8.93%	13.84%

(Continued on next page)

Figure V.A.1

Profitability and cost management demographic profile

	Medicine single specialty excluding general internal medicine			Surgical single specialty			Multispecialty all owners			Multispecialty, all owners, less than or equal to 50 percent, primary care			Multispecialty, all owners, greater than 50 percent primary care			Multispecialty, not hospital-owned, less than or equal to 50 percent, primary care		
	Better Performers	Others	All	Better Performers	Others	All	Better Performers	Others	All	Better Performers	Others	All	Better Performers	Others	All	Better Performers	Others	All
Practice description																		
Number of practices	36	187	223	46	228	274	55	270	325	17	79	96	40	167	207	15	66	81
Total provider FTE	15.50	12.47	13.05	12.65	11.00	11.70	45.38	36.50	39.62	83.85	62.00	68.08	31.83	25.95	26.05	83.85	58.70	62.70
Total physician FTE	13.00	8.50	9.00	8.30	6.00	6.23	35.27	25.40	27.00	69.62	49.20	52.49	21.08	18.00	18.40	56.04	49.00	49.20
Total NPP FTE	3.30	2.00	2.50	5.50	3.00	3.00	9.21	6.00	6.80	21.89	10.00	11.86	4.47	4.35	4.37	24.00	9.80	10.50
Total support staff FTE	72.43	32.50	35.15	54.01	29.00	30.75	167.80	115.77	135.72	417.51	259.98	264.80	115.35	84.85	92.25	417.51	255.96	260.01
Number of branch clinics	4	3	3	4	2	3	4	7	7	8	7	7	4	8	7	9	6	6
Square footage of all facilities	25,866	11,900	13,264	22,058	11,585	12,584	74,340	46,608	54,496	169,000	110,290	115,000	54,992	38,715	39,000	170,000	103,587	105,034
Net capitation revenue as a percent of total revenue	9.55%	2.83%	6.17%	*	6.55%	6.55%	7.16%	7.75%	7.71%	17.93%	9.21%	10.66%	7.47%	7.12%	7.16%	30.13%	9.44%	11.18%
Breakout of charges by payer																		
Medicare: fee-for-service	43.57%	37.00%	38.54%	25.00%	30.00%	29.00%	27.00%	25.00%	25.61%	33.61%	27.72%	29.25%	25.92%	22.34%	24.00%	33.95%	28.62%	30.13%
Medicare: managed care FFS	0.00%	0.00%	0.00%	0.00%	0.00%	0.00%	0.00%	0.00%	0.00%	0.00%	0.00%	0.00%	0.00%	0.00%	0.00%	0.00%	0.00%	0.00%
Medicare: capitated	0.00%	0.00%	0.00%	0.00%	0.00%	0.00%	0.00%	0.00%	0.00%	0.00%	0.00%	0.00%	0.00%	0.00%	0.00%	0.00%	0.00%	0.00%
Medicaid: fee-for-service	2.55%	3.00%	3.00%	2.19%	3.00%	2.87%	3.10%	5.00%	4.71%	4.90%	3.34%	4.00%	2.00%	5.93%	5.00%	4.40%	3.34%	3.90%
Medicaid: managed care FFS	0.00%	0.00%	0.00%	0.00%	0.00%	0.00%	0.00%	0.00%	0.00%	0.00%	0.00%	0.00%	0.00%	0.00%	0.00%	0.00%	0.00%	0.00%
Medicaid: capitated	0.00%	0.00%	0.00%	0.00%	0.00%	0.00%	0.00%	0.00%	0.00%	0.00%	0.00%	0.00%	0.00%	0.00%	0.00%	0.00%	0.00%	0.00%
Commercial: fee-for-service	24.50%	30.00%	30.00%	20.00%	27.20%	26.83%	40.60%	39.05%	39.13%	37.43%	41.30%	40.55%	40.67%	37.00%	37.00%	40.30%	40.50%	40.50%
Commercial: managed care FFS	10.99%	7.00%	7.00%	21.00%	16.00%	16.21%	2.28%	0.00%	0.00%	2.50%	0.00%	0.00%	2.10%	0.50%	0.90%	0.00%	0.00%	0.00%
Commercial: capitated	0.00%	0.00%	0.00%	0.00%	0.00%	0.00%	0.00%	0.00%	0.00%	0.00%	0.00%	0.00%	0.00%	0.00%	0.00%	0.00%	0.00%	0.00%
Workers' compensation	0.00%	0.01%	0.01%	9.20%	1.00%	1.00%	1.00%	0.60%	0.82%	1.07%	1.00%	1.00%	1.00%	0.50%	0.60%	1.20%	1.00%	1.00%
Charity care and prof courtesy	0.08%	0.00%	0.00%	1.00%	0.19%	0.20%	0.00%	0.00%	0.00%	0.00%	0.00%	0.00%	0.00%	0.00%	0.00%	0.00%	0.00%	0.00%
Self-pay	2.90%	3.00%	3.00%	2.56%	3.00%	3.00%	3.70%	3.80%	3.75%	3.50%	3.56%	3.56%	3.08%	3.89%	3.70%	3.05%	3.40%	3.10%
Other government payers	0.00%	0.00%	0.00%	0.00%	0.00%	0.00%	0.00%	0.00%	0.00%	0.00%	0.00%	0.00%	0.00%	0.00%	0.00%	0.00%	0.00%	0.00%
Geographic section																		
Eastern section	3.59%	18.83%	22.42%	3.28%	18.61%	21.90%	4.00%	19.08%	23.08%	3.13%	18.75%	21.88%	6.28%	16.91%	23.19%	3.70%	14.81%	18.52%
Midwest section	1.35%	17.94%	19.28%	4.38%	21.53%	25.91%	6.15%	26.46%	32.62%	7.29%	22.92%	30.21%	5.80%	27.54%	33.33%	8.64%	22.22%	30.86%
Southern section	8.97%	25.11%	34.08%	5.84%	24.09%	29.93%	4.00%	18.15%	22.15%	6.25%	20.83%	27.08%	3.86%	16.43%	20.29%	4.94%	23.46%	28.40%
Western section	2.24%	21.97%	24.22%	3.28%	18.98%	22.26%	2.77%	19.38%	22.15%	1.04%	19.79%	20.83%	3.38%	19.81%	23.19%	1.23%	20.99%	22.22%
Population designation																		
Nonmetropolitan (50,000 or less)	0.46%	3.67%	4.13%	1.50%	9.40%	10.90%	6.21%	28.88%	35.09%	3.13%	27.08%	30.21%	6.83%	30.73%	37.56%	3.70%	25.93%	29.63%
Metropolitan (50,000 to 250,000)	3.67%	26.61%	30.28%	6.39%	27.82%	34.21%	7.76%	26.71%	34.47%	13.54%	28.13%	41.67%	8.29%	23.41%	31.71%	13.58%	29.63%	43.21%
Metropolitan (250,001 to 1,000,000)	6.42%	31.19%	37.61%	4.89%	28.20%	33.08%	2.17%	19.88%	22.05%	1.04%	19.79%	20.83%	2.93%	19.02%	21.95%	1.23%	19.75%	20.99%
Metropolitan (1,000,001 or more)	5.50%	22.48%	27.98%	3.38%	18.42%	21.80%	0.93%	7.45%	8.39%	*	7.29%	7.29%	0.98%	7.80%	8.78%	*	6.17%	6.17%

(Continued on next page)

Figure V.A.1

Profitability and cost management demographic profile

	Multispecialty, not hospital-owned greater than 50 percent primary care			Multispecialty, hospital-owned less than or equal to 50 percent, primary care			Multispecialty, hospital-owned greater than 50 percent primary care			Anesthesiology with NPPs		
	Better Performers	Others	All	Better Performers	Others	All	Better Performers	Others	All	Better Performers	Others	All
Practice description												
Number of practices	22	105	127	4	11	15	17	63	80	2	70	72
Total provider FTE	34.50	23.50	26.00	209.55	122.35	122.35	49.08	27.30	28.60	25.30	25.00	25.00
Total physician FTE	21.08	18.00	18.40	154.61	97.90	98.21	16.00	21.00	19.25	8.30	15.92	15.67
Total NPP FTE	7.00	4.21	4.40	54.95	17.52	19.00	6.80	4.00	4.20	17.00	10.00	10.00
Total support staff FTE	128.80	92.85	94.00	739.51	426.00	433.83	78.18	79.00	78.59	16.68	4.50	4.75
Number of branch clinics	3	5	4	16	17	17	16	11	11	4	1	1
Square footage of all facilities	56,496	37,111	40,038	168,000	215,576	191,788	37,117	38,715	38,715	12,228	2,400	2,450
Net capitation revenue as a percent of total revenue	11.84%	7.24%	7.56%	8.51%	10.28%	10.28%	6.92%	7.45%	7.12%	*	12.33%	12.33%
Breakout of charges by payer												
Medicare: fee-for-service	25.15%	23.00%	23.25%	24.49%	25.14%	25.14%	24.00%	25.20%	25.00%	29.90%	27.00%	28.00%
Medicare: managed care FFS	0.00%	0.00%	0.00%	0.00%	0.00%	0.00%	0.00%	0.00%	0.00%	4.80%	0.00%	0.00%
Medicare: capitated	0.00%	0.00%	0.00%	0.00%	0.00%	0.00%	0.00%	0.00%	0.00%	0.00%	0.00%	0.00%
Medicaid: fee-for-service	1.79%	3.71%	3.05%	9.74%	6.00%	7.79%	6.90%	8.10%	8.00%	6.05%	6.82%	6.82%
Medicaid: managed care FFS	0.00%	0.00%	0.00%	0.00%	0.00%	0.00%	0.00%	0.00%	0.00%	0.00%	0.00%	0.00%
Medicaid: capitated	0.00%	0.00%	0.00%	0.00%	0.00%	0.00%	0.00%	0.00%	0.00%	0.00%	0.00%	0.00%
Commercial: fee-for-service	48.06%	38.03%	39.13%	4.76%	44.25%	42.00%	10.00%	38.00%	36.40%	20.47%	10.00%	10.00%
Commercial: managed care FFS	2.18%	2.50%	2.18%	40.42%	3.00%	11.00%	39.40%	0.00%	0.00%	29.54%	35.70%	35.70%
Commercial: capitated	0.00%	0.00%	0.00%	0.00%	0.00%	0.00%	0.43%	0.28%	0.35%	0.00%	0.00%	0.00%
Workers' compensation	0.85%	0.70%	0.70%	2.10%	0.77%	1.40%	0.00%	0.00%	0.00%	6.75%	2.39%	2.39%
Charity care and prof courtesy	0.00%	0.00%	0.00%	0.25%	0.00%	0.00%	0.00%	0.00%	0.00%	0.00%	0.00%	0.00%
Self-pay	3.04%	4.00%	3.82%	7.98%	4.65%	5.00%	4.24%	3.00%	3.00%	2.50%	3.00%	3.00%
Other government payers	0.00%	0.00%	0.00%	0.00%	0.00%	0.00%	0.00%	0.00%	0.00%	0.00%	0.40%	0.32%
Geographic section												
Eastern section	6.30%	16.54%	22.83%	6.67%	33.33%	40.00%	5.00%	18.75%	23.75%	1.39%	20.83%	22.22%
Midwest section	3.94%	22.05%	25.98%	*	26.67%	26.67%	10.00%	35.00%	45.00%	1.39%	25.00%	26.39%
Southern section	3.15%	20.47%	23.62%	13.33%	6.67%	20.00%	6.25%	8.75%	15.00%	*	37.50%	37.50%
Western section	3.94%	23.62%	27.56%	6.67%	6.67%	13.33%	*	16.25%	16.25%	*	13.89%	13.89%
Population designation												
Nonmetropolitan (50,000 or less)	5.60%	31.20%	36.80%	6.67%	26.67%	33.33%	8.75%	30.00%	38.75%	*	1.45%	1.45%
Metropolitan (50,000 to 250,000)	8.80%	26.40%	35.20%	6.67%	26.67%	33.33%	6.25%	20.00%	26.25%	*	42.03%	42.03%
Metropolitan (250,001 to 1,000,000)	3.20%	16.00%	19.20%	6.67%	13.33%	20.00%	2.50%	23.75%	26.25%	2.90%	37.68%	40.58%
Metropolitan (1,000,001 or more)	*	8.80%	8.80%	6.67%	6.67%	13.33%	3.75%	5.00%	8.75%	*	15.94%	15.94%

| Figure V.A.2 | Profitability and cost management indicators | | | |

Cardiology

	Better Performers	Others	All
Productivity			
Total gross charges per FTE physician	$2,799,759	$2,361,279	$2,442,373
Total RVUs per FTE physician	33,255	18,583	19,131
Physician work RVUs per FTE physician	12,988	9,263	9,774
Medical procedures inside practice to total gross charges ratio	34.82%	33.16%	33.51%
Medical procedures outside practice to total gross charges ratio	32.16%	36.92%	35.74%
Surgical procedures inside practice to total gross charges ratio	0.10%	0.16%	0.14%
Surgical procedures outside practice to total gross charges ratio	4.52%	3.83%	4.05%
Laboratory procedures to total gross charges ratio	0.28%	0.49%	0.41%
Radiology procedures to total gross charges ratio	20.12%	18.40%	18.75%
Total procedures per FTE physician	12,135	10,337	10,720
Patients per FTE physician	1,427	1,462	1,461
Encounters per FTE physician	6,126	4,767	5,322
Revenue			
Total medical revenue per FTE physician	$1,200,486	$985,772	$1,028,721
Total medical revenue after operating cost per FTE physician	$647,577	$489,486	$521,454
Total medical revenue after operating and NPP cost per FTE physician	$585,353	$459,511	$497,699
Cost management			
Total operating cost as a percent of total medical revenue	42.93%	49.87%	48.80%
Total operating cost per FTE physician	$539,241	$503,031	$518,066
Total operating and NPP cost as a percent of total medical revenue	48.07%	52.34%	51.70%
Total operating and NPP cost per FTE physician	$579,217	$538,446	$556,874
Total support staff cost per FTE physician	$293,152	$258,157	$263,748
– Total business operations support staff cost per FTE physician	$60,560	$56,547	$57,995
– Total front office support staff cost per FTE physician	$41,035	$45,413	$44,730
– Total clinical support staff cost per FTE physician	$52,312	$60,013	$56,383
– Total ancillary support staff cost per FTE physician	$41,602	$41,663	$41,663
Total general operating cost per FTE physician	$272,246	$242,789	$246,455
Total NPP cost per FTE physician	$24,335	$20,782	$21,399
Total physician cost per FTE physician	$560,904	$458,401	$491,390
Total support staff cost as a percent of total medical revenue	22.58%	25.93%	25.24%
– Information technology cost as a percent of total medical revenue	1.25%	1.28%	1.27%
– Professional liability cost as a percent of total medical revenue	1.82%	1.61%	1.64%
– Drug supply cost as a percent of total medical revenue	0.05%	3.93%	3.07%
– Medical/surgical supply cost as a percent of total medical revenue	0.86%	1.00%	0.97%
– Building and occupancy cost as a percent of total medical revenue	4.16%	4.82%	4.73%
Total NPP cost as a percent of total medical revenue	2.05%	2.14%	2.10%
Total physician cost as a percent of total medical revenue	48.55%	46.28%	47.19%
Operating cost per medical procedure inside the practice	$41.40	$54.84	$49.88
Provider cost per medical procedure inside the practice	$47.87	$40.87	$42.01
Operating cost per medical procedure outside the practice	$20.05	$21.20	$20.86
Provider cost per medical procedure outside the practice	$47.60	$44.31	$44.91
Operating cost per surgical procedure inside the practice	$107.80	$78.48	$98.13
Provider cost per surgical procedure inside the practice	$120.09	$79.46	$89.69
Operating cost per surgical procedure outside the practice	$94.40	$119.07	$107.81
Provider cost per surgical procedure outside the practice	$246.66	$258.08	$256.24
Operating cost per laboratory procedure	$6.28	$5.15	$5.28
Provider cost per laboratory procedure	$4.31	$3.88	$3.99
Operating cost per radiology procedure	$171.54	$160.69	$164.85
Provider cost per radiology procedure	$81.12	$82.99	$82.23

ᗡ—⚊ Key Indicator

Figure V.A.3	Profitability and cost management indicators		

Orthopedic surgery

	Better Performers	Others	All
Productivity			
Total gross charges per FTE physician	$2,796,815	$2,085,597	$2,219,916
Total RVUs per FTE physician	26,701	19,844	20,872
Physician work RVUs per FTE physician	11,451	8,366	8,755
Medical procedures inside practice to total gross charges ratio	18.90%	16.19%	16.63%
Medical procedures outside practice to total gross charges ratio	0.69%	0.63%	0.67%
Surgical procedures inside practice to total gross charges ratio	5.05%	6.54%	6.26%
Surgical procedures outside practice to total gross charges ratio	62.89%	61.75%	61.77%
Laboratory procedures to total gross charges ratio	1.53%	0.01%	0.01%
Radiology procedures to total gross charges ratio	10.87%	9.11%	9.15%
Total procedures per FTE physician	11,414	6,644	7,305
Patients per FTE physician	1,781	1,370	1,405
Encounters per FTE physician	4,534	3,864	4,023
Revenue			
Total medical revenue per FTE physician	$1,327,374	$986,887	$1,032,830
Total medical revenue after operating cost per FTE physician	$842,716	$520,040	$560,833
Total medical revenue after operating and NPP cost per FTE physician	$663,995	$480,664	$508,329
Cost management			
Total operating cost as a percent of total medical revenue	40.28%	47.36%	45.91%
Total operating cost per FTE physician	$487,061	$445,844	$470,206
Total operating and NPP cost as a percent of total medical revenue	43.76%	52.27%	50.64%
Total operating and NPP cost per FTE physician	$570,086	$520,765	$521,787
Total support staff cost per FTE physician	$268,655	$226,663	$233,172
− Total business operations support staff cost per FTE physician	$67,815	$57,528	$59,692
− Total front office support staff cost per FTE physician	$63,346	$53,732	$54,793
− Total clinical support staff cost per FTE physician	$42,628	$41,284	$41,467
− Total ancillary support staff cost per FTE physician	$31,766	$27,751	$28,728
Total general operating cost per FTE physician	$253,498	$220,157	$225,613
Total NPP cost per FTE physician	$47,925	$45,899	$46,663
Total physician cost per FTE physician	$621,834	$458,672	$488,635
Total support staff cost as a percent of total medical revenue	20.70%	23.00%	22.46%
− Information technology cost as a percent of total medical revenue	1.56%	1.32%	1.32%
− Professional liability cost as a percent of total medical revenue	2.34%	3.25%	3.06%
− Drug supply cost as a percent of total medical revenue	0.93%	1.74%	1.48%
− Medical/surgical supply cost as a percent of total medical revenue	1.54%	1.30%	1.35%
− Building and occupancy cost as a percent of total medical revenue	4.68%	5.76%	5.53%
Total NPP cost as a percent of total medical revenue	3.89%	4.02%	4.00%
Total physician cost as a percent of total medical revenue	52.08%	48.17%	48.72%
Operating cost per medical procedure inside the practice	$25.61	$44.50	$39.82
Provider cost per medical procedure inside the practice	$26.15	$29.59	$26.81
Operating cost per medical procedure outside the practice	$14.57	$18.14	$17.58
Provider cost per medical procedure outside the practice	$33.44	$35.35	$35.20
Operating cost per surgical procedure inside the practice	$69.27	$103.97	$96.47
Provider cost per surgical procedure inside the practice	$69.84	$71.38	$70.67
Operating cost per surgical procedure outside the practice	$185.23	$187.60	$187.60
Provider cost per surgical procedure outside the practice	$450.02	$378.15	$410.39
Operating cost per laboratory procedure	$5.33	$9.86	$9.58
Provider cost per laboratory procedure	$3.13	$3.91	$3.91
Operating cost per radiology procedure	$47.63	$49.94	$49.41
Provider cost per radiology procedure	$29.54	$25.69	$26.37

ℚ—ⴽ Key Indicator

From the *Performance and Practices of Successful Medical Groups, 2005 Report Based on 2004 Data.*
Reprinted with permission from the Medical Group Management Association, 104 Inverness Terrace East,
Englewood, Colorado 80112. www.mgma.com. Copyright 2005. Pages 142–160.

Figure V.A.4	Profitability and cost management indicators

Pediatrics

	Better Performers	Others	All
Productivity			
Total gross charges per FTE physician	$918,719	$744,087	$760,589
Total RVUs per FTE physician	14,026	11,664	12,227
Physician work RVUs per FTE physician	6,561	5,440	6,331
Medical procedures inside practice to total gross charges ratio	85.74%	87.07%	86.46%
Medical procedures outside practice to total gross charges ratio	4.60%	4.76%	4.76%
Surgical procedures inside practice to total gross charges ratio	1.79%	1.74%	1.74%
Surgical procedures outside practice to total gross charges ratio	1.15%	0.40%	1.09%
Laboratory procedures to total gross charges ratio	6.07%	4.45%	4.49%
Radiology procedures to total gross charges ratio	2.33%	1.18%	1.78%
Total procedures per FTE physician	17,107	13,033	13,682
Patients per FTE physician	2,968	2,498	2,508
Encounters per FTE physician	6,966	6,237	6,491
Revenue			
Total medical revenue per FTE physician	$669,972	$512,788	$538,569
Total medical revenue after operating cost per FTE physician	$285,871	$198,594	$221,883
Total medical revenue after operating and NPP cost per FTE physician	$259,984	$178,207	$198,083
Cost management			
Total operating cost as a percent of total medical revenue	55.14%	59.64%	59.18%
Total operating cost per FTE physician	$367,431	$312,055	$320,653
Total operating and NPP cost as a percent of total medical revenue	59.93%	67.14%	64.84%
Total operating and NPP cost per FTE physician	$411,116	$357,414	$365,754
Total support staff cost per FTE physician	$170,690	$147,732	$153,751
– Total business operations support staff cost per FTE physician	$41,783	$37,128	$37,174
– Total front office support staff cost per FTE physician	$33,712	$32,075	$32,322
– Total clinical support staff cost per FTE physician	$53,837	$54,258	$54,164
– Total ancillary support staff cost per FTE physician	$9,202	$7,212	$7,212
Total general operating cost per FTE physician	$190,097	$166,388	$171,246
Total NPP cost per FTE physician	$27,131	$21,736	$23,872
Total physician cost per FTE physician	$242,187	$172,580	$190,396
Total support staff cost as a percent of total medical revenue	26.95%	28.99%	28.77%
– Information technology cost as a percent of total medical revenue	2.11%	2.16%	2.14%
– Professional liability cost as a percent of total medical revenue	1.72%	1.98%	1.93%
– Drug supply cost as a percent of total medical revenue	11.56%	10.07%	10.27%
– Medical/surgical supply cost as a percent of total medical revenue	1.61%	2.09%	1.96%
– Building and occupancy cost as a percent of total medical revenue	6.28%	6.99%	6.96%
Total NPP cost as a percent of total medical revenue	4.34%	4.13%	4.28%
Total physician cost as a percent of total medical revenue	33.39%	35.16%	34.89%
Operating cost per medical procedure inside the practice	$24.04	$30.24	$28.04
Provider cost per medical procedure inside the practice	$15.19	$16.84	$16.83
Operating cost per medical procedure outside the practice	$17.24	$21.98	$20.76
Provider cost per medical procedure outside the practice	$28.97	$28.10	$28.92
Operating cost per surgical procedure inside the practice	$34.24	$37.53	$37.22
Provider cost per surgical procedure inside the practice	$24.36	$19.83	$21.54
Operating cost per surgical procedure outside the practice	$40.48	$47.87	$44.67
Provider cost per surgical procedure outside the practice	$76.28	$47.41	$65.62
Operating cost per laboratory procedure	$5.80	$7.81	$7.00
Provider cost per laboratory procedure	$5.37	$4.54	$5.01
Operating cost per radiology procedure	$47.29	$20.48	$22.85
Provider cost per radiology procedure	$19.88	$13.18	$13.18

ꝺ——ʞ Key Indicator

From the *Performance and Practices of Successful Medical Groups, 2005 Report Based on 2004 Data.*
Reprinted with permission from the Medical Group Management Association, 104 Inverness Terrace East,
Englewood, Colorado 80112. www.mgma.com. Copyright 2005. Pages 142–160.

Figure **V.A.5**	Profitability and cost management indicators			

Urology

	Better Performers	Others	All
Productivity			
Total gross charges per FTE physician	$1,921,591	$1,698,696	$1,757,344
Total RVUs per FTE physician	27,571	19,404	19,832
Physician work RVUs per FTE physician	10,045	9,788	9,916
Medical procedures inside practice to total gross charges ratio	15.73%	18.50%	17.07%
Medical procedures outside practice to total gross charges ratio	1.44%	2.24%	1.81%
Surgical procedures inside practice to total gross charges ratio	24.06%	16.74%	18.00%
Surgical procedures outside practice to total gross charges ratio	22.07%	34.03%	32.95%
Laboratory procedures to total gross charges ratio	2.09%	2.76%	2.64%
Radiology procedures to total gross charges ratio	3.75%	3.61%	3.65%
Total procedures per FTE physician	8,571	8,103	8,308
Patients per FTE physician	1,491	2,027	2,020
Encounters per FTE physician	4,303	5,167	4,709
Revenue			
Total medical revenue per FTE physician	$1,165,429	$914,960	$936,825
Total medical revenue after operating cost per FTE physician	$585,275	$421,592	$459,490
Total medical revenue after operating and NPP cost per FTE physician	$606,254	$442,641	$451,752
Cost management			
Total operating cost as a percent of total medical revenue	39.01%	50.93%	50.17%
Total operating cost per FTE physician	$492,992	$445,833	$452,939
Total operating and NPP cost as a percent of total medical revenue	44.19%	52.30%	51.96%
Total operating and NPP cost per FTE physician	$477,815	$472,319	$475,067
Total support staff cost per FTE physician	$211,942	$168,766	$177,796
– Total business operations support staff cost per FTE physician	$49,972	$45,713	$46,850
– Total front office support staff cost per FTE physician	$47,252	$44,312	$44,850
– Total clinical support staff cost per FTE physician	$42,319	$44,693	$44,036
– Total ancillary support staff cost per FTE physician	$19,752	$17,745	$17,745
Total general operating cost per FTE physician	$281,050	$279,858	$279,858
Total NPP cost per FTE physician	$23,554	$18,295	$20,566
Total physician cost per FTE physician	$568,733	$390,729	$435,200
Total support staff cost as a percent of total medical revenue	17.33%	18.66%	18.58%
– Information technology cost as a percent of total medical revenue	1.28%	1.34%	1.34%
– Professional liability cost as a percent of total medical revenue	1.04%	2.17%	2.03%
– Drug supply cost as a percent of total medical revenue	8.10%	8.41%	8.28%
– Medical/surgical supply cost as a percent of total medical revenue	3.27%	2.35%	2.41%
– Building and occupancy cost as a percent of total medical revenue	3.62%	5.57%	5.45%
Total NPP cost as a percent of total medical revenue	2.36%	1.84%	1.89%
Total physician cost as a percent of total medical revenue	47.85%	44.71%	45.05%
Operating cost per medical procedure inside the practice	$42.50	$59.05	$56.82
Provider cost per medical procedure inside the practice	$31.57	$31.81	$31.81
Operating cost per medical procedure outside the practice	$11.49	$17.25	$14.29
Provider cost per medical procedure outside the practice	$33.80	$34.81	$34.43
Operating cost per surgical procedure inside the practice	$141.26	$144.24	$144.24
Provider cost per surgical procedure inside the practice	$119.32	$87.81	$93.39
Operating cost per surgical procedure outside the practice	$124.16	$164.10	$147.03
Provider cost per surgical procedure outside the practice	$301.42	$318.08	$318.08
Operating cost per laboratory procedure	$6.15	$6.37	$6.37
Provider cost per laboratory procedure	$5.40	$5.78	$5.65
Operating cost per radiology procedure	$45.01	$75.81	$67.47
Provider cost per radiology procedure	$70.61	$59.66	$64.35

8——⋆ Key Indicator

From the *Performance and Practices of Successful Medical Groups, 2005 Report Based on 2004 Data*.
Reprinted with permission from the Medical Group Management Association, 104 Inverness Terrace East,
Englewood, Colorado 80112. www.mgma.com. Copyright 2005. Pages 142–160.

Figure **V.A.6**	Profitability and cost management indicators			

Multispecialty, primary and specialty care not hospital-owned

	Better Performers	Others	All
Productivity			
⊕ Total gross charges per FTE physician	$1,371,450	$1,094,961	$1,136,148
Total RVUs per FTE physician	15,704	12,288	12,808
Physician work RVUs per FTE physician	6,583	5,956	6,085
Medical procedures inside practice to total gross charges ratio	30.16%	37.96%	36.47%
Medical procedures outside practice to total gross charges ratio	8.73%	7.96%	8.28%
Surgical procedures inside practice to total gross charges ratio	11.55%	4.59%	4.97%
Surgical procedures outside practice to total gross charges ratio	16.39%	15.34%	15.65%
Laboratory procedures to total gross charges ratio	9.48%	9.80%	9.76%
Radiology procedures to total gross charges ratio	12.08%	9.87%	10.34%
Total procedures per FTE physician	12,354	11,204	11,273
Patients per FTE physician	1,722	1,422	1,486
Encounters per FTE physician	4,932	4,728	4,752
Revenue			
⊕ Total medical revenue per FTE physician	$760,749	$692,655	$713,722
Total medical revenue after operating cost per FTE physician	$350,630	$273,037	$286,218
Total medical revenue after operating and NPP cost per FTE physician	$336,086	$256,170	$266,579
Cost management			
⊕ Total operating cost as a percent of total medical revenue	54.96%	59.41%	59.03%
Total operating cost per FTE physician	$423,486	$413,388	$414,079
Total operating and NPP cost as a percent of total medical revenue	58.24%	62.80%	62.12%
Total operating and NPP cost per FTE physician	$449,720	$441,855	$444,058
Total support staff cost per FTE physician	$202,202	$199,328	$199,820
– Total business operations support staff cost per FTE physician	$46,364	$44,590	$44,611
– Total front office support staff cost per FTE physician	$39,512	$37,394	$37,717
– Total clinical support staff cost per FTE physician	$49,165	$46,940	$47,014
– Total ancillary support staff cost per FTE physician	$28,901	$27,328	$28,001
Total general operating cost per FTE physician	$217,684	$203,458	$209,254
Total NPP cost per FTE physician	$20,983	$18,486	$19,217
Total physician cost per FTE physician	$331,621	$250,688	$268,500
Total support staff cost as a percent of total medical revenue	25.19%	29.33%	28.39%
– Information technology cost as a percent of total medical revenue	1.46%	1.51%	1.47%
– Professional liability cost as a percent of total medical revenue	2.19%	2.10%	2.11%
– Drug supply cost as a percent of total medical revenue	5.27%	4.60%	4.69%
– Medical/surgical supply cost as a percent of total medical revenue	1.35%	1.50%	1.48%
– Building and occupancy cost as a percent of total medical revenue	5.05%	5.79%	5.77%
Total NPP cost as a percent of total medical revenue	2.78%	2.50%	2.51%
Total physician cost as a percent of total medical revenue	41.15%	37.13%	37.53%
Operating cost per medical procedure inside the practice	$32.00	$44.97	$41.61
Provider cost per medical procedure inside the practice	$23.73	$25.77	$25.37
Operating cost per medical procedure outside the practice	$15.77	$21.34	$20.09
Provider cost per medical procedure outside the practice	$34.55	$32.79	$32.99
Operating cost per surgical procedure inside the practice	$107.99	$88.49	$95.79
Provider cost per surgical procedure inside the practice	$64.00	$50.93	$53.88
Operating cost per surgical procedure outside the practice	$137.78	$122.60	$129.47
Provider cost per surgical procedure outside the practice	$236.27	$223.54	$226.99
Operating cost per laboratory procedure	$15.11	$13.49	$13.52
Provider cost per laboratory procedure	$9.91	$7.39	$7.53
Operating cost per radiology procedure	$77.91	$84.01	$81.20
Provider cost per radiology procedure	$55.96	$44.50	$47.02

⊕—⊼ Key Indicator

Figure V.A.7	Profitability and cost management indicators			

Multispecialty, primary care only, not hospital-owned

	Better Performers	Others	All
Productivity			
Total gross charges per FTE physician	$1,003,387	$736,355	$771,037
Total RVUs per FTE physician	9,259	7,739	7,836
Physician work RVUs per FTE physician	5,088	4,617	4,617
Medical procedures inside practice to total gross charges ratio	65.03%	58.01%	60.32%
Medical procedures outside practice to total gross charges ratio	8.14%	10.68%	9.48%
Surgical procedures inside practice to total gross charges ratio	3.67%	3.46%	3.67%
Surgical procedures outside practice to total gross charges ratio	3.16%	8.63%	6.61%
Laboratory procedures to total gross charges ratio	15.58%	8.48%	13.00%
Radiology procedures to total gross charges ratio	4.50%	4.14%	4.19%
Total procedures per FTE physician	15,896	9,294	9,898
Patients per FTE physician	2,668	2,143	2,211
Encounters per FTE physician	6,502	5,278	5,336
Revenue			
Total medical revenue per FTE physician	$614,295	$486,774	$513,530
Total medical revenue after operating cost per FTE physician	$252,123	$194,610	$217,315
Total medical revenue after operating and NPP cost per FTE physician	$216,910	$171,870	$180,282
Cost management			
Total operating cost as a percent of total medical revenue	56.53%	57.23%	57.23%
Total operating cost per FTE physician	$342,620	$282,184	$306,852
Total operating and NPP cost as a percent of total medical revenue	62.38%	62.92%	62.92%
Total operating and NPP cost per FTE physician	$367,298	$334,432	$340,391
Total support staff cost per FTE physician	$190,874	$154,071	$157,065
– Total business operations support staff cost per FTE physician	$42,125	$37,324	$38,770
– Total front office support staff cost per FTE physician	$39,893	$33,478	$34,712
– Total clinical support staff cost per FTE physician	$52,220	$42,502	$45,874
– Total ancillary support staff cost per FTE physician	$22,376	$14,307	$14,307
Total general operating cost per FTE physician	$162,733	$142,325	$145,374
Total NPP cost per FTE physician	$33,180	$25,395	$26,185
Total physician cost per FTE physician	$210,632	$176,368	$179,161
Total support staff cost as a percent of total medical revenue	30.08%	30.96%	30.84%
– Information technology cost as a percent of total medical revenue	1.95%	1.81%	1.82%
– Professional liability cost as a percent of total medical revenue	2.59%	2.28%	2.35%
– Drug supply cost as a percent of total medical revenue	3.12%	1.94%	2.29%
– Medical/surgical supply cost as a percent of total medical revenue	1.16%	1.61%	1.55%
– Building and occupancy cost as a percent of total medical revenue	6.25%	7.41%	7.26%
Total NPP cost as a percent of total medical revenue	5.85%	5.22%	5.31%
Total physician cost as a percent of total medical revenue	36.77%	37.12%	37.00%
Operating cost per medical procedure inside the practice	$30.54	$39.41	$33.85
Provider cost per medical procedure inside the practice	$19.35	$23.96	$21.82
Operating cost per medical procedure outside the practice	$17.42	$22.30	$18.96
Provider cost per medical procedure outside the practice	$23.78	$29.73	$28.52
Operating cost per surgical procedure inside the practice	$30.99	$47.79	$46.99
Provider cost per surgical procedure inside the practice	$20.28	$35.30	$32.46
Operating cost per surgical procedure outside the practice	$70.49	$109.74	$86.65
Provider cost per surgical procedure outside the practice	$152.35	$115.76	$143.18
Operating cost per laboratory procedure	$9.46	$11.46	$10.82
Provider cost per laboratory procedure	$5.00	$5.36	$5.24
Operating cost per radiology procedure	$60.73	$66.93	$66.87
Provider cost per radiology procedure	$19.77	$29.88	$27.43

ᴏ—ᴍ Key Indicator

Figure V.A.8	Profitability and cost management indicators			
Primary care, single specialties		**Better Performers**	**Others**	**All**
Productivity				
∞ Total gross charges per FTE physician		$813,581	$668,888	$694,542
Total RVUs per FTE physician		13,337	8,954	9,740
⚹ Physician work RVUs per FTE physician		6,489	4,306	4,542
Medical procedures inside practice to total gross charges ratio		81.44%	78.84%	78.96%
Medical procedures outside practice to total gross charges ratio		5.41%	6.12%	5.60%
Surgical procedures inside practice to total gross charges ratio		2.34%	3.48%	3.05%
Surgical procedures outside practice to total gross charges ratio		1.11%	3.10%	1.86%
Laboratory procedures to total gross charges ratio		7.08%	4.79%	5.68%
Radiology procedures to total gross charges ratio		3.97%	3.11%	3.37%
Total procedures per FTE physician		14,206	10,154	11,603
Patients per FTE physician		2,503	1,841	1,925
Encounters per FTE physician		6,966	4,918	5,184
Revenue				
∞ Total medical revenue per FTE physician		$563,415	$465,703	$498,780
Total medical revenue after operating cost per FTE physician		$248,894	$184,056	$196,657
⚹ Total medical revenue after operating and NPP cost per FTE physician		$239,951	$174,343	$187,630
Cost management				
∞ Total operating cost as a percent of total medical revenue		55.14%	60.11%	59.24%
Total operating cost per FTE physician		$333,339	$286,552	$290,343
Total operating and NPP cost as a percent of total medical revenue		60.03%	65.34%	64.41%
Total operating and NPP cost per FTE physician		$371,869	$326,855	$336,617
Total support staff cost per FTE physician		$166,849	$140,087	$146,472
– Total business operations support staff cost per FTE physician		$42,693	$28,059	$31,613
– Total front office support staff cost per FTE physician		$33,017	$35,618	$35,023
– Total clinical support staff cost per FTE physician		$51,944	$42,945	$44,508
– Total ancillary support staff cost per FTE physician		$13,017	$13,442	$13,229
Total general operating cost per FTE physician		$154,344	$141,508	$144,117
Total NPP cost per FTE physician		$28,197	$17,444	$20,393
Total physician cost per FTE physician		$212,689	$181,595	$189,566
Total support staff cost as a percent of total medical revenue		29.23%	30.96%	30.45%
– Information technology cost as a percent of total medical revenue		2.16%	1.48%	1.62%
– Professional liability cost as a percent of total medical revenue		1.62%	1.99%	1.92%
– Drug supply cost as a percent of total medical revenue		8.60%	2.73%	2.82%
– Medical/surgical supply cost as a percent of total medical revenue		1.79%	1.42%	1.57%
– Building and occupancy cost as a percent of total medical revenue		6.28%	7.32%	7.10%
Total NPP cost as a percent of total medical revenue		4.66%	3.64%	3.71%
Total physician cost as a percent of total medical revenue		39.10%	40.59%	40.35%
Operating cost per medical procedure inside the practice		$26.59	$39.21	$31.68
Provider cost per medical procedure inside the practice		$18.65	$28.81	$23.79
Operating cost per medical procedure outside the practice		$18.91	$23.85	$21.41
Provider cost per medical procedure outside the practice		$28.89	$35.13	$30.41
Operating cost per surgical procedure inside the practice		$37.55	$57.57	$51.77
Provider cost per surgical procedure inside the practice		$28.55	$39.96	$35.60
Operating cost per surgical procedure outside the practice		$44.57	$127.23	$61.71
Provider cost per surgical procedure outside the practice		$75.06	$155.91	$105.80
Operating cost per laboratory procedure		$8.31	$8.46	$8.42
Provider cost per laboratory procedure		$6.42	$5.57	$5.89
Operating cost per radiology procedure		$35.54	$49.04	$47.37
Provider cost per radiology procedure		$19.70	$22.69	$22.47

∞—⚹ Key Indicator

Figure V.A.9	Profitability and cost management indicators			

Medicine single specialty excluding general internal medicine

	Better Performers	Others	All
Productivity			
♋ Total gross charges per FTE physician	$2,421,379	$1,717,637	$1,865,934
Total RVUs per FTE physician	29,382	15,224	16,170
Physician work RVUs per FTE physician	11,185	7,975	8,486
Medical procedures inside practice to total gross charges ratio	34.15%	27.42%	29.78%
Medical procedures outside practice to total gross charges ratio	32.09%	27.36%	30.20%
Surgical procedures inside practice to total gross charges ratio	0.66%	0.89%	0.84%
Surgical procedures outside practice to total gross charges ratio	4.46%	5.00%	4.66%
Laboratory procedures to total gross charges ratio	0.40%	0.54%	0.48%
Radiology procedures to total gross charges ratio	20.41%	15.37%	17.55%
Total procedures per FTE physician	11,977	8,379	9,331
Patients per FTE physician	1,595	1,567	1,591
Encounters per FTE physician	6,658	4,213	4,552
Revenue			
♋ Total medical revenue per FTE physician	$1,118,550	$818,578	$908,622
Total medical revenue after operating cost per FTE physician	$582,430	$439,808	$475,014
Total medical revenue after operating and NPP cost per FTE physician	$559,685	$420,266	$459,511
Cost management			
♋ Total operating cost as a percent of total medical revenue	45.08%	46.43%	46.00%
Total operating cost per FTE physician	$526,237	$398,087	$425,234
Total operating and NPP cost as a percent of total medical revenue	47.60%	51.98%	51.31%
Total operating and NPP cost per FTE physician	$550,702	$455,329	$473,824
Total support staff cost per FTE physician	$270,113	$191,504	$205,659
− Total business operations support staff cost per FTE physician	$63,267	$46,678	$48,114
− Total front office support staff cost per FTE physician	$42,660	$34,816	$37,350
− Total clinical support staff cost per FTE physician	$49,920	$46,281	$46,667
− Total ancillary support staff cost per FTE physician	$38,169	$36,191	$36,853
Total general operating cost per FTE physician	$237,368	$192,339	$207,366
Total NPP cost per FTE physician	$21,566	$22,031	$22,031
Total physician cost per FTE physician	$515,943	$408,177	$438,190
Total support staff cost as a percent of total medical revenue	23.59%	20.68%	22.04%
− Information technology cost as a percent of total medical revenue	1.26%	1.20%	1.25%
− Professional liability cost as a percent of total medical revenue	1.86%	1.65%	1.67%
− Drug supply cost as a percent of total medical revenue	0.86%	3.46%	3.10%
− Medical/surgical supply cost as a percent of total medical revenue	0.93%	0.73%	0.75%
− Building and occupancy cost as a percent of total medical revenue	4.29%	4.24%	4.24%
Total NPP cost as a percent of total medical revenue	1.84%	2.39%	2.33%
Total physician cost as a percent of total medical revenue	48.70%	49.65%	48.92%
Operating cost per medical procedure inside the practice	$41.72	$58.06	$52.26
Provider cost per medical procedure inside the practice	$39.98	$46.93	$43.95
Operating cost per medical procedure outside the practice	$19.13	$23.17	$21.23
Provider cost per medical procedure outside the practice	$44.01	$46.53	$45.58
Operating cost per surgical procedure inside the practice	$156.28	$116.80	$124.43
Provider cost per surgical procedure inside the practice	$159.34	$106.43	$108.06
Operating cost per surgical procedure outside the practice	$94.40	$84.97	$91.87
Provider cost per surgical procedure outside the practice	$246.66	$203.39	$212.62
Operating cost per laboratory procedure	$7.00	$8.05	$7.87
Provider cost per laboratory procedure	$4.46	$5.72	$5.15
Operating cost per radiology procedure	$126.17	$96.83	$111.18
Provider cost per radiology procedure	$84.15	$61.12	$70.14

ଅ—⚊ Key Indicator

Figure V.A.10	Profitability and cost management indicators			

Surgical, single specialty

	Better Performers	Others	All
Productivity			
♀ Total gross charges per FTE physician	$2,470,492	$1,736,838	$1,823,027
Total RVUs per FTE physician	25,453	19,523	19,901
Physician work RVUs per FTE physician	10,787	8,790	8,798
Medical procedures inside practice to total gross charges ratio	17.25%	16.36%	16.38%
Medical procedures outside practice to total gross charges ratio	0.62%	1.45%	1.06%
Surgical procedures inside practice to total gross charges ratio	7.00%	11.78%	10.17%
Surgical procedures outside practice to total gross charges ratio	61.33%	58.01%	58.72%
Laboratory procedures to total gross charges ratio	2.09%	1.76%	1.87%
Radiology procedures to total gross charges ratio	7.49%	4.58%	5.56%
Total procedures per FTE physician	9,777	6,247	6,649
Patients per FTE physician	1,491	1,676	1,661
Encounters per FTE physician	4,533	3,972	4,079
Revenue			
♀ Total medical revenue per FTE physician	$1,218,403	$887,302	$936,715
Total medical revenue after operating cost per FTE physician	$660,211	$457,859	$493,804
Total medical revenue after operating and NPP cost per FTE physician	$598,126	$441,398	$468,956
Cost management			
♀ Total operating cost as a percent of total medical revenue	41.38%	47.70%	46.22%
Total operating cost per FTE physician	$489,416	$407,870	$434,143
Total operating and NPP cost as a percent of total medical revenue	46.54%	51.53%	50.21%
Total operating and NPP cost per FTE physician	$551,567	$462,675	$483,799
Total support staff cost per FTE physician	$246,909	$185,421	$203,807
– Total business operations support staff cost per FTE physician	$66,444	$48,606	$49,871
– Total front office support staff cost per FTE physician	$59,120	$45,007	$46,330
– Total clinical support staff cost per FTE physician	$44,078	$38,732	$39,719
– Total ancillary support staff cost per FTE physician	$30,562	$23,412	$25,282
Total general operating cost per FTE physician	$247,107	$213,910	$219,749
Total NPP cost per FTE physician	$49,216	$34,433	$39,430
Total physician cost per FTE physician	$565,073	$403,337	$436,034
Total support staff cost as a percent of total medical revenue	20.88%	21.44%	21.24%
– Information technology cost as a percent of total medical revenue	1.27%	1.35%	1.34%
– Professional liability cost as a percent of total medical revenue	2.29%	3.03%	2.84%
– Drug supply cost as a percent of total medical revenue	1.25%	3.01%	2.20%
– Medical/surgical supply cost as a percent of total medical revenue	1.89%	1.34%	1.54%
– Building and occupancy cost as a percent of total medical revenue	4.88%	5.60%	5.45%
Total NPP cost as a percent of total medical revenue	4.35%	3.83%	3.89%
Total physician cost as a percent of total medical revenue	50.43%	48.20%	48.58%
Operating cost per medical procedure inside the practice	$30.22	$53.93	$44.83
Provider cost per medical procedure inside the practice	$26.14	$31.42	$28.54
Operating cost per medical procedure outside the practice	$15.61	$17.63	$17.54
Provider cost per medical procedure outside the practice	$34.54	$35.51	$35.20
Operating cost per surgical procedure inside the practice	$101.79	$137.40	$128.04
Provider cost per surgical procedure inside the practice	$84.09	$85.90	$85.90
Operating cost per surgical procedure outside the practice	$176.25	$173.89	$175.26
Provider cost per surgical procedure outside the practice	$433.19	$372.36	$378.85
Operating cost per laboratory procedure	$4.75	$6.60	$6.57
Provider cost per laboratory procedure	$5.60	$5.57	$5.60
Operating cost per radiology procedure	$45.09	$60.19	$55.85
Provider cost per radiology procedure	$30.14	$35.84	$32.79

♀⟶• Key Indicator

Figure **V.A.11**	Profitability and cost management indicators			

Multispecialty, all owners

	Better Performers	Others	All
Productivity			
⚭ Total gross charges per FTE physician	$1,153,217	$855,918	$886,560
Total RVUs per FTE physician	12,359	10,460	10,791
Physician work RVUs per FTE physician	5,988	5,316	5,380
Medical procedures inside practice to total gross charges ratio	40.00%	47.95%	47.18%
Medical procedures outside practice to total gross charges ratio	7.77%	9.23%	8.77%
Surgical procedures inside practice to total gross charges ratio	6.60%	4.59%	4.82%
Surgical procedures outside practice to total gross charges ratio	13.45%	14.02%	13.72%
Laboratory procedures to total gross charges ratio	11.16%	8.36%	9.34%
Radiology procedures to total gross charges ratio	9.46%	5.61%	6.78%
Total procedures per FTE physician	12,397	9,446	10,101
Patients per FTE physician	1,839	1,564	1,584
Encounters per FTE physician	5,408	4,583	4,721
Revenue			
⚭ Total medical revenue per FTE physician	$669,276	$545,639	$582,307
Total medical revenue after operating cost per FTE physician	$285,358	$209,987	$236,021
Total medical revenue after operating and NPP cost per FTE physician	$258,688	$198,937	$217,069
Cost management			
⚭ Total operating cost as a percent of total medical revenue	55.95%	60.33%	59.59%
Total operating cost per FTE physician	$375,354	$346,487	$353,503
Total operating and NPP cost as a percent of total medical revenue	58.96%	64.33%	63.28%
Total operating and NPP cost per FTE physician	$407,550	$380,101	$389,636
Total support staff cost per FTE physician	$186,780	$171,037	$176,280
− Total business operations support staff cost per FTE physician	$44,366	$37,183	$39,442
− Total front office support staff cost per FTE physician	$40,070	$34,267	$35,458
− Total clinical support staff cost per FTE physician	$47,707	$46,400	$46,686
− Total ancillary support staff cost per FTE physician	$24,716	$20,698	$21,255
Total general operating cost per FTE physician	$188,236	$168,765	$171,553
Total NPP cost per FTE physician	$21,702	$18,817	$19,277
Total physician cost per FTE physician	$265,686	$218,714	$229,638
Total support staff cost as a percent of total medical revenue	27.63%	30.80%	30.45%
− Information technology cost as a percent of total medical revenue	1.52%	1.34%	1.40%
− Professional liability cost as a percent of total medical revenue	2.31%	2.28%	2.28%
− Drug supply cost as a percent of total medical revenue	3.09%	3.49%	3.42%
− Medical/surgical supply cost as a percent of total medical revenue	1.29%	1.54%	1.50%
− Building and occupancy cost as a percent of total medical revenue	5.62%	6.53%	6.38%
Total NPP cost as a percent of total medical revenue	2.91%	3.15%	3.13%
Total physician cost as a percent of total medical revenue	40.06%	40.35%	40.30%
Operating cost per medical procedure inside the practice	$30.64	$43.38	$40.10
Provider cost per medical procedure inside the practice	$23.08	$27.80	$26.17
Operating cost per medical procedure outside the practice	$18.06	$23.10	$21.83
Provider cost per medical procedure outside the practice	$32.28	$36.29	$35.46
Operating cost per surgical procedure inside the practice	$69.17	$78.47	$77.61
Provider cost per surgical procedure inside the practice	$54.13	$49.71	$50.70
Operating cost per surgical procedure outside the practice	$107.14	$144.61	$137.69
Provider cost per surgical procedure outside the practice	$206.32	$238.72	$226.14
Operating cost per laboratory procedure	$12.64	$13.04	$12.98
Provider cost per laboratory procedure	$7.27	$7.41	$7.40
Operating cost per radiology procedure	$76.22	$69.94	$72.95
Provider cost per radiology procedure	$43.41	$40.87	$41.27

ᗺ━━✖ Key Indicator

From the *Performance and Practices of Successful Medical Groups, 2005 Report Based on 2004 Data.*
Reprinted with permission from the Medical Group Management Association, 104 Inverness Terrace East,
Englewood, Colorado 80112. www.mgma.com. Copyright 2005. Pages 142–160.

Figure V.A.12	Profitability and cost management indicators			

Multispecialty, all owners, less than or equal to 50 percent primary care

	Better Performers	Others	All
Productivity			
⌘ Total gross charges per FTE physician	$1,572,198	$1,207,286	$1,299,613
Total RVUs per FTE physician	17,436	12,654	13,105
Physician work RVUs per FTE physician	6,913	5,956	6,286
Medical procedures inside practice to total gross charges ratio	25.45%	33.19%	30.82%
Medical procedures outside practice to total gross charges ratio	8.75%	8.61%	8.61%
Surgical procedures inside practice to total gross charges ratio	5.09%	5.18%	5.16%
Surgical procedures outside practice to total gross charges ratio	20.73%	18.31%	19.24%
Laboratory procedures to total gross charges ratio	9.23%	8.21%	8.36%
Radiology procedures to total gross charges ratio	13.88%	9.75%	10.53%
Total procedures per FTE physician	13,527	10,211	11,027
Patients per FTE physician	1,186	1,183	1,183
Encounters per FTE physician	4,539	4,503	4,503
Revenue			
⌘ Total medical revenue per FTE physician	$926,642	$760,749	$771,744
Total medical revenue after operating cost per FTE physician	$395,439	$295,316	$316,783
Total medical revenue after operating and NPP cost per FTE physician	$364,005	$275,220	$296,995
Cost management			
⌘ Total operating cost as a percent of total medical revenue	54.57%	59.92%	59.28%
Total operating cost per FTE physician	$478,827	$449,572	$457,350
Total operating and NPP cost as a percent of total medical revenue	56.86%	63.15%	62.08%
Total operating and NPP cost per FTE physician	$521,022	$465,902	$479,038
Total support staff cost per FTE physician	$230,189	$200,802	$203,711
− Total business operations support staff cost per FTE physician	$54,731	$43,679	$47,324
− Total front office support staff cost per FTE physician	$39,452	$34,162	$35,268
− Total clinical support staff cost per FTE physician	$52,394	$46,400	$47,563
− Total ancillary support staff cost per FTE physician	$31,819	$29,749	$30,743
Total general operating cost per FTE physician	$257,113	$224,688	$231,709
Total NPP cost per FTE physician	$23,931	$19,515	$19,900
Total physician cost per FTE physician	$362,893	$293,113	$304,805
Total support staff cost as a percent of total medical revenue	24.86%	28.72%	27.06%
− Information technology cost as a percent of total medical revenue	1.27%	1.37%	1.36%
− Professional liability cost as a percent of total medical revenue	2.03%	2.63%	2.43%
− Drug supply cost as a percent of total medical revenue	5.91%	7.26%	7.09%
− Medical/surgical supply cost as a percent of total medical revenue	1.37%	1.44%	1.43%
− Building and occupancy cost as a percent of total medical revenue	4.72%	5.47%	5.45%
Total NPP cost as a percent of total medical revenue	2.84%	2.51%	2.57%
Total physician cost as a percent of total medical revenue	43.24%	39.43%	40.22%
Operating cost per medical procedure inside the practice	$33.32	$48.87	$44.31
Provider cost per medical procedure inside the practice	$23.24	$27.80	$26.10
Operating cost per medical procedure outside the practice	$15.64	$22.23	$21.51
Provider cost per medical procedure outside the practice	$34.81	$36.95	$36.04
Operating cost per surgical procedure inside the practice	$107.99	$97.91	$98.17
Provider cost per surgical procedure inside the practice	$62.55	$59.07	$59.25
Operating cost per surgical procedure outside the practice	$102.57	$151.37	$141.08
Provider cost per surgical procedure outside the practice	$232.20	$289.29	$269.64
Operating cost per laboratory procedure	$15.14	$13.54	$13.63
Provider cost per laboratory procedure	$10.98	$7.42	$7.81
Operating cost per radiology procedure	$79.56	$88.82	$84.85
Provider cost per radiology procedure	$58.44	$46.44	$47.92

☐━━➤ Key Indicator

Figure V.A.13	Profitability and cost management indicators			

Multispecialty, all owners, greater than 50 percent primary care

	Better Performers	Others	All
Productivity			
⦵ Total gross charges per FTE physician	$940,024	$756,857	$797,276
Total RVUs per FTE physician	11,869	9,216	9,811
Physician work RVUs per FTE physician	5,947	4,931	5,050
Medical procedures inside practice to total gross charges ratio	50.81%	53.96%	52.17%
Medical procedures outside practice to total gross charges ratio	8.14%	9.00%	8.78%
Surgical procedures inside practice to total gross charges ratio	6.31%	4.63%	4.63%
Surgical procedures outside practice to total gross charges ratio	8.94%	11.16%	10.00%
Laboratory procedures to total gross charges ratio	13.23%	9.81%	10.80%
Radiology procedures to total gross charges ratio	7.02%	4.37%	4.88%
Total procedures per FTE physician	12,679	9,072	9,813
Patients per FTE physician	2,243	1,715	1,853
Encounters per FTE physician	6,095	4,711	4,935
Revenue			
⦵ Total medical revenue per FTE physician	$596,360	$504,449	$530,374
Total medical revenue after operating cost per FTE physician	$258,602	$192,254	$203,097
Total medical revenue after operating and NPP cost per FTE physician	$230,394	$174,216	$191,187
Cost management			
⦵ Total operating cost as a percent of total medical revenue	56.89%	61.67%	59.97%
Total operating cost per FTE physician	$343,948	$322,979	$330,147
Total operating and NPP cost as a percent of total medical revenue	59.11%	65.52%	64.20%
Total operating and NPP cost per FTE physician	$367,937	$354,760	$362,177
Total support staff cost per FTE physician	$176,110	$164,270	$166,938
− Total business operations support staff cost per FTE physician	$41,848	$35,909	$37,119
− Total front office support staff cost per FTE physician	$40,524	$34,740	$35,789
− Total clinical support staff cost per FTE physician	$44,859	$46,908	$46,600
− Total ancillary support staff cost per FTE physician	$18,144	$17,494	$17,957
Total general operating cost per FTE physician	$162,733	$154,335	$156,432
Total NPP cost per FTE physician	$17,036	$18,589	$18,393
Total physician cost per FTE physician	$228,838	$206,079	$210,062
Total support staff cost as a percent of total medical revenue	28.47%	32.62%	31.74%
− Information technology cost as a percent of total medical revenue	1.51%	1.42%	1.47%
− Professional liability cost as a percent of total medical revenue	2.27%	2.18%	2.20%
− Drug supply cost as a percent of total medical revenue	2.71%	2.87%	2.82%
− Medical/surgical supply cost as a percent of total medical revenue	1.38%	1.56%	1.55%
− Building and occupancy cost as a percent of total medical revenue	5.72%	7.24%	6.96%
Total NPP cost as a percent of total medical revenue	2.87%	3.38%	3.28%
Total physician cost as a percent of total medical revenue	39.69%	40.78%	40.28%
Operating cost per medical procedure inside the practice	$29.19	$40.93	$36.77
Provider cost per medical procedure inside the practice	$20.50	$28.47	$25.99
Operating cost per medical procedure outside the practice	$17.98	$24.12	$22.37
Provider cost per medical procedure outside the practice	$28.96	$36.92	$34.60
Operating cost per surgical procedure inside the practice	$48.83	$71.59	$64.77
Provider cost per surgical procedure inside the practice	$36.54	$43.07	$42.33
Operating cost per surgical procedure outside the practice	$93.92	$154.94	$126.95
Provider cost per surgical procedure outside the practice	$163.76	$223.16	$206.32
Operating cost per laboratory procedure	$11.12	$12.87	$11.93
Provider cost per laboratory procedure	$6.65	$7.54	$7.20
Operating cost per radiology procedure	$74.90	$63.99	$66.42
Provider cost per radiology procedure	$40.91	$33.63	$36.42

⦵——ᴋ Key Indicator

Figure **V.A.14**	Profitability and cost management indicators

Multispecialty, not hospital-owned, less than or equal to 50 percent primary care

	Better Performers	Others	All
Productivity			
☜ Total gross charges per FTE physician	$1,735,762	$1,281,287	$1,408,779
Total RVUs per FTE physician	17,436	12,654	13,154
Physician work RVUs per FTE physician	7,038	6,139	6,557
Medical procedures inside practice to total gross charges ratio	30.00%	32.13%	30.31%
Medical procedures outside practice to total gross charges ratio	8.75%	8.28%	8.42%
Surgical procedures inside practice to total gross charges ratio	7.92%	4.57%	4.99%
Surgical procedures outside practice to total gross charges ratio	19.77%	18.31%	19.12%
Laboratory procedures to total gross charges ratio	9.23%	8.32%	8.42%
Radiology procedures to total gross charges ratio	12.38%	10.87%	11.35%
Total procedures per FTE physician	13,656	11,006	11,147
Patients per FTE physician	1,186	1,183	1,183
Encounters per FTE physician	5,446	4,539	4,603
Revenue			
☜ Total medical revenue per FTE physician	$941,146	$771,744	$829,455
Total medical revenue after operating cost per FTE physician	$395,439	$309,256	$329,825
Total medical revenue after operating and NPP cost per FTE physician	$364,005	$293,160	$311,942
Cost management			
☜ Total operating cost as a percent of total medical revenue	57.36%	59.83%	59.33%
Total operating cost per FTE physician	$512,385	$462,386	$476,912
Total operating and NPP cost as a percent of total medical revenue	58.63%	63.19%	62.05%
Total operating and NPP cost per FTE physician	$539,858	$487,070	$502,626
Total support staff cost per FTE physician	$241,369	$202,697	$207,963
– Total business operations support staff cost per FTE physician	$55,771	$49,193	$51,655
– Total front office support staff cost per FTE physician	$39,962	$35,268	$37,616
– Total clinical support staff cost per FTE physician	$55,191	$47,563	$49,898
– Total ancillary support staff cost per FTE physician	$33,051	$30,640	$31,819
Total general operating cost per FTE physician	$269,365	$248,345	$256,715
Total NPP cost per FTE physician	$24,471	$19,366	$19,834
Total physician cost per FTE physician	$362,893	$297,000	$309,987
Total support staff cost as a percent of total medical revenue	25.31%	27.68%	26.92%
– Information technology cost as a percent of total medical revenue	1.36%	1.46%	1.39%
– Professional liability cost as a percent of total medical revenue	2.00%	2.62%	2.30%
– Drug supply cost as a percent of total medical revenue	5.75%	8.11%	7.44%
– Medical/surgical supply cost as a percent of total medical revenue	1.37%	1.43%	1.42%
– Building and occupancy cost as a percent of total medical revenue	4.91%	5.45%	5.44%
Total NPP cost as a percent of total medical revenue	2.84%	2.35%	2.43%
Total physician cost as a percent of total medical revenue	40.75%	37.24%	38.90%
Operating cost per medical procedure inside the practice	$36.97	$51.18	$46.16
Provider cost per medical procedure inside the practice	$23.24	$26.43	$25.80
Operating cost per medical procedure outside the practice	$15.64	$22.23	$20.96
Provider cost per medical procedure outside the practice	$32.75	$35.20	$34.15
Operating cost per surgical procedure inside the practice	$90.51	$100.83	$99.89
Provider cost per surgical procedure inside the practice	$57.99	$59.07	$58.53
Operating cost per surgical procedure outside the practice	$105.63	$146.41	$140.69
Provider cost per surgical procedure outside the practice	$232.20	$261.22	$260.69
Operating cost per laboratory procedure	$15.73	$13.71	$13.85
Provider cost per laboratory procedure	$9.90	$7.42	$7.52
Operating cost per radiology procedure	$84.01	$91.75	$91.53
Provider cost per radiology procedure	$59.56	$44.50	$48.36

☜—⚲ Key Indicator

Figure **V.A.15**	**Profitability and cost management indicators**			

Multispecialty, not hospital-owned, greater than 50 percent primary care

	Better Performers	Others	All
Productivity			
∞ Total gross charges per FTE physician	$1,064,351	$882,077	$901,739
Total RVUs per FTE physician	11,869	10,182	10,315
Physician work RVUs per FTE physician	6,056	5,122	5,252
Medical procedures inside practice to total gross charges ratio	49.96%	48.66%	48.66%
Medical procedures outside practice to total gross charges ratio	6.59%	9.37%	8.71%
Surgical procedures inside practice to total gross charges ratio	7.37%	4.43%	4.61%
Surgical procedures outside practice to total gross charges ratio	9.77%	10.10%	9.96%
Laboratory procedures to total gross charges ratio	13.35%	12.52%	12.61%
Radiology procedures to total gross charges ratio	7.09%	6.95%	7.00%
Total procedures per FTE physician	14,020	10,795	11,314
Patients per FTE physician	2,243	1,853	1,948
Encounters per FTE physician	6,292	4,891	5,018
Revenue			
∞ Total medical revenue per FTE physician	$652,673	$583,644	$596,297
Total medical revenue after operating cost per FTE physician	$269,595	$229,163	$239,319
Total medical revenue after operating and NPP cost per FTE physician	$248,738	$211,148	$219,786
Cost management			
∞ Total operating cost as a percent of total medical revenue	56.39%	59.05%	58.24%
Total operating cost per FTE physician	$370,706	$346,395	$356,710
Total operating and NPP cost as a percent of total medical revenue	59.87%	63.62%	62.43%
Total operating and NPP cost per FTE physician	$398,420	$379,487	$382,870
Total support staff per FTE physician	$176,110	$178,530	$177,610
– Total business operations support staff cost per FTE physician	$44,271	$39,153	$40,886
– Total front office support staff cost per FTE physician	$41,660	$34,723	$36,298
– Total clinical support staff cost per FTE physician	$45,269	$46,852	$46,720
– Total ancillary support staff cost per FTE physician	$18,485	$21,286	$20,698
Total general operating cost per FTE physician	$188,639	$164,928	$170,256
Total NPP cost per FTE physician	$20,573	$18,866	$18,991
Total physician cost per FTE physician	$240,077	$207,217	$212,025
Total support staff cost as a percent of total medical revenue	27.84%	31.10%	30.65%
– Information technology cost as a percent of total medical revenue	1.58%	1.73%	1.70%
– Professional liability cost as a percent of total medical revenue	2.34%	2.04%	2.14%
– Drug supply cost as a percent of total medical revenue	2.99%	3.13%	3.06%
– Medical/surgical supply cost as a percent of total medical revenue	1.33%	1.55%	1.53%
– Building and occupancy cost as a percent of total medical revenue	6.61%	6.46%	6.46%
Total NPP cost as a percent of total medical revenue	2.92%	3.11%	3.10%
Total physician cost as a percent of total medical revenue	38.55%	37.10%	37.13%
Operating cost per medical procedure inside the practice	$28.50	$38.89	$34.92
Provider cost per medical procedure inside the practice	$19.75	$23.96	$23.01
Operating cost per medical procedure outside the practice	$18.03	$21.99	$19.46
Provider cost per medical procedure outside the practice	$28.81	$32.16	$30.79
Operating cost per surgical procedure inside the practice	$73.07	$53.95	$54.48
Provider cost per surgical procedure inside the practice	$53.11	$37.51	$40.68
Operating cost per surgical procedure outside the practice	$95.56	$112.52	$105.52
Provider cost per surgical procedure outside the practice	$168.93	$192.69	$187.63
Operating cost per laboratory procedure	$10.82	$13.18	$12.38
Provider cost per laboratory procedure	$6.30	$7.29	$6.93
Operating cost per radiology procedure	$76.22	$66.81	$69.75
Provider cost per radiology procedure	$44.19	$37.04	$38.49

∞—× Key Indicator

From the *Performance and Practices of Successful Medical Groups, 2005 Report Based on 2004 Data.*
Reprinted with permission from the Medical Group Management Association, 104 Inverness Terrace East,
Englewood, Colorado 80112. www.mgma.com. Copyright 2005. Pages 142–160.

Figure V.A.16	Profitability and cost management indicators			

Multispecialty, hospital-owned, greater than 50 percent primary care

	Better Performers	Others	All
Productivity			
Total gross charges per FTE physician	$736,072	$647,602	$659,561
Total RVUs per FTE physician	10,153	8,334	9,062
Physician work RVUs per FTE physician	5,136	4,794	4,918
Medical procedures inside practice to total gross charges ratio	55.67%	61.55%	61.07%
Medical procedures outside practice to total gross charges ratio	9.79%	9.38%	9.38%
Surgical procedures inside practice to total gross charges ratio	4.05%	4.87%	4.81%
Surgical procedures outside practice to total gross charges ratio	6.73%	10.86%	10.14%
Laboratory procedures to total gross charges ratio	9.34%	3.94%	4.36%
Radiology procedures to total gross charges ratio	2.83%	2.83%	2.83%
Total procedures per FTE physician	10,060	6,963	7,659
Patients per FTE physician	1,568	1,831	1,715
Encounters per FTE physician	5,294	4,534	4,712
Revenue			
Total medical revenue per FTE physician	$472,395	$423,788	$437,228
Total medical revenue after operating cost per FTE physician	$183,387	$139,408	$161,250
Total medical revenue after operating and NPP cost per FTE physician	$165,805	$126,657	$147,623
Cost management			
Total operating cost as a percent of total medical revenue	57.52%	69.02%	64.47%
Total operating cost per FTE physician	$261,349	$297,244	$284,897
Total operating and NPP cost as a percent of total medical revenue	60.68%	71.13%	68.67%
Total operating and NPP cost per FTE physician	$278,724	$328,701	$324,040
Total support staff cost per FTE physician	$158,211	$151,582	$156,451
– Total business operations support staff cost per FTE physician	$31,677	$33,455	$33,163
– Total front office support staff cost per FTE physician	$36,305	$34,371	$34,600
– Total clinical support staff cost per FTE physician	$43,760	$46,698	$45,807
– Total ancillary support staff cost per FTE physician	$9,961	$9,461	$9,461
Total general operating cost per FTE physician	$118,398	$136,425	$133,429
Total NPP cost per FTE physician	$19,686	$16,820	$17,638
Total physician cost per FTE physician	$220,329	$204,465	$207,752
Total support staff cost as a percent of total medical revenue	32.62%	35.47%	34.41%
– Information technology cost as a percent of total medical revenue	1.29%	1.13%	1.19%
– Professional liability cost as a percent of total medical revenue	1.86%	2.74%	2.39%
– Drug supply cost as a percent of total medical revenue	3.01%	2.64%	2.64%
– Medical/surgical supply cost as a percent of total medical revenue	1.13%	1.64%	1.56%
– Building and occupancy cost as a percent of total medical revenue	6.27%	7.78%	7.56%
Total NPP cost as a percent of total medical revenue	4.16%	3.49%	3.53%
Total physician cost as a percent of total medical revenue	43.41%	49.09%	47.68%
Operating cost per medical procedure inside the practice	$32.05	$43.30	$39.44
Provider cost per medical procedure inside the practice	$25.75	$31.70	$29.97
Operating cost per medical procedure outside the practice	$22.64	$31.98	$26.97
Provider cost per medical procedure outside the practice	$40.87	$45.69	$44.59
Operating cost per surgical procedure inside the practice	$49.13	$72.80	$71.28
Provider cost per surgical procedure inside the practice	$41.46	$49.12	$44.92
Operating cost per surgical procedure outside the practice	$133.42	$219.88	$214.53
Provider cost per surgical procedure outside the practice	$187.45	$293.47	$254.32
Operating cost per laboratory procedure	$11.22	$10.78	$11.00
Provider cost per laboratory procedure	$9.71	$7.14	$7.85
Operating cost per radiology procedure	$42.41	$58.63	$56.86
Provider cost per radiology procedure	$21.67	$34.21	$33.55

꘎—꘎ Key Indicator

Productivity, Capacity and Staffing

This appendix contains articles and data from MGMA's *Performance and Practices of Successful Medical Groups* reports on productivity, capacity, and staffing:

- The Practices of Successful Medical Groups (from *Performance and Practices of Successful Medical Groups: 2003 Report Based on 2002 Data*, pages 114–116)
- MGMA Benchmarks: Better Performing Practices Comparison Exhibits (from *Performance and Practices of Successful Medical Groups: 2005 Report Based on 2004 Data*, pages 162–182)

The Practices of Successful Medical Groups

" Better performing groups are acutely aware that productivity is a key driver to group success. "

Bob Erra and Felipe Padilla, MBA

" The reality in medical group management is that any change in productivity will impact a practice's cost ratio more than any other influencing factor. "

Robert C. Bohlmann, FACMPE

The U.S. Department of Labor defines productivity as "a measure of efficiency which shows how effectively economic inputs are converted to economic outputs." In the manufacturing industry, the onus of productivity is on the machinery and equipment that produce the tangible outputs. In health care — part of the service industry — the burden of delivering outputs (for example, patient care) falls upon the efforts of individuals. Human productivity is rarely as predictable and reliable as machinery; the ability to maximize human potential and design systems that increase human production is notable and worthy of research.

The fields of study that influence human productivity span from psychology (what motivates people) and architecture (how the environment affects productivity) to business administration and human resource management. Rather than complete a lengthy research effort, Medical Group Management Association (MGMA) identifies practices that are high functioning and studies the elements that comprise outstanding performance. For the past five years, MGMA has selected better performers from its *Cost Survey Report* data in the area of Productivity, Capacity and Staffing through the following selection criteria:

■ Greater than the median for total gross charges per full-time equivalent (FTE) physician, plus one of the following:

■ For non-surgical specialties: Greater than the median for in-house professional procedures per square foot.

■ For surgical specialties: Greater than the median for total procedures per FTE physician.

This year, MGMA staff members conducted a qualitative analysis of better performing practices over the past five years to identify the characteristics, elements and systems that lead to increased productivity (see Executive Summary). The most common elements shared among better performers in this area were:

• Implementing effective recruitment and staffing techniques;

• Compensating physicians based on productivity;

• Improving patient flow;

• Using data to drive decision making;

• Employing technology to improve efficiency; and

• Providing adequate staffing and employee cross-training.

The primary similarity among better performing practices was the implementation of a productivity-based compensation plan, which in many cases was 100 percent productivity based. Linking pay to performance was also a common theme with support staff and employees, as was tying supervisor/manager compensation (whether they are administrators, physicians or billing managers) to the productivity of the staff reporting to them. Work ethic of physicians and staff was also identified as being important to practice performance. Interestingly, better performing practices have discovered ways to maintain high production levels while increasing employee and physician satisfaction.

The following two pages summarize the findings of the qualitative study. The behaviors and techniques that follow are by no means exhaustive, but they do provide a picture of the commonalities of high functioning practices.

(Continued on next page)

Management and Culture

Culture

☐ Promote and foster a sense of teamwork among employees, staff members and physicians by showing the interconnectedness of all processes and using a team approach for resolving issues

☐ Unify employees, physicians and staff members on key organizational values; organizational objectives and goals; and both short- and long-range planning. Make these goals visible via posting in offices and procedure rooms

☐ Recognize and reward employees for outstanding performance through off-site functions and other events that boost morale and encourage employee retention

Management

☐ Develop key management positions that are clearly defined and communicated throughout the organization

☐ Encourage physicians to spend time in business management activities by providing time for them to devote to these activities

☐ Regularly and systematically provide feedback to physicians regarding performance. Incorporate a systematic process that allows feedback to be provided on a regular basis

☐ Allow top producers — both providers and employees — to teach and mentor other members of the practice in specific tools and techniques that lead to increased performance

☐ Identify key indicators of practice success and collect data on these indicators on a regular basis. Use the data to drive decisions and as a source of internal benchmarking

Staffing

Staff Allocation

☐ Employ an optimal number of staff per physician with duties clearly outlined to maximize organizational effectiveness and leverage physician time for patient care

☐ Match nonphysician providers to specific physicians as opposed to rotating providers among physicians

☐ Expand the role of nonphysician providers (for example, nurse practitioners and physician assistants) to include making rounds to ease the burden on physicians. Ensure that role expansion is within their expertise and legal scope of practice

☐ Evaluate administrative and clerical positions; functions; and the knowledge, skills and abilities required to perform each set of tasks. Transfer appropriate tasks from administrative to clerical to maximize efficiency

☐ Cross-train employees, especially front office staff and business office staff

Recruitment and Retention

☐ Make physician recruitment a high priority. Recruit physicians with the highest standards that fit with organizational culture and work ethic

☐ Encourage retention and discourage turnover by hiring right. Formally assess employee attitudes, listen to employees and make employee satisfaction a high priority

☐ Be flexible with physician and employee schedules to promote higher quality of life for physicians and a diversity of appointment times for patients

Productivity

Performance Enhancement

☐ Measure productivity based on physician work relative value units (RVUs). RVUs offer a consistent and standardized measurement system for both internal and external comparability of providers

☐ Benchmark performance to track progress. Provide physicians and staff members with access to benchmarking reports regularly. Set goals to exceed external and internal benchmarking standards

☐ Automate all activities possible (for example, use an automated phone system to route calls for scheduling, prescription refills, referrals and appointment reminders). Eliminate activities that can be performed through use of technology (for example, do transcription and billing through EMR and physician orders through computerized physician order entry)

☐ Examine physical space and design facilities for effective patient flow. Focus on the time required of physicians and staff members to move between exam rooms, nursing stations and offices

☐ Provide daily patient briefings to physicians before their appointments to familiarize them with patient history and purpose of current visit

☐ Offer open access scheduling and extended hours to patients to maximize clinical capacity and productivity while increasing patient satisfaction and retention

☐ Empower supervisors and employee heads to be decision-makers. Create a decision-making model and guidelines so that decisions can be made more effectively and efficiently

(Continued on next page)

From the *Performance and Practices of Successful Medical Groups, 2003 Report Based on 2002 Data.*
Reprinted with permission from the Medical Group Management Association, 104 Inverness Terrace East, Englewood, Colorado 80112. www.mgma.com. Copyright 2003. Pages 114–116.

☐ Hold staff members accountable for their performance and hold managers responsible for the productivity of the individuals/ departments they supervise

Compensation Methodology

☐ Compensate physicians on a productivity basis that allows equal compensation for equal time and promotes greater production levels. Avoid compensation systems based purely on RVUs due to the lack of connection to cost concerns and the differences in acuity among physician patient panels

☐ Include measures of physician productivity, nonphysician provider productivity and cost containment as part of physician compensation structure

☐ Reward staff for performing at high levels by offering financial incentives, including profit sharing and quarterly bonuses

☐ Pay staff above market value and provide them with detailed performance data that links their productivity to organizational performance. Use benchmarking data to obtain comparison information

Other Ideas

• Strive for physicians to perform above median benchmarks. Some practices set expectations at the 75th and 90th percentiles in terms of productivity as well as compensation

• Create succession planning with defined partnership tracks for younger physicians. Offer senior or retiring physicians alternative schedules to assist in the transition and reduce the impact on practice productivity

• As appropriate and compliant, seek common information systems with hospitals to coordinate the sharing of patient information such as lab and other test results

Key Productivity, Capacity and Staffing Measurements

• Total gross charges per FTE physician

• Total medical revenue per FTE physician

• Physician work RVUs per FTE physician

• Patient encounters per FTE physician

• In-house professional procedures per square foot

• Total procedures per square foot

• Total procedures per FTE physician

• Total procedures per patient

• Total employed support staff per FTE physician

• Total employed support staff cost per FTE physician

• Total support staff cost as a percentage of total medical revenue

What to Avoid

☐ Treating staff as if they are not as valuable as physicians. Staff members and physicians alike must be acknowledged for their contributions to the organization

☐ Providing a single year-end bonus that is not linked to organizational outcomes. The more directly tied and timed incentives are to performance, the greater the value of the recognition and reinforcement of organizational values

☐ Over- or understaffing. Understaffing creates inefficiencies and higher turnover while overstaffing creates unnecessary costs and employee confusion. Evaluate your practice needs to strive for staff "right-sizing"

Other Standards

☐ ....

☐ ....

☐ ....

Notes

From the *Performance and Practices of Successful Medical Groups, 2003 Report Based on 2002 Data.*
Reprinted with permission from the Medical Group Management Association, 104 Inverness Terrace East,
Englewood, Colorado 80112. www.mgma.com. Copyright 2003. Pages 114–116.

Figure V.B.1

Productivity, capacity and staffing demographic profile

	Anesthesiology			Cardiology			Family practice			Gastroenterology			Internal medicine			OB/GYN		
	Better Performers	Others	All	Better Performers	Others	All	Better Performers	Others	All	Better Performers	Others	All	Better Performers	Others	All	Better Performers	Others	All
Practice description																		
Number of practices	33	82	115	15	74	89	11	38	49	3	18	21	2	16	18	9	46	55
Total provider FTE	31.00	24.85	25.00	25.00	15.80	17.00	7.65	6.73	6.78	12.00	11.00	11.50	12.00	8.85	8.85	8.00	8.00	8.00
Total physician FTE	13.00	20.13	18.00	14.50	11.00	11.50	5.00	5.00	5.00	9.00	8.55	8.60	9.50	6.50	6.50	5.00	5.33	5.00
Total NPP FTE	17.50	6.00	10.00	3.90	3.00	3.10	2.15	1.72	1.80	3.00	2.00	2.10	2.50	1.00	1.15	3.10	2.60	2.75
Total support staff FTE	5.00	4.00	4.20	119.16	60.76	66.40	30.65	25.00	26.65	52.50	34.00	35.00	46.68	30.50	30.50	33.40	28.30	29.00
Number of branch clinics	1	2	1	10	3	4	1	5	2	1	2	2	.	3	3	2	2	2
Square footage of all facilities	1,550	3,118	2,500	32,684	19,418	21,638	10,000	9,590	10,000	11,000	10,126	10,563	17,046	13,604	13,604	12,500	10,800	11,202
Net capitation revenue as a percent of total revenue	.	11.66%	11.66%	6.46%	1.38%	5.55%	5.83%	5.09%	5.09%	*	*	*	0.41%	4.82%	0.41%	*	19.40%	19.40%
Breakout of charges by payer																		
Medicare: fee-for-service	27.50%	26.00%	27.00%	48.00%	48.02%	48.00%	15.30%	13.50%	14.00%	36.00%	30.00%	30.69%	45.47%	51.51%	51.51%	6.00%	3.00%	3.24%
Medicare: managed care FFS	0.00%	0.00%	0.00%	0.00%	0.00%	0.00%	0.00%	0.00%	0.00%	0.00%	19.05%	19.05%	0.50%	0.00%	0.00%	0.00%	0.00%	0.00%
Medicare: capitated	0.00%	0.00%	0.00%	0.00%	0.00%	0.00%	0.00%	0.00%	0.00%	0.00%	0.00%	0.00%	0.00%	0.00%	0.00%	0.00%	0.00%	0.00%
Medicaid: fee-for-service	7.15%	5.82%	6.00%	3.00%	2.35%	2.61%	2.00%	4.35%	4.00%	1.00%	2.90%	2.55%	0.52%	1.45%	1.00%	6.40%	5.10%	6.05%
Medicaid: managed care FFS	0.00%	0.00%	0.00%	0.00%	0.00%	0.00%	0.00%	0.00%	0.00%	0.00%	0.00%	0.00%	0.00%	0.00%	0.00%	0.00%	0.00%	0.00%
Medicaid: capitated	0.00%	0.00%	0.00%	0.00%	0.00%	0.00%	0.00%	0.00%	0.00%	0.00%	0.00%	0.00%	0.00%	0.00%	0.00%	0.00%	0.00%	0.00%
Commercial: fee-for-service	9.70%	12.00%	11.60%	35.00%	21.00%	25.00%	8.80%	43.25%	37.69%	51.90%	38.50%	41.35%	10.88%	8.13%	8.13%	13.00%	40.00%	39.55%
Commercial: managed care FFS	35.53%	39.10%	38.00%	0.00%	19.50%	11.63%	60.00%	5.50%	14.30%	0.00%	12.00%	10.00%	40.67%	12.90%	12.90%	60.56%	28.00%	30.00%
Commercial: capitated	0.00%	0.00%	0.00%	0.00%	0.00%	0.00%	0.00%	0.00%	0.00%	0.00%	0.00%	0.00%	0.50%	0.00%	0.00%	0.00%	0.00%	0.00%
Workers' compensation	2.03%	2.50%	2.40%	0.00%	0.00%	0.00%	0.70%	0.20%	0.47%	0.02%	0.20%	0.11%	0.51%	0.00%	0.00%	0.00%	0.20%	0.25%
Charity care and prof courtesy	0.00%	0.00%	0.00%	0.10%	0.00%	0.00%	0.32%	0.05%	0.10%	0.01%	0.20%	0.00%	0.01%	0.00%	0.00%	0.29%	0.20%	0.25%
Self-pay	3.00%	3.43%	3.16%	2.50%	3.00%	2.92%	2.80%	5.10%	4.30%	4.70%	2.00%	2.00%	0.71%	2.12%	1.70%	4.60%	3.90%	3.95%
Other government payers	0.15%	0.20%	0.20%	0.00%	0.00%	0.00%	0.00%	0.00%	0.00%	0.00%	0.00%	0.00%	0.25%	0.00%	0.00%	0.10%	0.00%	0.00%
Geographic section																		
Eastern section	5.22%	15.65%	20.87%	3.37%	14.61%	17.98%	*	14.29%	14.29%	9.52%	9.52%	19.05%	5.56%	11.11%	16.67%	3.64%	18.18%	21.82%
Midwest section	5.22%	20.87%	26.09%	3.37%	22.47%	25.84%	14.29%	20.41%	34.69%	*	19.05%	19.05%	5.56%	16.67%	22.22%	5.45%	10.91%	16.36%
Southern section	16.52%	15.65%	32.17%	5.62%	31.46%	37.08%	4.08%	14.29%	18.37%	4.76%	38.10%	42.86%	*	50.00%	50.00%	5.45%	25.45%	30.91%
Western section	1.74%	19.13%	20.87%	4.49%	14.61%	19.10%	4.08%	28.57%	32.65%	*	19.05%	19.05%	*	11.11%	11.11%	1.82%	29.09%	30.91%
Population designation																		
Nonmetropolitan (50,000 or less)	*	4.50%	4.50%	*	4.55%	4.55%	10.87%	32.61%	43.48%	*	*	*	*	5.56%	5.56%	1.82%	16.36%	18.18%
Metropolitan (50,000 to 250,000)	16.22%	20.72%	36.94%	3.41%	27.27%	30.68%	4.35%	28.26%	32.61%	30.00%	30.00%	30.00%	*	50.00%	50.00%	9.09%	23.64%	32.73%
Metropolitan (250,001 to 1,000,000)	8.11%	29.73%	37.84%	10.23%	26.14%	36.36%	4.35%	8.70%	13.04%	15.00%	20.00%	35.00%	5.56%	16.67%	22.22%	5.45%	27.27%	32.73%
Metropolitan (1,000,001 or more)	5.41%	15.32%	20.72%	3.41%	25.00%	28.41%	2.17%	8.70%	10.87%	*	35.00%	35.00%	5.56%	16.67%	22.22%	*	16.36%	16.36%

(Continued on next page)

From the *Performance and Practices of Successful Medical Groups, 2005 Report Based on 2004 Data.* Reprinted with permission from the Medical Group Management Association, 104 Inverness Terrace East, Englewood, Colorado 80112. www.mgma.com. Copyright 2005. Pages 162–182.

Figure V.B.1 — Productivity, capacity and staffing demographic profile

	Orthopedic surgery			Pediatrics			Urology			Multispecialty, Primary and specialty care, not hospital-owned			Multispecialty, primary care only, not hospital-owned			Primary care single specialties		
	Better Performers	Others	All	Better Performers	Others	All	Better Performers	Others	All	Better Performers	Others	All	Better Performers	Others	All	Better Performers	Others	All
Practice description																		
Number of practices	29	85	114	14	57	71	17	52	69	28	146	174	6	42	48	44	186	230
Total provider FTE	20.00	12.00	14.25	10.75	8.08	8.64	7.72	7.00	7.00	105.04	45.65	51.00	17.84	11.82	12.50	9.00	6.75	7.27
Total physician FTE	11.15	7.00	8.53	7.13	6.00	6.00	6.00	5.00	5.33	71.53	34.84	38.15	8.75	8.45	8.45	6.00	5.00	5.09
Total NPP FTE	6.00	3.70	4.75	2.75	1.70	2.00	1.75	1.00	1.30	18.60	8.00	8.60	5.09	3.00	3.00	2.50	1.25	1.50
Total support staff FTE	91.00	37.84	48.40	43.13	23.75	25.15	56.44	21.22	24.50	453.80	178.17	192.35	72.15	39.74	41.36	27.85	21.00	22.56
Number of branch clinics	4	2	2	2	2	2	2	3	3	8	5	6	3	4	4	2	2	2
Square footage of all facilities	32,236	15,749	18,656	13,147	10,258	10,700	15,790	10,000	10,389	129,855	70,712	76,326	19,024	17,275	17,525	10,000	10,000	10,000
Net capitation revenue as a percent of total revenue	7.90%	9.75%	9.29%	7.70%	10.94%	10.37%	25.17%	1.90%	3.71%	12.40%	8.68%	9.80%	6.20%	7.32%	7.16%	9.22%	10.10%	9.37%
Breakout of charges by payer																		
Medicare: fee-for-service	21.00%	23.50%	22.32%	0.00%	0.00%	0.00%	40.09%	42.50%	42.00%	28.54%	26.00%	26.00%	30.31%	22.57%	23.00%	0.00%	12.89%	10.42%
Medicare: managed care FFS	0.00%	0.00%	0.00%	0.00%	0.00%	0.00%	0.04%	0.00%	0.00%	0.00%	0.00%	0.00%	0.00%	0.00%	0.00%	0.00%	0.00%	0.00%
Medicare: capitated	0.00%	0.00%	0.00%	0.00%	0.00%	0.00%	0.00%	0.00%	0.00%	0.00%	0.00%	0.00%	0.00%	0.00%	0.00%	0.00%	0.00%	0.00%
Medicaid: fee-for-service	2.00%	2.40%	2.00%	6.00%	2.25%	2.75%	3.00%	2.00%	2.10%	4.00%	3.00%	3.09%	0.58%	5.00%	4.00%	3.00%	3.20%	3.00%
Medicaid: managed care FFS	0.00%	0.00%	0.00%	0.00%	0.00%	0.00%	0.00%	0.00%	0.00%	0.00%	0.00%	0.00%	0.00%	0.00%	0.00%	0.00%	0.00%	0.00%
Medicaid: capitated	0.00%	0.00%	0.00%	0.00%	0.00%	0.00%	0.00%	0.00%	0.00%	0.00%	0.00%	0.00%	0.00%	0.00%	0.00%	0.00%	0.00%	0.00%
Commercial: fee-for-service	19.00%	27.90%	23.72%	17.82%	36.25%	34.50%	17.75%	20.24%	20.00%	39.00%	40.60%	40.46%	24.00%	37.00%	34.80%	19.00%	32.50%	32.00%
Commercial: managed care FFS	26.59%	21.16%	22.00%	42.55%	20.00%	22.20%	16.20%	15.00%	15.00%	9.00%	0.00%	0.00%	16.14%	1.00%	2.28%	24.40%	17.50%	18.40%
Commercial: capitated	0.00%	0.00%	0.00%	0.00%	0.00%	0.00%	0.00%	0.00%	0.00%	0.00%	0.00%	0.00%	0.00%	0.00%	0.00%	0.00%	0.00%	0.00%
Workers' compensation	10.00%	10.00%	10.00%	0.00%	0.00%	0.00%	0.05%	0.10%	0.10%	1.00%	1.00%	1.00%	0.14%	1.00%	1.00%	0.00%	0.00%	0.00%
Charity care and prof courtesy	1.00%	0.10%	0.19%	0.00%	0.00%	0.00%	0.09%	0.54%	0.26%	0.00%	0.00%	0.00%	1.00%	0.00%	0.49%	0.00%	0.00%	0.00%
Self-pay	2.20%	2.91%	2.70%	2.50%	4.20%	4.00%	2.00%	2.00%	2.00%	3.00%	3.20%	3.15%	4.38%	5.00%	5.05%	4.00%	3.00%	3.00%
Other government payers	0.00%	0.00%	0.00%	0.00%	0.00%	0.00%	0.00%	0.00%	0.00%	0.00%	0.00%	0.00%	0.00%	0.00%	0.00%	0.00%	0.00%	0.00%
Geographic section																		
Eastern section	5.26%	14.04%	19.30%	1.41%	30.99%	32.39%	2.90%	23.19%	26.09%	2.87%	16.09%	18.97%	4.17%	25.00%	29.17%	3.91%	26.52%	30.43%
Midwest section	5.26%	21.93%	27.19%	*	11.27%	11.27%	4.35%	14.49%	18.84%	4.60%	25.29%	29.89%	*	22.92%	22.92%	3.04%	14.35%	17.39%
Southern section	8.77%	14.91%	23.68%	11.27%	15.49%	26.76%	14.49%	18.84%	33.33%	4.60%	22.41%	27.01%	6.25%	12.50%	18.75%	6.52%	23.04%	29.57%
Western section	6.14%	23.68%	29.82%	7.04%	22.54%	29.58%	2.90%	18.84%	21.74%	4.02%	20.11%	24.14%	2.08%	27.08%	29.17%	5.65%	16.96%	22.61%
Population designation																		
Nonmetropolitan (50,000 or less)	0.93%	15.74%	16.67%	1.45%	11.59%	13.04%	*	4.48%	4.48%	2.87%	28.16%	31.03%	4.44%	40.00%	44.44%	3.13%	19.64%	22.77%
Metropolitan (50,000 to 250,000)	5.56%	27.78%	33.33%	2.90%	31.88%	34.78%	10.45%	32.84%	43.28%	7.47%	32.76%	40.23%	2.22%	26.67%	28.89%	5.36%	27.68%	33.04%
Metropolitan (250,001 to 1,000,000)	12.04%	19.44%	31.48%	4.35%	20.29%	24.64%	7.46%	23.88%	31.34%	4.60%	16.09%	20.69%	4.44%	15.56%	20.00%	4.91%	25.45%	30.36%
Metropolitan (1,000,001 or more)	8.33%	10.19%	18.52%	11.59%	15.94%	27.54%	7.46%	13.43%	20.90%	1.15%	6.90%	8.05%	2.22%	4.44%	6.67%	5.80%	8.04%	13.84%

(Continued on next page)

Figure V.B.1 — Productivity, capacity and staffing demographic profile

	Medicine single specialty excluding general internal medicine			Surgical single specialty			Multispecialty all owners			Multispecialty, all owners, less than or equal to 50 percent, primary care			Multispecialty, all owners, greater than 50 percent primary care			Multispecialty, not hospital-owned, less than or equal to 50 percent, primary care		
	Better Performers	Others	All	Better Performers	Others	All	Better Performers	Others	All	Better Performers	Others	All	Better Performers	Others	All	Better Performers	Others	All
Practice description																		
Number of practices	37	186	223	66	208	274	45	280	325	16	80	96	27	180	207	14	67	81
Total provider FTE	13.10	13.00	13.05	15.60	10.55	11.70	52.00	35.92	39.62	135.00	62.70	68.08	48.04	24.60	26.05	105.45	59.78	62.70
Total physician FTE	10.47	8.55	9.00	9.57	6.00	6.23	40.00	24.70	27.00	89.01	49.10	52.49	38.00	17.64	18.40	67.53	48.45	49.20
Total NPP FTE	3.00	2.20	2.50	5.00	3.00	3.00	9.60	6.05	6.80	33.00	10.00	11.86	6.50	4.26	4.37	26.44	10.00	10.50
Total support staff FTE	53.98	32.55	35.15	62.25	27.00	30.75	212.81	115.77	135.72	504.76	254.16	264.80	174.00	83.63	92.25	439.51	232.49	260.01
Number of branch clinics	3	3	3	3	2	3	7	7	7	13	7	7	9	6	7	11	6	6
Square footage of all facilities	18,895	12,472	13,264	24,925	11,000	12,584	78,376	49,500	54,496	174,128	105,034	115,000	76,451	37,802	39,000	148,000	103,000	105,034
Net capitation revenue as a percent of total revenue	6.46%	5.20%	6.17%	16.54%	5.63%	6.55%	9.80%	7.60%	7.71%	11.39%	10.66%	10.66%	6.37%	7.24%	7.16%	15.42%	9.96%	11.18%
Breakout of charges by payer																		
Medicare: fee-for-service	45.64%	35.00%	38.54%	26.70%	30.00%	29.00%	28.51%	25.00%	25.61%	33.90%	28.54%	29.25%	23.75%	24.00%	24.00%	33.32%	29.05%	30.13%
Medicare: managed care FFS	0.00%	0.00%	0.00%	0.00%	0.00%	0.00%	0.00%	0.00%	0.00%	0.00%	0.00%	0.00%	0.00%	0.00%	0.00%	0.00%	0.00%	0.00%
Medicare: capitated	0.00%	0.00%	0.00%	0.00%	0.00%	0.00%	0.00%	0.00%	0.00%	0.00%	0.00%	0.00%	0.00%	0.00%	0.00%	0.00%	0.00%	0.00%
Medicaid: fee-for-service	2.00%	3.00%	3.00%	2.10%	3.00%	2.87%	2.50%	5.10%	4.71%	4.00%	3.64%	4.00%	1.66%	5.59%	5.00%	4.00%	3.55%	3.90%
Medicaid: managed care FFS	0.00%	0.00%	0.00%	0.00%	0.00%	0.00%	0.00%	0.00%	0.00%	0.00%	0.00%	0.00%	0.00%	0.00%	0.00%	0.00%	0.00%	0.00%
Medicaid: capitated	0.00%	0.00%	0.00%	0.00%	0.00%	0.00%	0.00%	0.00%	0.00%	0.00%	0.00%	0.00%	0.00%	0.00%	0.00%	0.00%	0.00%	0.00%
Commercial: fee-for-service	35.28%	29.00%	30.00%	22.50%	27.20%	26.83%	38.07%	39.21%	39.13%	40.60%	40.50%	40.55%	36.92%	37.00%	37.00%	39.00%	40.55%	40.50%
Commercial: managed care FFS	0.75%	8.00%	7.00%	21.70%	15.60%	16.21%	2.28%	0.00%	0.00%	0.00%	0.00%	0.00%	7.89%	0.00%	0.90%	0.00%	0.00%	0.00%
Commercial: capitated	0.00%	0.00%	0.00%	0.00%	0.00%	0.00%	0.00%	0.00%	0.00%	0.00%	0.00%	0.00%	0.00%	0.00%	0.00%	0.00%	0.00%	0.00%
Workers' compensation	0.00%	0.04%	0.01%	6.10%	1.00%	1.00%	1.00%	0.70%	0.82%	1.80%	1.00%	1.00%	0.81%	0.55%	0.60%	1.80%	1.00%	1.00%
Charity care and prof courtesy	0.00%	0.00%	0.00%	0.25%	0.20%	0.20%	0.00%	0.00%	0.00%	0.00%	0.00%	0.00%	0.00%	0.00%	0.00%	0.00%	0.00%	0.00%
Self-pay	2.03%	3.00%	3.00%	2.19%	3.00%	3.00%	3.00%	3.95%	3.75%	3.00%	3.86%	3.56%	2.95%	3.90%	3.70%	3.00%	3.56%	3.10%
Other government payers	0.00%	0.00%	0.00%	0.00%	0.00%	0.00%	0.00%	0.00%	0.00%	0.00%	0.00%	0.00%	0.00%	0.00%	0.00%	0.00%	0.00%	0.00%
Geographic section																		
Eastern section	4.93%	17.49%	22.42%	5.84%	16.06%	21.90%	2.77%	20.31%	23.08%	4.17%	17.71%	21.88%	2.90%	20.29%	23.19%	3.70%	14.81%	18.52%
Midwest section	3.14%	16.14%	19.28%	6.93%	18.98%	25.91%	3.69%	28.92%	32.62%	6.25%	23.96%	30.21%	3.38%	29.95%	33.33%	6.17%	24.69%	30.86%
Southern section	5.38%	28.70%	34.08%	8.03%	21.90%	29.93%	4.00%	18.15%	22.15%	3.13%	23.96%	27.08%	4.35%	15.94%	20.29%	3.70%	24.69%	28.40%
Western section	3.14%	21.08%	24.22%	3.28%	18.98%	22.26%	3.38%	18.77%	22.15%	3.13%	17.71%	20.83%	2.42%	20.77%	23.19%	3.70%	18.52%	22.22%
Population designation																		
Nonmetropolitan (50,000 or less)	0.46%	3.67%	4.13%	1.50%	9.40%	10.90%	3.42%	31.68%	35.09%	5.21%	25.00%	30.21%	2.44%	35.12%	37.56%	3.70%	25.93%	29.63%
Metropolitan (50,000 to 250,000)	4.13%	26.15%	30.28%	6.39%	27.82%	34.21%	5.59%	28.88%	34.47%	9.38%	32.29%	41.67%	4.39%	27.32%	31.71%	11.11%	32.10%	43.21%
Metropolitan (250,001 to 1,000,000)	6.88%	30.73%	37.61%	10.53%	22.56%	33.08%	3.11%	18.94%	22.05%	1.04%	19.79%	20.83%	2.93%	19.02%	21.95%	1.23%	19.75%	20.99%
Metropolitan (1,000,001 or more)	5.50%	22.48%	27.98%	6.02%	15.79%	21.80%	1.86%	6.52%	8.39%	1.04%	6.25%	7.29%	3.41%	5.37%	8.78%	1.23%	4.94%	6.17%

(Continued on next page)

Figure V.B.1

Productivity, capacity and staffing demographic profile

	Multispecialty, not hospital-owned greater than 50 percent primary care			Multispecialty, hospital-owned less than or equal to 50 percent, primary care			Multispecialty, hospital-owned greater than 50 percent primary care			Anesthesiology with NPPs		
	Better Performers	Others	All	Better Performers	Others	All	Better Performers	Others	All	Better Performers	Others	All
Practice description												
Number of practices	16	111	127	2	13	15	13	67	80	20	52	72
Total provider FTE	47.00	22.68	26.00	209.55	122.35	122.35	21.75	30.78	28.60	29.00	24.93	25.00
Total physician FTE	36.38	18.00	18.40	154.61	97.90	98.21	11.20	21.00	19.25	9.25	16.90	15.67
Total NPP FTE	7.00	4.37	4.40	54.95	17.52	19.00	2.50	4.60	4.20	17.25	6.52	10.00
Total support staff FTE	169.90	94.00	94.00	739.51	426.00	433.83	78.18	79.00	78.59	4.35	5.00	4.75
Number of branch clinics	6	4	4	20	15	17	14	10	11	1	2	1
Square footage of all facilities	78,206	39,000	40,038	321,592	177,373	191,788	21,834	38,936	38,715	1,275	3,389	2,450
Net capitation revenue as a percent of total revenue	11.76%	7.24%	7.56%	0.65%	11.36%	10.28%	2.04%	7.13%	7.12%	*	12.33%	12.33%
Breakout of charges by payer												
Medicare: fee-for-service	23.00%	23.50%	23.25%	29.30%	25.14%	25.14%	25.60%	24.50%	25.00%	27.00%	28.45%	28.00%
Medicare: managed care FFS	0.00%	0.00%	0.00%	0.00%	0.00%	0.00%	0.00%	0.00%	0.00%	0.00%	0.00%	0.00%
Medicare: capitated	0.00%	0.00%	0.00%	0.00%	0.00%	0.00%	0.00%	0.00%	0.00%	0.00%	0.00%	0.00%
Medicaid: fee-for-service	1.00%	3.81%	3.05%	9.95%	6.00%	7.79%	8.00%	7.50%	8.00%	9.40%	6.26%	6.82%
Medicaid: managed care FFS	0.00%	0.00%	0.00%	0.00%	0.00%	0.00%	0.00%	0.00%	0.00%	0.00%	0.00%	0.00%
Medicaid: capitated	0.00%	0.00%	0.00%	0.00%	0.00%	0.00%	0.00%	0.00%	0.00%	0.00%	0.00%	0.00%
Commercial: fee-for-service	35.76%	39.21%	39.13%	24.10%	42.00%	42.00%	45.22%	34.60%	36.40%	9.40%	11.80%	10.00%
Commercial: managed care FFS	10.00%	1.00%	2.18%	27.00%	11.00%	11.00%	0.00%	0.00%	0.00%	38.00%	35.41%	35.70%
Commercial: capitated	0.00%	0.00%	0.00%	0.00%	0.00%	0.00%	0.00%	0.00%	0.00%	0.00%	0.00%	0.00%
Workers' compensation	0.29%	0.70%	0.70%	2.10%	1.13%	1.40%	0.30%	0.39%	0.35%	2.50%	2.35%	2.39%
Charity care and prof courtesy	0.00%	0.00%	0.00%	0.25%	0.00%	0.00%	0.00%	0.00%	0.00%	0.00%	0.00%	0.00%
Self-pay	2.90%	4.00%	3.82%	7.30%	4.97%	5.00%	2.80%	3.80%	3.00%	3.00%	3.17%	3.00%
Other government payers	0.00%	0.00%	0.00%	0.00%	0.00%	0.00%	0.00%	0.00%	0.00%	0.00%	0.41%	0.32%
Geographic section												
Eastern section	2.36%	20.47%	22.83%	6.67%	33.33%	40.00%	2.50%	21.25%	23.75%	5.56%	16.67%	22.22%
Midwest section	3.15%	22.83%	25.98%	*	26.67%	26.67%	8.75%	36.25%	45.00%	4.17%	22.22%	26.39%
Southern section	3.94%	19.69%	23.62%	6.67%	13.33%	20.00%	5.00%	10.00%	15.00%	15.28%	22.22%	37.50%
Western section	3.15%	24.41%	27.56%	*	13.33%	13.33%	*	16.25%	16.25%	2.78%	11.11%	13.89%
Population designation												
Nonmetropolitan (50,000 or less)	2.40%	34.40%	36.80%	6.67%	26.67%	33.33%	5.00%	33.75%	38.75%		1.45%	1.45%
Metropolitan (50,000 to 250,000)	4.00%	31.20%	35.20%	6.67%	26.67%	33.33%	3.75%	22.50%	26.25%	15.94%	26.09%	42.03%
Metropolitan (250,001 to 1,000,000)	4.00%	15.20%	19.20%	*	20.00%	20.00%	3.75%	22.50%	26.25%	7.25%	33.33%	40.58%
Metropolitan (1,000,001 or more)	2.40%	6.40%	8.80%	*	13.33%	13.33%	3.75%	5.00%	8.75%	5.80%	10.14%	15.94%

Figure V.B.2	Productivity, capacity and staffing indicators			

Anesthesiology

	Better Performers	Others	All
Productivity			
ꙮ Total gross charges per FTE physician	$1,585,147	$939,020	$1,175,582
Total RVUs per FTE physician	1,299	1,140	1,220
Physician work RVUs per FTE physician	1,675	361	847
Patients per FTE physician	1,429	916	1,044
Encounters per FTE physician	1,753	1,101	1,299
Total procedures per FTE physician	1,843	1,163	1,453
Staffing			
ꙮ Total support staff FTE per FTE physician	0.54	0.28	0.36
– Total business operations support staff FTE per FTE physician	0.39	0.34	0.37
– Total front office support staff FTE per FTE physician	0.14	0.13	0.14
– Total clinical support staff FTE per FTE physician	0.16	0.08	0.10
– Total ancillary support staff FTE per FTE physician	0.39	0.04	0.06
Primary care physicians per FTE physician	*	1.00	1.00
Nonsurgical physicians per FTE physician	1.00	1.00	1.00
Surgical specialty physicians per FTE physician	1.00	1.00	1.00
Total NPPs per FTE physician	2.00	0.42	0.87
Capacity			
ꙮ ASA units per FTE physician	21,061.50	10,859.47	13,726.57
Inside med/surg procedures per FTE physician	577.19	589.82	589.82
Inside med/surg procedures per FTE clinical support staff	3,040.50	6,779.79	4,514.67
Inside med/surg gross charges per FTE physician	$104,454	$666,739	$553,243
Medical procedures inside practice per FTE physician	210	83	111
Medical procedures outside practice per FTE physician	54	30	39
Surgical procedures inside practice per FTE physician	785	819	792
Surgical procedures outside practice per FTE physician	1,753	989	1,162
Laboratory procedures per FTE physician	*	1	1
Radiology procedures per FTE physician	111	6	7
Square feet per FTE physician	141	118	128
Cost			
ꙮ Total operating cost per FTE physician	$88,716	$63,110	$67,508
Total operating and NPP cost per FTE physician	$390,585	$147,182	$238,100
Total operating cost as a percent of total medical revenue	12.21%	11.82%	11.92%
Total operating and NPP cost as a percent of total medical revenue	48.19%	27.97%	40.00%
Total support staff cost per FTE physician	$25,063	$16,144	$18,889
Total general operating cost per FTE physician	$60,031	$43,275	$47,815
Total NPP cost per FTE physician	$295,238	$55,103	$135,423
Total physician cost per FTE physician	$435,898	$387,308	$400,200
– Total physician compensation	$385,603	$334,017	$342,902
– Total physician benefit cost	$58,429	$58,360	$58,429
Revenue			
ꙮ Total medical revenue per FTE physician	$762,641	$473,578	$535,435
Total medical revenue after operating cost per FTE physician	$637,385	$416,623	$462,667
Total medical revenue after operating and NPP cost per FTE physician	$383,652	$401,340	$393,669

ꙮ—⚲ Key Indicator

Figure **V.B.3**	Productivity, capacity and staffing indicators			

Cardiology

		Better Performers	Others	All
Productivity				
♀	Total gross charges per FTE physician	$2,841,825	$2,296,504	$2,442,373
	Total RVUs per FTE physician	30,001	17,919	19,131
	Physician work RVUs per FTE physician	10,254	9,347	9,774
	Patients per FTE physician	1,697	1,405	1,461
	Encounters per FTE physician	5,537	4,855	5,322
	Total procedures per FTE physician	11,862	10,337	10,720
Staffing				
♀	Total support staff FTE per FTE physician	5.88	5.34	5.46
	– Total business operations support staff FTE per FTE physician	1.54	1.22	1.24
	– Total front office support staff FTE per FTE physician	1.61	1.64	1.63
	– Total clinical support staff FTE per FTE physician	1.51	1.49	1.50
	– Total ancillary support staff FTE per FTE physician	0.91	0.82	0.83
	Primary care physicians per FTE physician	0.53	0.26	0.26
	Nonsurgical physicians per FTE physician	1.00	1.00	1.00
	Surgical specialty physicians per FTE physician	0.10	0.23	0.17
	Total NPPs per FTE physician	0.22	0.25	0.25
Capacity				
♀	Inside med/surg procedures per square foot	3.03	2.09	2.27
	Inside med/surg procedures per FTE physician	6,363.51	4,027.38	4,488.50
	Inside med/surg procedures per FTE clinical support staff	4,299.49	3,207.28	3,360.25
	Inside med/surg gross charges per FTE physician	$1,209,284	$695,742	$737,131
	Medical procedures inside practice per FTE physician	6,339	3,937	4,469
	Medical procedures outside practice per FTE physician	3,653	3,812	3,763
	Surgical procedures inside practice per FTE physician	13	6	6
	Surgical procedures outside practice per FTE physician	115	81	85
	Laboratory procedures per FTE physician	690	544	588
	Radiology procedures per FTE physician	1,233	917	941
	Square feet per FTE physician	1,705	1,992	1,959
Cost				
♀	Total operating cost per FTE physician	$547,349	$503,031	$518,066
	Total operating and NPP cost per FTE physician	$568,514	$548,058	$556,874
	Total operating cost as a percent of total medical revenue	49.07%	48.28%	48.80%
	Total operating and NPP cost as a percent of total medical revenue	53.37%	51.40%	51.70%
	Total support staff cost per FTE physician	$297,191	$251,830	$263,748
	Total general operating cost per FTE physician	$272,246	$242,789	$246,455
	Total NPP cost per FTE physician	$21,165	$21,634	$21,399
	Total physician cost per FTE physician	$530,376	$475,447	$491,390
	– Total physician compensation	$470,098	$415,659	$425,802
	– Total physician benefit cost	$67,880	$59,305	$60,139
Revenue				
♀	Total medical revenue per FTE physician	$1,166,809	$1,016,370	$1,028,721
	Total medical revenue after operating cost per FTE physician	$592,518	$502,221	$521,454
	Total medical revenue after operating and NPP cost per FTE physician	$558,001	$490,275	$497,699

Ⴝ—⋗ Key Indicator

From the *Performance and Practices of Successful Medical Groups, 2005 Report Based on 2004 Data.*
Reprinted with permission from the Medical Group Management Association, 104 Inverness Terrace East,
Englewood, Colorado 80112. www.mgma.com. Copyright 2005. Pages 162–182.

Figure **V.B.4**	Productivity, capacity and staffing indicators		
Family practice			
	Better Performers	**Others**	**All**
Productivity			
☺ Total gross charges per FTE physician	$804,810	$618,293	$673,400
Total RVUs per FTE physician	11,080	9,509	10,298
Physician work RVUs per FTE physician	5,398	4,474	5,123
Patients per FTE physician	2,419	2,483	2,446
Encounters per FTE physician	6,841	5,675	5,891
Total procedures per FTE physician	13,253	8,901	10,121
Staffing			
☺ Total support staff FTE per FTE physician	5.59	4.45	4.59
– Total business operations support staff FTE per FTE physician	1.25	1.01	1.03
– Total front office support staff FTE per FTE physician	1.93	1.53	1.57
– Total clinical support staff FTE per FTE physician	1.94	1.43	1.54
– Total ancillary support staff FTE per FTE physician	0.49	0.39	0.44
Primary care physicians per FTE physician	1.00	1.00	1.00
Nonsurgical physicians per FTE physician	*	0.49	0.49
Surgical specialty physicians per FTE physician	1.00	*	1.00
Total NPPs per FTE physician	0.38	0.33	0.33
Capacity			
☺ Inside med/surg procedures per square foot	4.74	3.09	3.66
Inside med/surg procedures per FTE physician	8,212.62	5,889.41	6,570.50
Inside med/surg procedures per FTE clinical support staff	4,311.81	3,725.74	3,994.66
Inside med/surg gross charges per FTE physician	$576,870	$426,606	$453,491
Medical procedures inside practice per FTE physician	7,523	5,563	6,095
Medical procedures outside practice per FTE physician	403	300	344
Surgical procedures inside practice per FTE physician	516	262	309
Surgical procedures outside practice per FTE physician	20	71	47
Laboratory procedures per FTE physician	5,292	2,308	2,641
Radiology procedures per FTE physician	440	225	251
Square feet per FTE physician	2,024	1,838	1,900
Cost			
☺ Total operating cost per FTE physician	$349,623	$265,636	$287,816
Total operating and NPP cost per FTE physician	$402,137	$312,821	$336,617
Total operating cost as a percent of total medical revenue	56.93%	57.84%	57.63%
Total operating and NPP cost as a percent of total medical revenue	66.50%	64.19%	64.32%
Total support staff cost per FTE physician	$177,348	$152,924	$156,161
Total general operating cost per FTE physician	$168,233	$123,296	$130,753
Total NPP cost per FTE physician	$31,819	$30,603	$30,704
Total physician cost per FTE physician	$184,149	$157,641	$166,847
– Total physician compensation	$167,241	$143,019	$144,924
– Total physician benefit cost	$26,190	$23,473	$23,473
Revenue			
☺ Total medical revenue per FTE physician	$572,609	$470,847	$504,336
Total medical revenue after operating cost per FTE physician	$235,930	$203,406	$214,377
Total medical revenue after operating and NPP cost per FTE physician	$192,619	$177,786	$187,630

☺—↳ Key Indicator

Figure **V.B.5**	Productivity, capacity and staffing indicators			

Orthopedic surgery

	Better Performers	Others	All
Productivity			
Total gross charges per FTE physician	$2,885,492	$1,939,910	$2,219,916
Total RVUs per FTE physician	26,701	18,623	20,872
Physician work RVUs per FTE physician	13,017	8,185	8,755
Patients per FTE physician	1,920	1,213	1,405
Encounters per FTE physician	5,658	3,665	4,023
Total procedures per FTE physician	11,579	6,358	7,305
Staffing			
Total support staff FTE per FTE physician	6.46	5.17	5.48
– Total business operations support staff FTE per FTE physician	1.68	1.35	1.44
– Total front office support staff FTE per FTE physician	2.58	1.86	2.03
– Total clinical support staff FTE per FTE physician	1.34	1.23	1.24
– Total ancillary support staff FTE per FTE physician	0.86	0.72	0.76
Primary care physicians per FTE physician	0.03	0.11	0.09
Nonsurgical physicians per FTE physician	0.10	0.13	0.11
Surgical specialty physicians per FTE physician	0.93	0.96	0.96
Total NPPs per FTE physician	0.64	0.50	0.53
Capacity			
Total procedures per FTE physician	11,579.43	6,357.77	7,304.56
Inside med/surg procedures per FTE physician	6,342.89	3,734.42	4,210.87
Inside med/surg procedures per FTE clinical support staff	4,068.04	3,223.25	3,381.72
Inside med/surg gross charges per FTE physician	$615,895	$412,754	$472,104
Medical procedures inside practice per FTE physician	5,354	3,286	3,703
Medical procedures outside practice per FTE physician	101	81	91
Surgical procedures inside practice per FTE physician	790	537	611
Surgical procedures outside practice per FTE physician	965	698	804
Laboratory procedures per FTE physician	1,569	19	19
Radiology procedures per FTE physician	2,403	1,638	1,799
Square feet per FTE physician	2,496	2,273	2,311
Cost			
Total operating cost per FTE physician	$537,128	$437,233	$470,206
Total operating and NPP cost per FTE physician	$584,121	$501,771	$521,787
Total operating cost as a percent of total medical revenue	44.00%	46.24%	45.91%
Total operating and NPP cost as a percent of total medical revenue	48.05%	51.42%	50.64%
Total support staff cost per FTE physician	$277,946	$219,524	$233,172
Total general operating cost per FTE physician	$257,443	$216,240	$225,613
Total NPP cost per FTE physician	$43,143	$47,294	$46,663
Total physician cost per FTE physician	$610,890	$456,009	$488,635
– Total physician compensation	$538,037	$376,699	$417,282
– Total physician benefit cost	$70,168	$62,808	$65,086
Revenue			
Total medical revenue per FTE physician	$1,309,988	$986,084	$1,032,830
Total medical revenue after operating cost per FTE physician	$729,776	$514,797	$560,833
Total medical revenue after operating and NPP cost per FTE physician	$639,363	$476,314	$508,329

⛓—✱ Key Indicator

From the *Performance and Practices of Successful Medical Groups, 2005 Report Based on 2004 Data.*
Reprinted with permission from the Medical Group Management Association, 104 Inverness Terrace East, Englewood, Colorado 80112. www.mgma.com. Copyright 2005. Pages 162–182.

Figure V.B.6	Productivity, capacity and staffing indicators			

Pediatrics		Better Performers	Others	All
Productivity				
∽	Total gross charges per FTE physician	$970,959	$740,656	$760,589
	Total RVUs per FTE physician	13,681	11,617	12,227
	Physician work RVUs per FTE physician	6,489	5,842	6,331
	Patients per FTE physician	2,504	2,508	2,508
	Encounters per FTE physician	7,064	5,575	6,491
	Total procedures per FTE physician	18,459	12,939	13,682
Staffing				
∽	Total support staff FTE per FTE physician	4.88	4.00	4.03
	– Total business operations support staff FTE per FTE physician	1.12	1.00	1.00
	– Total front office support staff FTE per FTE physician	1.58	1.29	1.33
	– Total clinical support staff FTE per FTE physician	1.74	1.60	1.67
	– Total ancillary support staff FTE per FTE physician	0.44	0.19	0.20
	Primary care physicians per FTE physician	1.00	1.00	1.00
	Nonsurgical physicians per FTE physician	*	0.35	0.35
	Surgical specialty physicians per FTE physician	*	0.24	0.24
	Total NPPs per FTE physician	0.32	0.29	0.30
Capacity				
∽	Inside med/surg procedures per square foot	10.11	5.64	7.08
	Inside med/surg procedures per FTE physician	15,981.12	10,078.28	10,963.93
	Inside med/surg procedures per FTE clinical support staff	9,393.79	5,702.51	6,479.79
	Inside med/surg gross charges per FTE physician	$931,672	$618,149	$661,090
	Medical procedures inside practice per FTE physician	15,812	9,871	10,782
	Medical procedures outside practice per FTE physician	280	341	340
	Surgical procedures inside practice per FTE physician	241	136	166
	Surgical procedures outside practice per FTE physician	28	25	28
	Laboratory procedures per FTE physician	2,254	1,548	1,662
	Radiology procedures per FTE physician	559	206	221
	Square feet per FTE physician	1,579	1,644	1,619
Cost				
∽	Total operating cost per FTE physician	$407,483	$300,068	$320,653
	Total operating and NPP cost per FTE physician	$443,439	$349,368	$365,754
	Total operating cost as a percent of total medical revenue	59.59%	59.01%	59.18%
	Total operating and NPP cost as a percent of total medical revenue	63.90%	65.26%	64.84%
	Total support staff cost per FTE physician	$179,818	$143,760	$153,751
	Total general operating cost per FTE physician	$218,890	$163,516	$171,246
	Total NPP cost per FTE physician	$25,571	$21,049	$23,872
	Total physician cost per FTE physician	$231,942	$167,190	$190,396
	– Total physician compensation	$196,008	$140,009	$165,830
	– Total physician benefit cost	$28,424	$19,467	$20,100
Revenue				
∽	Total medical revenue per FTE physician	$682,296	$505,120	$538,569
	Total medical revenue after operating cost per FTE physician	$273,633	$201,104	$221,883
	Total medical revenue after operating and NPP cost per FTE physician	$242,500	$188,042	$198,083

∽——↘ Key Indicator

Figure V.B.7	Productivity, capacity and staffing indicators		

Urology

	Better Performers	Others	All
Productivity			
Total gross charges per FTE physician	$2,192,339	$1,568,670	$1,757,344
Total RVUs per FTE physician	27,571	17,033	19,832
Physician work RVUs per FTE physician	10,967	8,543	9,916
Patients per FTE physician	2,131	1,764	2,020
Encounters per FTE physician	5,393	4,257	4,709
Total procedures per FTE physician	11,253	6,383	8,308
Staffing			
Total support staff FTE per FTE physician	6.10	3.90	4.39
– Total business operations support staff FTE per FTE physician	1.62	1.00	1.00
– Total front office support staff FTE per FTE physician	2.05	1.57	1.70
– Total clinical support staff FTE per FTE physician	1.79	1.32	1.38
– Total ancillary support staff FTE per FTE physician	0.76	0.33	0.42
Primary care physicians per FTE physician	0.98	1.00	1.00
Nonsurgical physicians per FTE physician	0.11	0.04	0.08
Surgical specialty physicians per FTE physician	1.00	1.00	1.00
Total NPPs per FTE physician	0.27	0.17	0.21
Capacity			
Total procedures per FTE physician	11,253.00	6,383.07	8,307.52
Inside med/surg procedures per FTE physician	5,165.40	3,602.32	4,101.33
Inside med/surg procedures per FTE clinical support staff	3,351.36	2,976.33	3,111.09
Inside med/surg gross charges per FTE physician	$782,848	$562,898	$631,139
Medical procedures inside practice per FTE physician	3,675	2,690	2,942
Medical procedures outside practice per FTE physician	444	255	341
Surgical procedures inside practice per FTE physician	1,431	1,043	1,121
Surgical procedures outside practice per FTE physician	858	439	497
Laboratory procedures per FTE physician	4,590	1,923	2,378
Radiology procedures per FTE physician	408	244	302
Square feet per FTE physician	2,817	1,757	1,956
Cost			
Total operating cost per FTE physician	$605,050	$422,915	$452,939
Total operating and NPP cost per FTE physician	$598,685	$443,596	$475,067
Total operating cost as a percent of total medical revenue	54.27%	49.69%	50.17%
Total operating and NPP cost as a percent of total medical revenue	55.57%	50.13%	51.96%
Total support staff cost per FTE physician	$263,060	$160,414	$177,796
Total general operating cost per FTE physician	$341,991	$250,069	$279,858
Total NPP cost per FTE physician	$21,618	$19,418	$20,566
Total physician cost per FTE physician	$490,698	$399,713	$435,200
– Total physician compensation	$410,668	$373,165	$388,572
– Total physician benefit cost	$57,453	$56,701	$57,027
Revenue			
Total medical revenue per FTE physician	$1,118,077	$882,555	$936,825
Total medical revenue after operating cost per FTE physician	$512,605	$431,569	$459,490
Total medical revenue after operating and NPP cost per FTE physician	$445,327	$458,274	$451,752

ᴤ—ᴋ Key Indicator

Figure V.B.8	Productivity, capacity and staffing indicators			
Multispecialty, primary and specialty care, not hospital-owned		Better Performers	Others	All
Productivity				
⌽ Total gross charges per FTE physician		$1,448,244	$1,050,428	$1,136,148
Total RVUs per FTE physician		13,870	12,288	12,808
Physician work RVUs per FTE physician		6,167	6,056	6,085
Patients per FTE physician		1,277	1,556	1,486
Encounters per FTE physician		5,314	4,604	4,752
Total procedures per FTE physician		12,491	11,146	11,273
Staffing				
⌽ Total support staff FTE per FTE physician		5.66	5.14	5.25
– Total business operations support staff FTE per FTE physician		1.34	1.27	1.29
– Total front office support staff FTE per FTE physician		1.63	1.56	1.58
– Total clinical support staff FTE per FTE physician		1.72	1.53	1.55
– Total ancillary support staff FTE per FTE physician		1.01	0.78	0.81
Primary care physicians per FTE physician		0.43	0.51	0.51
Nonsurgical physicians per FTE physician		0.32	0.26	0.29
Surgical specialty physicians per FTE physician		0.23	0.23	0.23
Total NPPs per FTE physician		0.27	0.21	0.22
Capacity				
⌽ Inside med/surg procedures per square foot		3.20	2.44	2.68
Inside med/surg procedures per FTE physician		6,661.36	5,443.31	5,582.24
Inside med/surg procedures per FTE clinical support staff		4,160.64	3,707.41	3,775.86
Inside med/surg gross charges per FTE physician		$603,340	$452,308	$492,971
Medical procedures inside practice per FTE physician		5,589	4,904	5,169
Medical procedures outside practice per FTE physician		745	705	720
Surgical procedures inside practice per FTE physician		612	361	383
Surgical procedures outside practice per FTE physician		254	188	195
Laboratory procedures per FTE physician		3,938	3,631	3,688
Radiology procedures per FTE physician		713	616	638
Square feet per FTE physician		2,020	2,141	2,088
Cost				
⌽ Total operating cost per FTE physician		$507,226	$400,578	$414,079
Total operating and NPP cost per FTE physician		$530,908	$422,816	$444,058
Total operating cost as a percent of total medical revenue		58.27%	59.14%	59.03%
Total operating and NPP cost as a percent of total medical revenue		61.62%	62.34%	62.12%
Total support staff cost per FTE physician		$234,361	$192,918	$199,820
Total general operating cost per FTE physician		$265,204	$197,628	$209,254
Total NPP cost per FTE physician		$21,163	$18,393	$19,217
Total physician cost per FTE physician		$317,558	$253,262	$268,500
– Total physician compensation		$275,235	$226,295	$233,598
– Total physician benefit cost		$38,314	$35,624	$35,814
Revenue				
⌽ Total medical revenue per FTE physician		$849,338	$678,003	$713,722
Total medical revenue after operating cost per FTE physician		$368,061	$272,901	$286,218
Total medical revenue after operating and NPP cost per FTE physician		$336,129	$257,792	$266,579

⌽—⅃ Key Indicator

Figure V.B.9	Productivity, capacity and staffing indicators			

Primary care, single specialties

	Better Performers	Others	All
Productivity			
♔ Total gross charges per FTE physician	$850,308	$640,013	$694,542
Total RVUs per FTE physician	11,794	8,626	9,740
Physician work RVUs per FTE physician	5,742	4,265	4,542
Patients per FTE physician	2,408	1,846	1,925
Encounters per FTE physician	6,731	4,845	5,184
Total procedures per FTE physician	14,765	10,127	11,603
Staffing			
♔ Total support staff FTE per FTE physician	4.60	3.81	4.00
– Total business operations support staff FTE per FTE physician	1.17	0.72	0.85
– Total front office support staff FTE per FTE physician	1.65	1.37	1.43
– Total clinical support staff FTE per FTE physician	1.75	1.39	1.49
– Total ancillary support staff FTE per FTE physician	0.40	0.42	0.42
Primary care physicians per FTE physician	1.00	1.00	1.00
Nonsurgical physicians per FTE physician	*	0.37	0.37
Surgical specialty physicians per FTE physician	1.00	0.19	0.24
Total NPPs per FTE physician	0.45	0.22	0.25
Capacity			
♔ Inside med/surg procedures per square foot	6.50	3.34	4.00
Inside med/surg procedures per FTE physician	11,712.25	5,971.93	6,992.24
Inside med/surg procedures per FTE clinical support staff	6,122.41	4,322.09	4,511.27
Inside med/surg gross charges per FTE physician	$740,409	$474,708	$548,737
Medical procedures inside practice per FTE physician	11,556	5,642	6,844
Medical procedures outside practice per FTE physician	358	342	342
Surgical procedures inside practice per FTE physician	218	196	201
Surgical procedures outside practice per FTE physician	28	27	28
Laboratory procedures per FTE physician	2,123	2,040	2,067
Radiology procedures per FTE physician	431	230	251
Square feet per FTE physician	1,643	1,726	1,701
Cost			
♔ Total operating cost per FTE physician	$374,546	$271,985	$290,343
Total operating and NPP cost per FTE physician	$406,214	$318,762	$336,617
Total operating cost as a percent of total medical revenue	60.85%	58.96%	59.24%
Total operating and NPP cost as a percent of total medical revenue	65.72%	64.14%	64.41%
Total support staff cost per FTE physician	$177,661	$137,100	$146,472
Total general operating cost per FTE physician	$196,514	$132,241	$144,117
Total NPP cost per FTE physician	$30,008	$17,460	$20,393
Total physician cost per FTE physician	$212,147	$183,312	$189,566
– Total physician compensation	$186,503	$158,242	$165,636
– Total physician benefit cost	$19,171	$25,448	$24,863
Revenue			
♔ Total medical revenue per FTE physician	$614,909	$456,968	$498,780
Total medical revenue after operating cost per FTE physician	$251,148	$192,089	$196,657
Total medical revenue after operating and NPP cost per FTE physician	$205,073	$179,513	$187,630

♔—✖ Key Indicator

Figure V.B.10	Productivity, capacity and staffing indicators			

Medicine single specialty, excluding general internal medicine

	Better Performers	Others	All
Productivity			
Total gross charges per FTE physician	$2,794,029	$1,635,532	$1,865,934
Total RVUs per FTE physician	20,025	15,224	16,170
Physician work RVUs per FTE physician	9,574	8,266	8,486
Patients per FTE physician	1,405	1,638	1,591
Encounters per FTE physician	4,986	4,332	4,552
Total procedures per FTE physician	11,632	8,153	9,331
Staffing			
Total support staff FTE per FTE physician	5.46	4.20	4.49
– Total business operations support staff FTE per FTE physician	1.47	1.06	1.13
– Total front office support staff FTE per FTE physician	1.61	1.39	1.46
– Total clinical support staff FTE per FTE physician	1.56	1.19	1.34
– Total ancillary support staff FTE per FTE physician	0.86	0.74	0.75
Primary care physicians per FTE physician	1.00	1.00	1.00
Nonsurgical physicians per FTE physician	1.00	1.00	1.00
Surgical specialty physicians per FTE physician	0.18	1.00	0.78
Total NPPs per FTE physician	0.25	0.25	0.25
Capacity			
Inside med/surg procedures per square foot	3.03	1.98	2.24
Inside med/surg procedures per FTE physician	5,854.88	3,586.52	3,937.10
Inside med/surg procedures per FTE clinical support staff	3,898.93	2,906.48	3,213.92
Inside med/surg gross charges per FTE physician	$1,076,173	$566,731	$637,901
Medical procedures inside practice per FTE physician	5,831	3,484	3,854
Medical procedures outside practice per FTE physician	3,451	2,140	2,302
Surgical procedures inside practice per FTE physician	81	80	81
Surgical procedures outside practice per FTE physician	84	124	122
Laboratory procedures per FTE physician	805	452	607
Radiology procedures per FTE physician	1,054	861	941
Square feet per FTE physician	1,678	1,642	1,658
Cost			
Total operating cost per FTE physician	$539,241	$388,796	$425,234
Total operating and NPP cost per FTE physician	$568,514	$452,726	$473,824
Total operating cost as a percent of total medical revenue	51.81%	45.04%	46.00%
Total operating and NPP cost as a percent of total medical revenue	54.14%	49.06%	51.31%
Total support staff cost per FTE physician	$294,452	$189,698	$205,659
Total general operating cost per FTE physician	$270,786	$184,545	$207,366
Total NPP cost per FTE physician	$22,405	$21,833	$22,031
Total physician cost per FTE physician	$522,882	$415,975	$438,190
– Total physician compensation	$456,825	$365,209	$380,124
– Total physician benefit cost	$63,834	$53,192	$55,344
Revenue			
Total medical revenue per FTE physician	$1,157,059	$828,123	$908,622
Total medical revenue after operating cost per FTE physician	$581,689	$451,743	$475,014
Total medical revenue after operating and NPP cost per FTE physician	$526,539	$433,846	$459,511

⊖—⋌ Key Indicator

Figure V.B.11	Productivity, capacity and staffing indicators		

Surgical single specialty

	Better Performers	Others	All
Productivity			
○ Total gross charges per FTE physician	$2,615,509	$1,679,099	$1,823,027
Total RVUs per FTE physician	26,701	18,114	19,901
Physician work RVUs per FTE physician	11,364	8,202	8,798
Patients per FTE physician	1,978	1,500	1,661
Encounters per FTE physician	5,442	3,643	4,079
Total procedures per FTE physician	10,018	5,454	6,649
Staffing			
○ Total support staff FTE per FTE physician	6.36	4.43	4.79
– Total business operations support staff FTE per FTE physician	1.64	1.08	1.24
– Total front office support staff FTE per FTE physician	2.28	1.60	1.75
– Total clinical support staff FTE per FTE physician	1.50	1.17	1.25
– Total ancillary support staff FTE per FTE physician	0.83	0.55	0.66
Primary care physicians per FTE physician	0.08	0.62	0.24
Nonsurgical physicians per FTE physician	0.10	0.14	0.11
Surgical specialty physicians per FTE physician	1.00	1.00	1.00
Total NPPs per FTE physician	0.46	0.46	0.46
Capacity			
○ Total procedures per FTE physician	10,018.23	5,453.72	6,648.97
Inside med/surg procedures per FTE physician	5,998.94	3,204.44	3,898.61
Inside med/surg procedures per FTE clinical support staff	3,419.47	2,723.03	3,023.67
Inside med/surg gross charges per FTE physician	$701,256	$396,364	$521,418
Medical procedures inside practice per FTE physician	4,843	2,519	3,119
Medical procedures outside practice per FTE physician	132	145	143
Surgical procedures inside practice per FTE physician	878	571	672
Surgical procedures outside practice per FTE physician	858	614	682
Laboratory procedures per FTE physician	2,844	1,138	1,910
Radiology procedures per FTE physician	1,832	599	1,020
Square feet per FTE physician	2,697	1,866	2,036
Cost			
○ Total operating cost per FTE physician	$553,880	$392,298	$434,143
Total operating and NPP cost per FTE physician	$584,121	$447,196	$483,799
Total operating cost as a percent of total medical revenue	47.75%	46.02%	46.22%
Total operating and NPP cost as a percent of total medical revenue	51.64%	49.74%	50.21%
Total support staff cost per FTE physician	$272,242	$173,185	$203,807
Total general operating cost per FTE physician	$276,952	$198,930	$219,749
Total NPP cost per FTE physician	$39,430	$39,374	$39,430
Total physician cost per FTE physician	$547,851	$399,292	$436,034
– Total physician compensation	$483,683	$343,673	$379,864
– Total physician benefit cost	$67,951	$55,569	$57,617
Revenue			
○ Total medical revenue per FTE physician	$1,236,599	$845,365	$936,715
Total medical revenue after operating cost per FTE physician	$615,101	$453,675	$493,804
Total medical revenue after operating and NPP cost per FTE physician	$577,742	$434,724	$468,956

♀—⚲ Key Indicator

Figure V.B.12	Productivity, capacity and staffing indicators			

Multispecialty, all owners

	Better Performers	Others	All
Productivity			
Total gross charges per FTE physician	$1,241,842	$824,902	$886,560
Total RVUs per FTE physician	12,920	10,528	10,791
Physician work RVUs per FTE physician	6,395	5,312	5,380
Patients per FTE physician	1,532	1,584	1,584
Encounters per FTE physician	5,446	4,567	4,721
Total procedures per FTE physician	12,768	9,553	10,101
Staffing			
Total support staff FTE per FTE physician	5.53	4.62	4.71
– Total business operations support staff FTE per FTE physician	1.29	1.06	1.10
– Total front office support staff FTE per FTE physician	1.62	1.49	1.52
– Total clinical support staff FTE per FTE physician	1.61	1.50	1.51
– Total ancillary support staff FTE per FTE physician	0.84	0.59	0.62
Primary care physicians per FTE physician	0.54	0.68	0.66
Nonsurgical physicians per FTE physician	0.30	0.25	0.26
Surgical specialty physicians per FTE physician	0.18	0.23	0.22
Total NPPs per FTE physician	0.25	0.22	0.22
Capacity			
Inside med/surg procedures per square foot	3.69	2.52	2.80
Inside med/surg procedures per FTE physician	7,304.17	5,394.75	5,592.71
Inside med/surg procedures per FTE clinical support staff	4,224.84	3,549.47	3,730.49
Inside med/surg gross charges per FTE physician	$602,529	$434,584	$468,972
Medical procedures inside practice per FTE physician	6,480	4,883	5,111
Medical procedures outside practice per FTE physician	629	637	637
Surgical procedures inside practice per FTE physician	585	276	322
Surgical procedures outside practice per FTE physician	194	160	167
Laboratory procedures per FTE physician	3,833	2,866	3,101
Radiology procedures per FTE physician	664	471	521
Square feet per FTE physician	2,041	1,929	1,950
Cost			
Total operating cost per FTE physician	$433,511	$339,186	$353,503
Total operating and NPP cost per FTE physician	$473,180	$371,447	$389,636
Total operating cost as a percent of total medical revenue	58.93%	59.63%	59.59%
Total operating and NPP cost as a percent of total medical revenue	62.71%	63.58%	63.28%
Total support staff cost per FTE physician	$208,931	$169,524	$176,280
Total general operating cost per FTE physician	$224,688	$159,069	$171,553
Total NPP cost per FTE physician	$21,163	$19,048	$19,277
Total physician cost per FTE physician	$267,169	$221,899	$229,638
– Total physician compensation	$236,229	$189,997	$199,589
– Total physician benefit cost	$30,034	$31,955	$31,906
Revenue			
Total medical revenue per FTE physician	$750,768	$551,005	$582,307
Total medical revenue after operating cost per FTE physician	$301,779	$221,740	$236,021
Total medical revenue after operating and NPP cost per FTE physician	$255,011	$209,636	$217,069

◖──✳ Key Indicator

Figure V.B.13	Productivity, capacity and staffing indicators

Multispecialty, all owners, less than or equal to 50 percent, primary care

	Better Performers	Others	All
Productivity			
☿ Total gross charges per FTE physician	$1,513,073	$1,200,646	$1,299,613
Total RVUs per FTE physician	17,436	12,359	13,105
Physician work RVUs per FTE physician	6,583	6,068	6,286
Patients per FTE physician	1,095	1,208	1,183
Encounters per FTE physician	4,851	4,487	4,503
Total procedures per FTE physician	12,824	10,441	11,027
Staffing			
☿ Total support staff FTE per FTE physician	5.66	5.11	5.30
– Total business operations support staff FTE per FTE physician	1.53	1.31	1.34
– Total front office support staff FTE per FTE physician	1.62	1.39	1.50
– Total clinical support staff FTE per FTE physician	1.72	1.44	1.44
– Total ancillary support staff FTE per FTE physician	1.01	0.86	0.88
Primary care physicians per FTE physician	0.38	0.38	0.38
Nonsurgical physicians per FTE physician	0.38	0.36	0.36
Surgical specialty physicians per FTE physician	0.25	0.27	0.26
Total NPPs per FTE physician	0.33	0.20	0.22
Capacity			
☿ Inside med/surg procedures per square foot	2.95	2.32	2.47
Inside med/surg procedures per FTE physician	7,121.88	5,199.42	5,443.31
Inside med/surg procedures per FTE clinical support staff	4,069.61	3,549.47	3,597.64
Inside med/surg gross charges per FTE physician	$608,332	$449,169	$490,414
Medical procedures inside practice per FTE physician	5,772	4,786	4,874
Medical procedures outside practice per FTE physician	730	711	724
Surgical procedures inside practice per FTE physician	738	327	373
Surgical procedures outside practice per FTE physician	312	238	259
Laboratory procedures per FTE physician	4,089	3,104	3,293
Radiology procedures per FTE physician	814	636	682
Square feet per FTE physician	2,244	2,189	2,212
Cost			
☿ Total operating cost per FTE physician	$538,746	$442,523	$457,350
Total operating and NPP cost per FTE physician	$569,704	$461,125	$479,038
Total operating cost as a percent of total medical revenue	58.15%	59.43%	59.28%
Total operating and NPP cost as a percent of total medical revenue	61.81%	62.08%	62.08%
Total support staff cost per FTE physician	$238,667	$199,347	$203,711
Total general operating cost per FTE physician	$302,519	$220,351	$231,709
Total NPP cost per FTE physician	$24,201	$19,448	$19,900
Total physician cost per FTE physician	340,938	302,421	304,805
– Total physician compensation	290,084	261,073	268,845
– Total physician benefit cost	35,688	35,624	35,624
Revenue			
☿ Total medical revenue per FTE physician	893,951	748,744	771,744
Total medical revenue after operating cost per FTE physician	389,339	308,824	316,783
Total medical revenue after operating and NPP cost per FTE physician	346,772	290,391	296,995

ჟ—⚹ Key Indicator

Figure V.B.14	Productivity, capacity and staffing indicators

Multispecialty, all owners, greater than 50 percent primary care

	Better Performers	Others	All
Productivity			
✿ Total gross charges per FTE physician	$966,147	$742,922	$797,276
Total RVUs per FTE physician	10,460	9,509	9,811
Physician work RVUs per FTE physician	6,113	4,947	5,050
Patients per FTE physician	1,933	1,839	1,853
Encounters per FTE physician	5,294	4,711	4,935
Total procedures per FTE physician	13,151	9,289	9,813
Staffing			
✿ Total support staff FTE per FTE physician	4.86	4.50	4.60
– Total business operations support staff FTE per FTE physician	1.27	1.00	1.05
– Total front office support staff FTE per FTE physician	1.60	1.52	1.53
– Total clinical support staff FTE per FTE physician	1.46	1.53	1.53
– Total ancillary support staff FTE per FTE physician	0.60	0.50	0.51
Primary care physicians per FTE physician	0.86	0.84	0.85
Nonsurgical physicians per FTE physician	0.25	0.18	0.19
Surgical specialty physicians per FTE physician	0.10	0.17	0.16
Total NPPs per FTE physician	0.17	0.22	0.21
Capacity			
✿ Inside med/surg procedures per square foot	4.02	2.76	3.14
Inside med/surg procedures per FTE physician	8,141.42	5,600.53	5,719.31
Inside med/surg procedures per FTE clinical support staff	4,619.99	3,753.19	3,785.32
Inside med/surg gross charges per FTE physician	$592,883	$439,281	$461,258
Medical procedures inside practice per FTE physician	7,280	5,217	5,341
Medical procedures outside practice per FTE physician	563	585	581
Surgical procedures inside practice per FTE physician	640	259	286
Surgical procedures outside practice per FTE physician	97	112	110
Laboratory procedures per FTE physician	4,142	2,707	2,983
Radiology procedures per FTE physician	585	372	411
Square feet per FTE physician	1,748	1,882	1,865
Cost			
✿ Total operating cost per FTE physician	$353,503	$321,763	$330,147
Total operating and NPP cost per FTE physician	$373,154	$354,760	$362,177
Total operating cost as a percent of total medical revenue	56.95%	60.28%	59.97%
Total operating and NPP cost as a percent of total medical revenue	59.11%	64.53%	64.20%
Total support staff cost per FTE physician	$174,800	$166,173	$166,938
Total general operating cost per FTE physician	$166,323	$151,526	$156,432
Total NPP cost per FTE physician	$16,670	$18,682	$18,393
Total physician cost per FTE physician	233,272	206,851	210,062
– Total physician compensation	199,697	177,696	182,908
– Total physician benefit cost	31,671	29,616	30,103
Revenue			
✿ Total medical revenue per FTE physician	611,361	515,244	530,374
Total medical revenue after operating cost per FTE physician	243,466	197,361	203,097
Total medical revenue after operating and NPP cost per FTE physician	230,676	183,487	191,187

❍——★ Key Indicator

Figure V.B.15 Productivity, capacity and staffing indicators

Multispecialty, not hospital-owned, less than or equal to 50 percent primary care

	Better Performers	*Others*	*All*
Productivity			
Total gross charges per FTE physician	$1,545,356	$1,261,565	$1,408,779
Total RVUs per FTE physician	17,159	12,826	13,154
Physician work RVUs per FTE physician	6,627	6,442	6,557
Patients per FTE physician	1,106	1,205	1,183
Encounters per FTE physician	5,158	4,582	4,603
Total procedures per FTE physician	12,824	11,018	11,147
Staffing			
Total support staff FTE per FTE physician	5.66	5.34	5.49
– Total business operations support staff FTE per FTE physician	1.53	1.35	1.38
– Total front office support staff FTE per FTE physician	1.62	1.52	1.57
– Total clinical support staff FTE per FTE physician	1.79	1.49	1.55
– Total ancillary support staff FTE per FTE physician	1.09	0.88	0.89
Primary care physicians per FTE physician	0.38	0.38	0.38
Nonsurgical physicians per FTE physician	0.38	0.37	0.37
Surgical specialty physicians per FTE physician	0.25	0.26	0.26
Total NPPs per FTE physician	0.33	0.21	0.22
Capacity			
Inside med/surg procedures per square foot	3.04	2.32	2.47
Inside med/surg procedures per FTE physician	7,130.38	5,420.68	5,471.33
Inside med/surg procedures per FTE clinical support staff	3,851.02	3,559.37	3,559.37
Inside med/surg gross charges per FTE physician	$627,646	$470,381	$510,867
Medical procedures inside practice per FTE physician	5,772	4,865	5,068
Medical procedures outside practice per FTE physician	720	785	759
Surgical procedures inside practice per FTE physician	738	361	379
Surgical procedures outside practice per FTE physician	312	252	261
Laboratory procedures per FTE physician	4,089	3,367	3,585
Radiology procedures per FTE physician	779	674	702
Square feet per FTE physician	2,145	2,294	2,235
Cost			
Total operating cost per FTE physician	$557,785	$460,933	$476,912
Total operating and NPP cost per FTE physician	$586,731	$482,386	$502,626
Total operating cost as a percent of total medical revenue	58.81%	59.41%	59.33%
Total operating and NPP cost as a percent of total medical revenue	61.96%	62.05%	62.05%
Total support staff cost per FTE physician	$238,667	$203,427	$207,963
Total general operating cost per FTE physician	$304,325	$234,048	$256,715
Total NPP cost per FTE physician	$22,705	$19,515	$19,834
Total physician cost per FTE physician	$340,938	$307,936	$309,987
– Total physician compensation	$290,084	$268,162	$271,021
– Total physician benefit cost	$35,688	$37,982	$37,264
Revenue			
Total medical revenue per FTE physician	$893,951	$770,522	$829,455
Total medical revenue after operating cost per FTE physician	$389,339	$318,245	$329,825
Total medical revenue after operating and NPP cost per FTE physician	$346,772	$307,385	$311,942

Key Indicator

From the *Performance and Practices of Successful Medical Groups, 2005 Report Based on 2004 Data.*
Reprinted with permission from the Medical Group Management Association, 104 Inverness Terrace East, Englewood, Colorado 80112. www.mgma.com. Copyright 2005. Pages 162–182.

Figure V.B.16	Productivity, capacity and staffing indicators			
Multispecialty, not hospital-owned, greater than 50 percent primary care		Better Performers	Others	All
Productivity				
⚷	Total gross charges per FTE physician	$1,238,287	$866,394	$901,739
	Total RVUs per FTE physician	12,808	10,184	10,315
	Physician work RVUs per FTE physician	6,226	5,146	5,252
	Patients per FTE physician	1,964	1,948	1,948
	Encounters per FTE physician	5,106	5,018	5,018
	Total procedures per FTE physician	14,374	11,038	11,314
Staffing				
⚷	Total support staff FTE per FTE physician	5.04	4.88	4.89
	– Total business operations support staff FTE per FTE physician	1.28	1.11	1.13
	– Total front office support staff FTE per FTE physician	1.80	1.58	1.59
	– Total clinical support staff FTE per FTE physician	1.45	1.53	1.52
	– Total ancillary support staff FTE per FTE physician	0.78	0.62	0.65
	Primary care physicians per FTE physician	0.81	0.82	0.82
	Nonsurgical physicians per FTE physician	0.30	0.19	0.19
	Surgical specialty physicians per FTE physician	0.10	0.16	0.16
	Total NPPs per FTE physician	0.18	0.23	0.22
Capacity				
⚷	Inside med/surg procedures per square foot	4.18	2.78	3.20
	Inside med/surg procedures per FTE physician	8,477.01	5,687.71	6,011.99
	Inside med/surg procedures per FTE clinical support staff	4,698.41	3,816.82	4,022.80
	Inside med/surg gross charges per FTE physician	$665,799	$441,770	$484,392
	Medical procedures inside practice per FTE physician	7,391	5,341	5,516
	Medical procedures outside practice per FTE physician	544	708	660
	Surgical procedures inside practice per FTE physician	599	323	332
	Surgical procedures outside practice per FTE physician	97	128	122
	Laboratory procedures per FTE physician	4,444	3,775	3,778
	Radiology procedures per FTE physician	610	543	563
	Square feet per FTE physician	1,952	1,927	1,927
Cost				
⚷	Total operating cost per FTE physician	$369,901	$346,395	$356,710
	Total operating and NPP cost per FTE physician	$395,613	$380,158	$382,870
	Total operating cost as a percent of total medical revenue	56.96%	58.78%	58.24%
	Total operating and NPP cost as a percent of total medical revenue	59.11%	62.61%	62.43%
	Total support staff cost per FTE physician	$189,828	$177,504	$177,610
	Total general operating cost per FTE physician	$199,306	$160,711	$170,256
	Total NPP cost per FTE physician	$17,036	$19,116	$18,991
	Total physician cost per FTE physician	$223,536	$209,239	$212,025
	– Total physician compensation	$202,054	$183,459	$190,122
	– Total physician benefit cost	$29,305	$30,853	$30,631
Revenue				
⚷	Total medical revenue per FTE physician	$715,826	$583,644	$596,297
	Total medical revenue after operating cost per FTE physician	$279,495	$236,244	$239,319
	Total medical revenue after operating and NPP cost per FTE physician	$251,890	$213,007	$219,786

⚷—⚹ Key Indicator

Figure **V.B.17**	Productivity, capacity and staffing indicators			

Multispecialty, hospital-owned, greater than 50 percent, primary care

	Better Performers	Others	All
Productivity			
☤ Total gross charges per FTE physician	$750,686	$630,981	$659,561
Total RVUs per FTE physician	10,254	8,631	9,062
Physician work RVUs per FTE physician	5,074	4,892	4,918
Patients per FTE physician	1,584	1,831	1,715
Encounters per FTE physician	5,294	4,567	4,712
Total procedures per FTE physician	12,098	6,781	7,659
Staffing			
☤ Total support staff FTE per FTE physician	4.11	4.01	4.02
– Total business operations support staff FTE per FTE physician	0.78	0.84	0.84
– Total front office support staff FTE per FTE physician	1.57	1.39	1.45
– Total clinical support staff FTE per FTE physician	1.59	1.54	1.55
– Total ancillary support staff FTE per FTE physician	0.31	0.28	0.29
Primary care physicians per FTE physician	1.00	0.90	1.00
Nonsurgical physicians per FTE physician	0.15	0.17	0.15
Surgical specialty physicians per FTE physician	0.10	0.16	0.15
Total NPPs per FTE physician	0.13	0.20	0.19
Capacity			
☤ Inside med/surg procedures per square foot	3.77	2.68	3.01
Inside med/surg procedures per FTE physician	7,304.17	5,132.11	5,399.38
Inside med/surg procedures per FTE clinical support staff	4,541.57	3,443.08	3,608.92
Inside med/surg gross charges per FTE physician	$523,266	$422,938	$453,238
Medical procedures inside practice per FTE physician	6,081	4,838	4,976
Medical procedures outside practice per FTE physician	619	489	508
Surgical procedures inside practice per FTE physician	349	241	254
Surgical procedures outside practice per FTE physician	45	91	79
Laboratory procedures per FTE physician	3,631	873	1,266
Radiology procedures per FTE physician	320	183	197
Square feet per FTE physician	1,711	1,822	1,818
Cost			
☤ Total operating cost per FTE physician	$314,106	$280,323	$284,897
Total operating and NPP cost per FTE physician	$336,111	$322,887	$324,040
Total operating cost as a percent of total medical revenue	63.83%	66.75%	64.47%
Total operating and NPP cost as a percent of total medical revenue	67.59%	68.81%	68.67%
Total support staff cost per FTE physician	$164,270	$154,691	$156,451
Total general operating cost per FTE physician	$160,236	$120,118	$133,429
Total NPP cost per FTE physician	$18,849	$17,517	$17,638
Total physician cost per FTE physician	$226,924	$204,465	$207,752
– Total physician compensation	$189,873	$172,984	$178,192
– Total physician benefit cost	$25,276	$28,782	$27,844
Revenue			
☤ Total medical revenue per FTE physician	$509,002	$418,752	$437,228
Total medical revenue after operating cost per FTE physician	$196,033	$155,761	$161,250
Total medical revenue after operating and NPP cost per FTE physician	$172,159	$142,876	$147,623

Ꮗ—ᵏ Key Indicator

From the *Performance and Practices of Successful Medical Groups, 2005 Report Based on 2004 Data.*
Reprinted with permission from the Medical Group Management Association, 104 Inverness Terrace East,
Englewood, Colorado 80112. www.mgma.com. Copyright 2005. Pages 162–182.

Figure V.B.18	Productivity, capacity and staffing indicators			

Anesthesiology with NPPs

	Better Performers	Others	All
Productivity			
Total gross charges per FTE physician	$1,874,886	$1,215,866	$1,345,552
Total RVUs per FTE physician	1,299	22,109	4,989
Physician work RVUs per FTE physician	1,675	1,119	1,119
Patients per FTE physician	1,922	1,024	1,119
Encounters per FTE physician	1,898	1,248	1,430
Total procedures per FTE physician	1,878	1,318	1,605
Staffing			
Total support staff FTE per FTE physician	0.57	0.38	0.39
– Total business operations support staff FTE per FTE physician	0.49	0.39	0.39
– Total front office support staff FTE per FTE physician	0.14	0.14	0.14
– Total clinical support staff FTE per FTE physician	0.16	0.11	0.15
– Total ancillary support staff FTE per FTE physician	0.39	0.04	0.06
Primary care physicians per FTE physician	*	1.00	1.00
Nonsurgical physicians per FTE physician	1.00	1.00	1.00
Surgical specialty physicians per FTE physician	1.00	1.00	1.00
Total NPPs per FTE physician	2.10	0.51	0.87
Capacity			
ASA units per FTE physician	22,676.78	12,331.16	15,325.66
Inside med/surg procedures per FTE physician	744.18	823.46	744.18
Inside med/surg procedures per FTE clinical support staff	3,777.58	4,221.13	3,777.58
Inside med/surg gross charges per FTE physician	$114,418	$713,756	$707,791
Medical procedures inside practice per FTE physician	280	152	216
Medical procedures outside practice per FTE physician	51	58	51
Surgical procedures inside practice per FTE physician	785	974	953
Surgical procedures outside practice per FTE physician	1,835	1,108	1,321
Laboratory procedures per FTE physician	*	1	1
Radiology procedures per FTE physician	94	23	41
Square feet per FTE physician	200	141	150
Cost			
Total operating cost per FTE physician	$93,230	$69,099	$77,228
Total operating and NPP cost per FTE physician	$435,410	$178,824	$231,905
Total operating cost as a percent of total medical revenue	12.10%	12.34%	12.34%
Total operating and NPP cost as a percent of total medical revenue	49.60%	32.07%	39.22%
Total support staff cost per FTE physician	$26,658	$24,288	$24,288
Total general operating cost per FTE physician	$68,789	$49,417	$52,926
Total NPP cost per FTE physician	$349,437	$65,573	$130,687
Total physician cost per FTE physician	$417,674	$408,423	$409,071
– Total physician compensation	$377,873	$347,927	$355,353
– Total physician benefit cost	$58,429	$61,784	$60,386
Revenue			
Total medical revenue per FTE physician	$862,023	$561,044	$623,569
Total medical revenue after operating cost per FTE physician	$734,553	$489,669	$546,833
Total medical revenue after operating and NPP cost per FTE physician	$405,004	$377,453	$385,171

ȣ——ʍ Key Indicator

From the *Performance and Practices of Successful Medical Groups, 2005 Report Based on 2004 Data.*
Reprinted with permission from the Medical Group Management Association, 104 Inverness Terrace East,
Englewood, Colorado 80112. www.mgma.com. Copyright 2005. Pages 162–182.

Accounts Receivable and Collections

This appendix contains articles and data from MGMA's *Performance and Practices of Successful Medical Groups* reports on accounts receivable and collections:

- Benchmarking Accounts Receivable: A Dashboard (from *Performance and Practices of Successful Medical Groups: 2005 Report Based on 2004 Data*, pages 95–98)

- The Practices of Successful Medical Groups (from *Performance and Practices of Successful Medical Groups: 2003 Report Based on 2002 Data*, pages 138–140)

- Selecting a Billing Service: Interviewing Vendors (from *Performance and Practices of Successful Medical Groups: 2004 Report Based on 2003 Data*, pages 91–94)

- MGMA Benchmarks: Better Performing Practices Comparison Exhibits (from *Performance and Practices of Successful Medical Groups: 2005 Report Based on 2004 Data*, pages 184–194)

Benchmarking Accounts Receivable — a Dashboard

Introduction

Assessing the economic health of a practice includes measuring a number of key Accounts Receivable (A/R) factors. Tracking these components allows a practice to recognize patterns, identify issues and validate presumptions with facts.

This Best Practice A/R Dashboard provides an approach to visually keep track of key indicators in A/R and identifies areas in which to look to improve performance. The Best Practice Benchmarks can be found in the Accounts Receivable and Collections — Demographic Profile and Key Indicators section of this report.

Total medical revenue per full-time equivalent (FTE) physician

	Actual	Best Practice Benchmark	Variance
Jan.			
Feb.			
March			
April			
May			
June			
July			
Aug.			
Sept.			
Oct.			
Nov.			
Dec.			

Total medical revenue after operating cost per FTE physician

	Actual	Best Practice Benchmark	Variance
Jan.			
Feb.			
March			
April			
May			
June			
July			
Aug.			
Sept.			
Oct.			
Nov.			
Dec.			

(Continued on next page)

Total medical revenue after operating and NPP cost per FTE physician			
	Actual	Best Practice Benchmark	Variance
Jan.			
Feb.			
March			
April			
May			
June			
July			
Aug.			
Sept.			
Oct.			
Nov.			
Dec.			

Months gross FFS charges in A/R			
	Actual	Best Practice Benchmark	Variance
Jan.			
Feb.			
March			
April			
May			
June			
July			
Aug.			
Sept.			
Oct.			
Nov.			
Dec.			

Percent of total A/R 120+ days			
	Actual	Best Practice Benchmark	Variance
Jan.			
Feb.			
March			
April			
May			
June			
July			
Aug.			
Sept.			
Oct.			
Nov.			
Dec.			

(Continued on next page)

Bad debts due to FFS activity per FTE physician

	Actual	Best Practice Benchmark	Variance
Jan.			
Feb.			
March			
April			
May			
June			
July			
Aug.			
Sept.			
Oct.			
Nov.			
Dec.			

General accounting support staff per FTE physician

	Actual	Best Practice Benchmark	Variance
Jan.			
Feb.			
March			
April			
May			
June			
July			
Aug.			
Sept.			
Oct.			
Nov.			
Dec.			

General accounting support staff cost per FTE physician

	Actual	Best Practice Benchmark	Variance
Jan.			
Feb.			
March			
April			
May			
June			
July			
Aug.			
Sept.			
Oct.			
Nov.			
Dec.			

(Continued on next page)

From the *Performance and Practices of Successful Medical Groups, 2005 Report Based on 2004 Data.*
Reprinted with permission from the Medical Group Management Association, 104 Inverness Terrace East,
Englewood, Colorado 80112. www.mgma.com. Copyright 2005. Pages 95–98.

Factors impeding A/R performance and ideas to help

Many factors contribute to A/R performance. By measuring and tracking key elements, a practice administrator can see the areas that need improvement as well as areas that have improved. The ideas presented below list areas that impede A/R performance and suggest ways to improve it.

Slow payers and high denial rates

Diligent review and audits of payer performance enhances the objective of obtaining a desirable benchmark-driven A/R. Payers may be viewed as adversaries but are integral to the practice. Establishing a rapport and engaging with them allows the practice the potential of positive responses from payers, which equates to more timely payment and less denials.

Some ideas to consider:
- Review claims that were denied and identify the reasons. Communicate with the payer to address the denials and create processes to correct errors;
- Monitor payer relationships and contracts;
- Meet with payers regularly; and
- Assign claims by payer to billing staff so that one person becomes familiar with the payer terms and methods.

Process efficiency

A medical practice cannot operate without efficient processes. Ineffective and outdated functions affect many aspects of a practice including its A/R performance. It's important to review the processes within the practice and involve key staff members to help identify positive processes as well as gaps or inefficiencies.

Some ideas to consider:
- Review patient encounter information to identify insufficient or inaccurate capture of data;
- Confirm insurance status of each patient at check-in;
- Review patient account balances at time of appointment scheduling;
- Examine the billing strategy, specifically the billing cycle (bills sent out the same time each month or bills dispersed throughout the month) and the procedures for handling late payments;
- Cross train staff on the A/R process;
- Set performance standards and expectations of the billing staff;
- Provide financial counseling and payment plans to patients; and
- Define the elements of a clean claim and build processes around them.

Staff and training

A knowledgeable and dedicated staff will assist the practice in achieving its goals. Providing a comfortable and challenging work environment along with the opportunity for staff to improve their skills will help move the practice forward and achieve its benchmarks. Investing time and money into the staff sends the message that the practice values them and wants them to succeed.

Some ideas to consider:
- Identify current staff resources and develop a thorough job description that sets the level of responsibility and expectations for each employee;
- Provide continuing education and training in areas such as coding;
- Create a policy handbook so that all rules and procedures are documented;
- Cross train staff so that processes run smoothly regardless of vacations or sick time; and
- Recognize and reward staff for achieving goals.

Coding

Over- or under-coding can cause A/R discrepancies and staff frustration. It's important that the practice have coding rules and guidelines that are communicated to physicians and staff to eliminate errors and improve collections.

Some ideas to consider:
- Conduct regular audits that examine physician coding procedures to identify issues and create plans to correct them;
- Bring in a coding consultant or hire a certified coding professional. Either approach will reduce coding errors because the consultant or professional will work with physicians to improve their coding knowledge; and
- Redesign the charge ticket to list the top-20 current procedural terminology (CPT) codes on the front or create a coding template for physicians to capture accurate information during the patient encounter.

Technology

Many advances in technology for the health care industry can provide a more effective process and improve efficiency in the practice.

Some ideas to consider:
- Submit claims electronically;
- View and verify claims via the Internet;
- Convert paper documents to online documents via document imaging;
- Implement electronic health records (EHR); and
- Create a Web site that allows patients to update information, schedule appointments and view account balances.

Content contributors

J. Dennis Mock. Accounts Receivable Management for the Medical Practice, 1995.

Medical Group Management Association Performance and Practices of Successful Medical Groups: 2003 Report Based on 2002 Data, 2004, p. 139-140.

The Practices of Successful Medical Groups

" *Successful medical groups in accounts receivable develop systems to manage contractual relationships, measure key indicators, create accountability, and educate and motivate staff through all aspects of the revenue cycle.* "

Marilyn Happold-Latham, MBA, FACMPE, and Mickey O'Neal, CPA

In an era of declining reimbursement and increasing costs, many administrators view accounts receivable (A/R) management as the most effective means of maintaining or improving financial performance. Medical practices that excel in A/R management despite current negative environmental conditions possess a fundamental component of successful practice management.

Identifying these practices and studying their techniques is valuable for organizations seeking to improve financial performance. MGMA has identified A/R performance criteria from its *Cost Survey Report* data to select better performing medical groups. To be acknowledged as an MGMA better performer in A/R, a practice must meet the following performance indicators:

■ Less than the median for percent of total A/R over 120 days;

■ Greater than the median for adjusted fee-for-service collection percentage; and

■ Less than the median for months gross fee-for-service charges in A/R.

This year, MGMA conducted a five-year qualitative analysis of better performing practices (see Executive Summary). MGMA studied the featured practices and noted and quantified common better performance factors. The results of this study reveal that better performers most frequently:

• Implement sound billing and collection methods;

• Ensure measures are taken to improve physician coding;

• Use electronic billing and claims submission;

• Collect copayments, deductibles and outstanding balances prior to visit;

• Monitor payer performance;

• Maintain close relationships with payers; and

• Verify patient insurance eligibility.

Successful medical groups exhibit a number of behaviors that stem from the organization's value system and surround the entire A/R management activity. These behaviors become culturally instilled and influence decision making and overall performance. The common values noted among better performing groups are:

• Possessing and continually fostering a culture that supports A/R objectives;

• Constantly seeking to improve the methods or patient account processes that maximize collections; and

• Establishing goals, monitoring performance and actively addressing A/R management problems early.

A deeper understanding of these cultural and operational indicators can assist groups in their pursuit of best practices. Following are the results of the qualitative analysis of better performing A/R practice groups.

(Continued on next page)

Management and Culture

☐ Involve each member of the staff in A/R management

☐ Measure A/R performance on a regular basis. Communicate A/R performance results to physicians and staff members to reinforce its importance in overall organizational performance

☐ Tie salary bonuses to A/R performance. Withhold an appropriate percentage of revenue each quarter and reward staff for achieving high collection percentages and keeping days in A/R low

☐ Provide thorough training of the staff and make training or continuing education a regular job requirement. Send the staff to training seminars to stay up to date on changes, especially in coding

☐ Provide physicians and staff members with updates on regulatory changes to ensure compliance and proper documentation of patient encounters

☐ Involve physicians in the billing process to ensure that staff members understand the importance of the process and the value of their roles

☐ Provide regular training to physicians to promote their understanding of the A/R process, minimize denials and reduce delays in the revenue cycle

Process

Staff Involvement

☐ Employ talented individuals in the billing office and reward experience

☐ Set performance standards and expectations for billing staff

☐ Cross-train staff on the A/R process

☐ Define the elements of a clean claim and build training programs for billing staff around those elements

☐ Have the staff establish rapport with patients early to reduce patient stress caused by large payment obligations

☐ Employ a certified coder or encourage appropriate staff members to pursue such credentials to enhance their technical qualifications

Payer Relations and Contracting

☐ Manage payer relationships and contracts. Regularly monitor performance and quickly take action on problems

☐ Meet with payers regularly to build rapport, create understanding of policies and ease the resolution of problems. Review outstanding performance issues (such as zero payments, denials and delayed payments) and coding concerns (such as bundling actions) taken by the payer

☐ Ensure that payer contracts explain: what constitutes a clean claim; timely submission and payment; payment amounts by procedure; the appeals process; and contract termination causes and methods

☐ Assign claims to billing staff by payer to build rapport and facilitate understanding of payer terms and methods

☐ Thoroughly document all interactions with payer organizations and their representatives to aid in the resolution of problems

Patient Scheduling

☐ Review patient account balances at scheduling. Request payment of outstanding balances via credit card

☐ Verify eligibility, copayments and deductibles prior to the provision of services

☐ Verify referral approval or pre-authorization before scheduling appointments

☐ For large payment obligations, assign patients to a financial counselor and arrange a payment plan prior to services being rendered

☐ Verify that referrals have been authorized 72 hours prior to appointments. Reschedule patients for whom proper referrals are not received

The Visit

☐ Confirm the insurance status of patients every time they visit

☐ Use verification resources provided by payers to ensure payment for services

☐ Follow up on any missing or unverified information

☐ Collect the copayment or deductible at the time of service

☐ Develop coding templates for physicians to assist in proper documentation and ensure appropriate information is provided to the billing staff

☐ To the extent possible, keep billing and clinical areas and functions physically separated to allow for a more focused clinical experience for patients and a cohesive environment for billing staff

(Continued on next page)

Billing and Collections

☐ Post charges for all E&M and office visits on the date of service

☐ Audit insurer payments to ensure they match contracted terms

☐ Follow up on outstanding claims early to reduce the need for more aggressive tactics later

☐ Prioritize claims for follow up by amount and age

☐ Establish structured payment in response to patient needs

☐ If available, use the practice's billing system software application to assist in patient and payer contact management, payment auditing and A/R performance monitoring

☐ Appropriately document all follow-up actions on outstanding claims or patient balances. Documentation will help avoid having to start the collection process over if staff turnover or other issues delay payments

Other Ideas

• Use outside consultants to provide objective, expert coding evaluations and relevant training to billing staff and physicians

• Establish quality improvement committees, with staff members and physicians, to address organizational and process issues. Assign key staff members to monitor improvement progress

• Set 24-hour dictation and transcription standards

• For surgery practices, do not wait until the patient is discharged to submit claims. Bill within 5 days of surgeries

• Understand the factors that can influence or distort A/R performance (for example, increasing the fee schedule, adding providers or boosting patient volume may lower collection percentages)

• Conduct lag reports to match the date a claim is paid with the date the service was provided (for capitation environments)

Key A/R Measurements

• Total A/R (also standardized per FTE Physician)

• Days in A/R (Aging Reports)

• Gross Collection Percentage

• Gross FFS Charges per FTE Physician

• Adjustments to FFS Charges (also standardize per FTE Physician)

• Adjusted Collections Percent

• Payer Mix as a Percent of Charges/Collections

• Aged Accounts by Payer

• Business Office Support Staff per FTE Physician

• Business Office Support Staff Cost per FTE Physician

• Time to Generate a Claim (include both ambulatory and hospital encounters)

• Claim Turnaround

• EOB Review (to determine denial rates, audit payers and assess fee schedules)

What to Avoid

☐ Skimping on staff resources. Adequate staff members must be dedicated to A/R management. Appropriate skill sets should be recruited and sufficient, on-going training provided

☐ Viewing payers as adversaries. Payers are organizations with which your practice does business. Establish rapport with payer representatives. Be diligent about contracting and contract management and hold them accountable for poor performance

☐ Collecting insufficient or inaccurate patient and encounter information. Most denials can be tracked to missing or improper information submitted as part of the claim

☐ Allowing physicians to take a "hands-off" approach to A/R management. Physicians should be involved, but their roles clearly defined

Other Standards

☐ _____
_____
_____
_____

☐ _____
_____
_____
_____

☐ _____
_____
_____

Notes

Selecting a Billing Service: Interviewing Vendors

Introduction and summary

Transitioning to an outside billing service or replacing an existing service requires research, analysis and support from leadership.

Interviewing potential vendors should be the first step in the process and in some ways the most daunting. The information presented here explains why you need to be selective and suggests key questions to ask of each vendor that will lead to an informed decision.

Objectives

- Find the "right" billing service
- Improve profitability and efficiency

Challenges

- Determining the appropriate vendor and the best fit for the practice
- Managing the due diligence process
- Interviewing the vendors to get the information necessary to make an informed decision

Philosophy and helpful considerations

- Start with a review of your existing billing service contract (if you are currently outsourcing the service)
- Select the vendors objectively
- Evaluate at least three vendors
- Obtain legal review before signing a new contract

Key metrics

- Billing expense as a percent of total operating cost
- Billing expense as a percent of total medical revenue
- Potential downtime during the transition
- Impact on practice operations

Body of Knowledge reference

- Planning and Marketing
- Financial Management
- Business and Clinical Operations

(Continued on next page)

Key audiences

- Billing and collections staff
- Administrator / Chief executive officer
- Group physicians

Involved staff

- Administrator / CEO
- Managing partner / President
- Staff

Industry applicability

Elements of this best practice can be applied in most practices.

Management difficulty

Medium / High — the process must be managed and involve all leaders of the practice.

Process duration and time factors

Three to six months

- Availability of vendors for interview and on-site visits
- Existing contract expiration

Key obstacles to avoid

- Selecting the wrong billing service for the practice
- Interviewing too few vendors
- Permitting too much subjectivity in evaluating vendors
- Accepting inadequacies of a service in exchange for lowest cost

Key organizational attitudes

- Devote appropriate time to vendor selection to improve decision making
- Make the most of your time with each vendor

The process to select a billing service includes the following:

Before interviewing vendors

1. Review your current contract if considering a change in vendors.

   ☐ Address each of these contract clauses:

   ○ Inadequate notice

   ○ Ownership of data and its format

   ○ Automatic contract extensions

   ○ Written notice requirements

   ○ Termination options

   ○ Continuation beyond termination

   ○ Start and end dates

   ○ Potential penalties

   ○ Health Insurance Portability and Accountability Act (HIPAA) compliance

Interview process

1. Evaluate at least three companies.

   ☐ Obtain recommendations from other practice managers.

   ☐ Decide if the vendor needs to be in-state or limited to a specific regional area.

   ☐ Research each vendor and ask the following questions:

   Background — general questions

   ○ How many years in business?

   ○ In business under any other name? If yes, what name? Why was the name changed?

   ○ What compliance plan is in place?

   ○ What necessary HIPAA regulations are in place?

   ○ Has the company ever been investigated in a fraud or abuse case? If yes, what was the outcome?

○ What is the in-house audit system?

○ Are periodic audits done by an outside firm?

○ Is there a current auditor's report or summary available?

○ How many certified coders are on staff?

○ What type of training is provided?

○ How often is training done?

○ How are hiring and background-checks performed?

○ Does the company carry errors and omissions insurance?

○ Does the company offer bookkeeping services?

○ How many clients does the company have with our specialty?

Billing questions

○ What insurance companies are billed electronically?

○ Are insurance payments posted electronically? If yes, from what companies?

○ Are there any exceptions to billing electronically?

○ How is information transmitted back and forth between the practice and billing service? Is the information sent on paper, disk or electronically?

○ How is the work load distributed? Is one person responsible for an account, or do several people work on it?

○ Are there any billing processes that the company does not supply?

○ Do you handle all billing-related and ancillary documentation to insurance companies and private-pay patients? If no, what is not handled?

(Continued on next page)

○ What is the procedure for deposits — lock boxes or other?

○ How often are claims submitted to insurance companies?

○ How often are statements sent to patients?

○ Who is responsible for CPT*, HCPCS** and ICD-9*** coding?

○ What is the process/policy for handling problems such as incomplete billing information?

○ How are electronic rejections handled?

○ How are charges batched? Are charges confirmed against a service log?

Payment posting/ follow-up questions

○ How are returned claims and statements handled, and who is responsible for them?

○ Are payments posted line by line or by the total amount of the claim?

○ How are zero payments (deductibles) posted?

○ What is the average denial rate?

○ How are denied claims posted and tracked?

○ What services are provided to resolve denials?

○ How are rejections tracked and resolved?

○ How often are reports run for credit balances?

○ How are credit balances handled?

○ Who reviews reports and makes the decisions regarding bad debt, write-offs, etc? What are the standards followed?

○ Is there a threshold below which a balance is not billed?

○ Are small balances kept on the books or are they written off?

Data entry questions

○ What is the data entry process?

○ Is there a required format for encounter forms?

○ What types of forms and data is the practice required to submit? Can a sample be provided of the types of forms the practice needs to complete?

○ How are data entries verified and audited?

○ From the time data is received, how much time is needed to process the claim?

○ Who has ownership of the data if the contract is terminated?

Reports questions

○ What types of standard reports are provided?

○ Can customized reports be provided?

○ Can an aged report be completed by "billing date" and "date of service"?

○ Can the practice access the computer terminal to perform queries, update records, schedule appointments, generate demand reports, demand statements and create superbills?

○ Can one report (same page, tabular style) be generated showing a patient's name, insurance provider, charge payment, adjustment and balance?

○ Can a report show the names, amounts and reasons for bad-debt write-offs and full adjustments?

Costs questions

○ How are fees determined?

○ If payment is by percentage, is it determined by the amount billed or by the amount collected?

○ Is there an additional charge for paper claims?

○ Is there an extra cost for adding a new physician to the system?

○ How is physician credentialing handled?

○ What is the conversion process and the costs involved?

○ Approximately how long will the conversion process take?

○ Is a conversion schedule provided?

○ How are old accounts receivable from the previous billing company handled?

○ Does the practice generally require additional staff to handle the conversion?

Computers/software questions

○ What is the security system and who has access?

○ Are regularly scheduled virus checks performed?

○ What are the back-up procedures and where are the back-ups stored (on-site or off-site)?

○ How are yearly computer system updates handled for CPT, HCPCS and ICD-9 codes?

○ Can the software track a patient's demographics?

○ How would the system handle the following situation? A patient changes insurance companies, and there are outstanding balances on Plan A and new charges on Plan B.

(Continued on next page)

From the *Performance and Practices of Successful Medical Groups, 2004 Report Based on 2003 Data.*
Reprinted with permission from the Medical Group Management Association, 104 Inverness Terrace East,
Englewood, Colorado 80112. www.mgma.com. Copyright 2004. Pages 91–94.

- ○ Can the system handle two primary insurances and differentiate which needs to be billed by date of service?

- ○ Is the practice required to pay for a software license?

- ○ Is an Application Service Provider (ASP) model required?

- ○ Does the practice have to pay for any software or hardware updates or maintenance?

- ○ Is the practice required to pay for any hardware? If so, does the practice retain the license and hardware, if the agreement ends?

- ○ What billing software is used and is it the latest version?

Collections questions

- ○ Is there a separate department that handles collections?

- ○ Can reports be generated showing the patient's name, the provider of the services, insurance company, charges and reason for insurance rejection?

- ○ What is the collection procedure for private-pay patients?

- ○ Who calls patients with a past-due balance?

- ○ If the practice does not provide the service with information in a timely manner, is the account written off as a bad debt or as an insurance adjustment?

- ○ How are services provided but not billable due to timeliness documented?

- ○ Is there a charge to document services not billable to the insurance company or patient?

- ○ Can a sample of collection letters be provided?

- ☐ What process is followed to turn an account over to collections?

- ☐ If an account is turned over to a collection agency, are the "regular rate" fees subtracted from the amount due to you when payment is collected?

- ☐ Narrow the search to the two top vendors that best meet your needs.

2. Conduct an on-site visit for the two vendors to gather specific information.

- ☐ Use the questions in step two to validate answers.

- ☐ Ask to meet and talk with staff who will be assigned to your account.

- ☐ Determine if the vendor culture fits your needs.

3. Check references

- ☐ Contact medical practices that currently use the service and ask the following questions:

  - ○ Has the billing service carried out its commitment?

  - ○ Was the conversion process handled smoothly?

  - ○ Have you encountered any hidden costs or surprises?

  - ○ Does the customer service department meet your needs most of the time?

  - ○ How helpful is the company in meeting your individual needs?

  - ○ What, if any, problems have you experienced?

  - ○ Does the company stay up-to-date on industry changes?

  - ○ Would you recommend the service?

Select a vendor

1. Review the contract.

- ☐ Compare potential contract with the existing contract.

- ☐ Highlight items in the existing contract that you were not pleased with and determine if the potential contract addresses these issues.

- ☐ Ask for changes if necessary.

2. Conduct a legal review of the contract.

- ☐ Ask your lawyer to review the contract.

- ☐ Ask for updates where appropriate.

Content contributor

Christina Moschella, FACMPE, *MGMA Connexion*, "Be choosy: Selecting a billing service," Vol. 3, Issue 4, April 2003.

*   Current procedural terminology

**   Common Procedure Coding System

***   International Classification of Diseases — 9th revision

Notes:

Figure V.C.1 — Accounts receivable and collections demographic profile

	Anesthesiology			Cardiology			Family practice			Gastroenterology			Internal medicine		
	Better Performers	Others	All	Better Performers	Others	All	Better Performers	Others	All	Better Performers	Others	All	Better Performers	Others	All
Practice description															
Number of practices	17	98	115	13	76	89	7	42	49	3	18	21	2	16	18
Total provider FTE	37.38	24.85	25.00	18.00	15.80	17.00	6.40	6.78	6.78	11.75	11.40	11.50	6.00	9.00	8.85
Total physician FTE	21.75	16.90	18.00	12.50	11.34	11.50	6.00	5.00	5.00	8.50	8.80	8.60	5.00	7.50	6.50
Total NPP FTE	10.10	9.72	10.00	5.00	3.00	3.10	1.24	1.81	1.80	2.00	2.10	2.10	2.00	1.00	1.15
Total support staff FTE	4.50	4.15	4.20	76.40	65.80	66.40	26.65	26.50	26.65	20.30	37.40	35.00	25.45	32.00	30.50
Number of branch clinics	1	1	1	3	4	4	1	3	4	2	2	2	*	3	3
Square footage of all facilities	3,247	2,500	2,500	20,793	22,054	21,638	10,000	9,965	10,000	8,100	11,749	10,563	7,040	14,500	13,604
Net capitation revenue as a percent of total revenue	*	11.66%	11.66%	*	5.55%	5.55%	2.17%	5.97%	5.09%	*	*	*	0.41%	4.82%	0.41%
Breakout of charges by payer															
Medicare: fee-for-service	28.95%	27.00%	27.00%	49.00%	47.00%	48.00%	12.00%	14.50%	14.00%	16.40%	31.38%	30.69%	51.50%	51.51%	51.51%
Medicare: managed care FFS	0.00%	0.00%	0.00%	0.00%	0.00%	0.00%	1.00%	0.00%	0.00%	15.00%	0.00%	0.00%	0.50%	0.00%	0.00%
Medicare: capitated	0.00%	0.00%	0.00%	0.00%	0.00%	0.00%	0.00%	0.00%	0.00%	0.00%	0.00%	0.00%	0.00%	0.00%	0.00%
Medicaid: fee-for-service	5.10%	6.82%	6.00%	1.87%	2.98%	2.61%	4.00%	4.00%	4.00%	1.50%	2.90%	2.55%	0.50%	1.45%	1.00%
Medicaid: managed care FFS	0.00%	0.00%	0.00%	0.00%	0.00%	0.00%	0.00%	0.00%	0.00%	0.00%	0.00%	0.00%	0.00%	0.00%	0.00%
Medicaid: capitated	0.00%	0.00%	0.00%	0.00%	0.00%	0.00%	0.00%	0.00%	0.00%	0.00%	0.00%	0.00%	0.00%	0.00%	0.00%
Commercial: fee-for-service	4.44%	13.00%	11.60%	33.98%	22.95%	25.00%	47.30%	25.30%	37.69%	8.00%	51.90%	41.35%	11.50%	8.13%	8.13%
Commercial: managed care FFS	44.16%	37.04%	38.00%	10.35%	15.32%	11.63%	11.00%	18.25%	14.30%	50.47%	7.00%	10.00%	34.00%	12.90%	12.90%
Commercial: capitated	0.00%	0.00%	0.00%	0.00%	0.00%	0.00%	0.00%	0.00%	0.00%	0.00%	0.00%	0.00%	0.50%	0.00%	0.00%
Workers' compensation	3.05%	2.37%	2.40%	0.00%	0.00%	0.00%	1.00%	0.30%	0.47%	0.00%	0.00%	0.00%	0.50%	0.00%	0.00%
Charity care and prof courtesy	0.00%	0.00%	0.00%	0.00%	0.00%	0.00%	0.30%	0.10%	0.10%	1.00%	0.01%	0.11%	0.00%	0.00%	0.00%
Self-pay	2.60%	3.50%	3.16%	4.00%	2.90%	2.92%	8.00%	4.02%	4.30%	2.00%	2.00%	2.00%	0.50%	2.12%	1.70%
Other government payers	0.46%	0.15%	0.20%	0.00%	0.00%	0.00%	0.00%	0.00%	0.00%	0.00%	0.00%	0.00%	0.50%	0.00%	0.00%
Geographic section															
Eastern section	3.48%	17.39%	20.87%	4.49%	13.48%	17.98%	2.04%	12.24%	14.29%	*	19.05%	19.05%	*	16.67%	16.67%
Midwest section	4.35%	21.74%	26.09%	3.37%	22.47%	25.84%	2.04%	32.65%	34.69%	9.52%	9.52%	19.05%	5.56%	16.67%	22.22%
Southern section	4.35%	27.83%	32.17%	3.37%	33.71%	37.08%	2.04%	16.33%	18.37%	4.76%	38.10%	42.86%	5.56%	44.44%	50.00%
Western section	2.61%	18.26%	20.87%	3.37%	15.73%	19.10%	8.16%	24.49%	32.65%	*	19.05%	19.05%	*	11.11%	11.11%
Population designation															
Nonmetropolitan (50,000 or less)	*	4.50%	4.50%	2.27%	2.27%	4.55%	8.70%	34.78%	43.48%	*	*	*	*	5.56%	5.56%
Metropolitan (50,000 to 250,000)	6.31%	30.63%	36.94%	3.41%	27.27%	30.68%	4.35%	28.26%	32.61%	5.00%	25.00%	30.00%	*	50.00%	50.00%
Metropolitan (250,001 to 1,000,000)	5.41%	32.43%	37.84%	3.41%	32.95%	36.36%	*	13.04%	13.04%	5.00%	30.00%	35.00%	11.11%	11.11%	22.22%
Metropolitan (1,000,001 or more)	2.70%	18.02%	20.72%	5.68%	22.73%	28.41%	2.17%	8.70%	10.87%	5.00%	30.00%	35.00%	*	22.22%	22.22%

(Continued on next page)

Figure V.C.1

Accounts receivable and collections demographic profile

	OB/GYN			Orthopedic surgery			Pediatrics			Urology			Multispecialty, primary and specialty care, not hospital-owned		
	Better Performers	Others	All	Better Performers	Others	All	Better Performers	Others	All	Better Performers	Others	All	Better Performers	Others	All
Practice description															
Number of practices	7	48	55	18	96	114	4	67	71	9	60	69	31	143	174
Total provider FTE	10.25	7.75	8.00	18.75	14.13	14.25	8.20	8.64	8.64	7.72	7.00	7.00	49.50	51.50	51.00
Total physician FTE	7.25	5.00	5.00	7.80	8.73	8.53	6.65	6.00	6.00	5.10	5.37	5.33	38.30	38.00	38.15
Total NPP FTE	2.75	2.75	2.75	5.00	4.63	4.75	2.80	2.00	2.00	2.17	1.00	1.30	8.00	8.82	8.60
Total support staff FTE	33.60	28.30	29.00	42.20	50.00	48.40	28.50	23.75	25.15	31.25	24.14	24.50	163.50	194.33	192.35
Number of branch clinics	2	2	2	2	3	2	1	2	2	2	3	3	8	6	6
Square footage of all facilities	13,000	10,800	11,202	16,850	18,813	18,656	8,128	11,000	10,700	9,503	10,700	10,389	62,480	79,788	76,326
Net capitation revenue as a percent of total revenue	*	19.40%	19.40%	*	9.29%	9.29%	*	10.37%	10.37%	*	3.71%	3.71%	7.16%	11.18%	9.80%
Breakout of charges by payer															
Medicare: fee-for-service	3.00%	3.50%	3.24%	24.00%	22.15%	22.32%	0.00%	0.00%	0.00%	36.19%	42.00%	42.00%	26.00%	26.00%	26.00%
Medicare: managed care FFS	0.00%	0.00%	0.00%	0.00%	0.00%	0.00%	0.00%	0.00%	0.00%	0.00%	0.00%	0.00%	0.00%	0.00%	0.00%
Medicare: capitated	0.00%	0.00%	0.00%	0.00%	0.00%	0.00%	0.00%	0.00%	0.00%	0.00%	0.00%	0.00%	0.00%	0.00%	0.00%
Medicaid: fee-for-service	2.00%	6.10%	6.05%	2.80%	2.00%	2.00%	1.05%	3.00%	2.75%	1.00%	2.80%	2.10%	1.90%	4.00%	3.09%
Medicaid: managed care FFS	0.00%	0.00%	0.00%	0.00%	0.00%	0.00%	0.00%	0.00%	0.00%	0.00%	0.00%	0.00%	0.00%	0.00%	0.00%
Medicaid: capitated	0.00%	0.00%	0.00%	0.00%	0.00%	0.00%	0.00%	0.00%	0.00%	0.00%	0.00%	0.00%	0.00%	0.00%	0.00%
Commercial: fee-for-service	64.00%	29.21%	39.55%	28.00%	23.36%	23.72%	44.25%	34.50%	34.50%	38.42%	20.00%	20.00%	43.46%	40.41%	40.46%
Commercial: managed care FFS	0.00%	33.00%	30.00%	24.00%	21.66%	22.00%	42.50%	22.20%	22.20%	10.00%	15.00%	15.00%	0.00%	0.00%	0.00%
Commercial: capitated	0.00%	0.00%	0.00%	0.00%	0.00%	0.00%	0.00%	0.00%	0.00%	0.00%	0.00%	0.00%	0.00%	0.00%	0.00%
Workers' compensation	0.00%	0.00%	0.00%	9.20%	10.00%	10.00%	0.00%	0.00%	0.00%	0.17%	0.08%	0.10%	0.50%	1.00%	1.00%
Charity care and prof courtesy	0.00%	0.29%	0.25%	0.04%	0.20%	0.19%	0.00%	0.00%	0.00%	0.00%	0.57%	0.26%	0.00%	0.00%	0.00%
Self-pay	2.01%	4.42%	3.95%	3.00%	2.70%	2.70%	3.00%	4.00%	4.00%	2.56%	2.00%	2.00%	2.90%	3.40%	3.15%
Other government payers	0.00%	0.00%	0.00%	0.00%	0.00%	0.00%	0.00%	0.00%	0.00%	0.00%	0.00%	0.00%	0.00%	0.00%	0.00%
Geographic section															
Eastern section	5.45%	16.36%	21.82%	3.51%	15.79%	19.30%	2.82%	29.58%	32.39%	5.80%	20.29%	26.09%	4.60%	14.37%	18.97%
Midwest section	*	16.36%	16.36%	2.63%	24.56%	27.19%	*	11.27%	11.27%	2.90%	15.94%	18.84%	5.75%	24.14%	29.89%
Southern section	3.64%	27.27%	30.91%	6.14%	17.54%	23.68%	1.41%	25.35%	26.76%	2.90%	30.43%	33.33%	3.45%	23.56%	27.01%
Western section	3.64%	27.27%	30.91%	3.51%	26.32%	29.82%	1.41%	28.17%	29.58%	1.45%	20.29%	21.74%	4.02%	20.11%	24.14%
Population designation															
Nonmetropolitan (50,000 or less)	*	18.18%	18.18%	1.85%	14.81%	16.67%	*	13.04%	13.04%	1.49%	2.99%	4.48%	4.60%	26.44%	31.03%
Metropolitan (50,000 to 250,000)	5.45%	27.27%	32.73%	7.41%	25.93%	33.33%	*	34.78%	34.78%	4.48%	38.81%	43.28%	4.60%	35.63%	40.23%
Metropolitan (250,001 to 1,000,000)	7.27%	25.45%	32.73%	5.56%	25.93%	31.48%	1.45%	23.19%	24.64%	4.48%	26.87%	31.34%	5.75%	14.94%	20.69%
Metropolitan (1,000,001 or more)	*	16.36%	16.36%	1.85%	16.67%	18.52%	2.90%	24.64%	27.54%	2.99%	17.91%	20.90%	2.87%	5.17%	8.05%

(Continued on next page)

From the *Performance and Practices of Successful Medical Groups, 2005 Report Based on 2004 Data.*
Reprinted with permission from the Medical Group Management Association, 104 Inverness Terrace East,
Englewood, Colorado 80112. www.mgma.com. Copyright 2005. Pages 184–194.

Figure V.C.1

Accounts receivable and collections demographic profile

	Multispecialty, primary care only, not hospital-owned			Primary care single specialties			Medicine single specialty excluding general internal medicine			Surgical single specialty			Multispecialty, all owners		
	Better Performers	Others	All	Better Performers	Others	All	Better Performers	Others	All	Better Performers	Others	All	Better Performers	Others	All
Practice description															
Number of practices	9	39	48	22	208	230	30	193	223	43	231	274	61	264	325
Total provider FTE	12.00	13.00	12.50	7.88	7.23	7.27	12.95	13.20	13.05	10.20	12.00	11.70	39.62	39.84	39.62
Total physician FTE	8.00	8.63	8.45	6.00	5.00	5.09	7.30	9.15	9.00	6.00	6.50	6.23	27.00	27.19	27.00
Total NPP FTE	3.63	2.84	3.00	1.60	1.48	1.50	2.80	2.35	2.50	3.00	3.40	3.00	7.00	6.65	6.80
Total support staff FTE	35.62	52.47	41.36	25.90	22.28	22.56	37.08	35.00	35.15	30.50	31.00	30.75	136.94	135.46	135.72
Number of branch clinics	2	4	4	1	2	2	3	3	3	3	3	3	8	7	7
Square footage of all facilities	15,700	20,647	17,525	9,000	10,000	10,000	13,124	13,328	13,264	10,900	12,668	12,584	43,716	60,000	54,496
Net capitation revenue as a percent of total revenue	6.58%	8.63%	7.16%	0.41%	9.39%	9.37%	4.22%	6.31%	6.17%	0.03%	7.37%	6.55%	6.37%	9.95%	7.71%
Breakout of charges by payer															
Medicare: fee-for-service	34.00%	23.00%	23.00%	8.12%	10.42%	10.42%	41.87%	38.10%	38.54%	33.81%	28.00%	29.00%	24.28%	25.85%	25.61%
Medicare: managed care FFS	0.00%	0.00%	0.00%	0.00%	0.00%	0.00%	0.14%	0.00%	0.00%	0.00%	0.00%	0.00%	0.00%	0.00%	0.00%
Medicare: capitated	0.00%	0.00%	0.00%	0.00%	0.00%	0.00%	0.00%	0.00%	0.00%	0.00%	0.00%	0.00%	0.00%	0.00%	0.00%
Medicaid: fee-for-service	1.00%	4.80%	4.00%	1.05%	3.70%	3.00%	1.69%	3.00%	3.00%	2.00%	3.00%	2.87%	1.82%	5.74%	4.71%
Medicaid: managed care FFS	0.00%	0.00%	0.00%	0.00%	0.00%	0.00%	0.00%	0.00%	0.00%	0.00%	0.00%	0.00%	0.00%	0.00%	0.00%
Medicaid: capitated	0.00%	0.00%	0.00%	0.00%	0.00%	0.00%	0.00%	0.00%	0.00%	0.00%	0.00%	0.00%	0.00%	0.00%	0.00%
Commercial: fee-for-service	35.50%	34.80%	34.80%	38.50%	31.40%	32.00%	24.86%	30.00%	30.00%	32.00%	24.90%	26.83%	42.07%	39.00%	39.13%
Commercial: managed care FFS	6.00%	2.28%	2.28%	0.53%	20.00%	18.40%	22.00%	6.60%	7.00%	16.00%	16.70%	16.21%	16.00%	0.00%	0.00%
Commercial: capitated	0.00%	0.00%	0.00%	0.00%	0.00%	0.00%	0.00%	0.00%	0.00%	0.00%	0.00%	0.00%	0.00%	0.00%	0.00%
Workers' compensation	0.14%	1.00%	1.00%	0.00%	0.00%	0.00%	0.00%	0.01%	0.01%	0.43%	2.00%	1.00%	0.34%	1.00%	0.82%
Charity care and prof courtesy	0.53%	0.49%	0.49%	0.00%	0.00%	0.00%	0.11%	0.00%	0.00%	0.20%	0.20%	0.20%	0.00%	0.00%	0.00%
Self-pay	5.00%	5.00%	5.00%	2.80%	3.00%	3.00%	2.80%	3.00%	3.00%	2.50%	3.00%	3.00%	3.00%	3.87%	3.75%
Other government payers	0.00%	0.00%	0.00%	0.00%	0.00%	0.00%	0.00%	0.00%	0.00%	0.00%	0.00%	0.00%	0.00%	0.00%	0.00%
Geographic section															
Eastern section	8.33%	20.83%	29.17%	2.17%	28.26%	30.43%	3.14%	19.28%	22.42%	5.47%	16.42%	21.90%	4.31%	18.77%	23.08%
Midwest section	4.17%	18.75%	22.92%	1.74%	15.65%	17.39%	3.14%	16.14%	19.28%	2.92%	22.99%	25.91%	6.15%	26.46%	32.62%
Southern section	2.08%	16.67%	18.75%	3.04%	26.52%	29.57%	4.04%	30.04%	34.08%	4.74%	25.18%	29.93%	3.38%	18.77%	22.15%
Western section	4.17%	25.00%	29.17%	2.61%	20.00%	22.61%	3.14%	21.08%	24.22%	2.55%	19.71%	22.26%	4.92%	17.23%	22.15%
Population designation															
Nonmetropolitan (50,000 or less)	6.67%	37.78%	44.44%	1.34%	21.43%	22.77%	1.38%	2.75%	4.13%	1.13%	9.77%	10.90%	4.04%	31.06%	35.09%
Metropolitan (50,000 to 250,000)	4.44%	24.44%	28.89%	3.13%	29.91%	33.04%	4.13%	26.15%	30.28%	4.14%	30.08%	34.21%	5.90%	28.57%	34.47%
Metropolitan (250,001 to 1,000,000)	4.44%	15.56%	20.00%	3.13%	27.23%	30.36%	3.67%	33.94%	37.61%	6.02%	27.07%	33.08%	6.21%	15.84%	22.05%
Metropolitan (1,000,001 or more)	4.44%	2.22%	6.67%	1.79%	12.05%	13.84%	4.59%	23.39%	27.98%	4.89%	16.92%	21.80%	2.80%	5.59%	8.39%

(Continued on next page)

Figure V.C.2	Accounts receivable and collections indicators			

Anesthesiology

	Better Performers	Others	All
Accounts receivable management			
Percent of total A/R 120+ days	8.27%	15.79%	14.12%
Percent of total A/R 0-30 days	65.30%	49.61%	52.34%
Percent of total A/R 31-60 days	15.00%	17.18%	16.90%
Percent of total A/R 61-90 days	6.31%	8.37%	7.75%
Percent of total A/R 91-120 days	3.90%	5.53%	5.13%
− Re-aged: 0-30 days in A/R	67.98%	50.80%	58.11%
− Re-aged: 31-60 days in A/R	15.09%	18.75%	18.52%
− Re-aged: 61-90 days in A/R	5.23%	7.75%	6.97%
− Re-aged: 91-120 days in A/R	3.75%	6.02%	5.07%
− Re-aged: 120+ days in A/R	7.97%	15.55%	11.02%
− Not re-aged: 0-30 days in A/R	65.30%	49.37%	52.08%
− Not re-aged: 31-60 days in A/R	14.47%	17.04%	16.90%
− Not re-aged: 61-90 days in A/R	7.03%	8.71%	8.55%
− Not re-aged: 91-120 days in A/R	3.90%	5.41%	5.10%
− Not re-aged: 120+ days in A/R	9.89%	16.14%	14.12%
Total A/R per FTE physician	$128,986	$161,006	$160,798
Charges			
Months gross FFS charges in A/R	1.23	1.79	1.71
Days gross FFS charges in A/R	37.47	54.32	51.91
Gross FFS charges per FTE physician	$1,294,851	$1,188,554	$1,206,767
Gross FFS collection percentage	47.14%	45.88%	46.07%
Adjustments to FFS charges per FTE physician	$618,950	$570,039	$583,535
Adjusted FFS charges per FTE physician	$628,448	$576,224	$583,094
Collections			
Adjusted FFS collection percentage	97.96%	94.57%	95.37%
Bad debts due to FFS activity per FTE physician	$16,211	$33,802	$30,011
Staffing			
Patient accounting support staff per FTE physician	0.37	0.32	0.33
General accounting support staff per FTE physician	0.05	0.03	0.03
Patient accounting support staff cost per FTE physician	$12,543	$12,750	$12,583
General accounting support staff cost per FTE physician	$3,411	$1,500	$1,538
Revenue			
Total medical revenue per FTE physician	$622,582	$528,718	$535,435
Total medical revenue after operating cost per FTE physician	$543,052	$453,604	$462,667
Total medical revenue after operating and NPP cost per FTE physician	$425,895	$386,690	$393,669

8—ᴋ Key Indicator

Figure V.C.3	Accounts receivable and collections indicators			

Cardiology

	Better Performers	Others	All
Accounts receivable management			
∞ Percent of total A/R 120+ days	10.00%	18.53%	17.16%
Percent of total A/R 0-30 days	66.63%	56.66%	57.73%
Percent of total A/R 31-60 days	13.26%	12.80%	12.91%
Percent of total A/R 61-90 days	6.57%	6.66%	6.61%
Percent of total A/R 91-120 days	3.68%	4.46%	4.20%
− Re-aged: 0-30 days in A/R	66.63%	52.67%	56.66%
− Re-aged: 31-60 days in A/R	16.38%	11.61%	11.76%
− Re-aged: 61-90 days in A/R	6.04%	6.35%	6.33%
− Re-aged: 91-120 days in A/R	2.93%	4.35%	3.82%
− Re-aged: 120+ days in A/R	7.44%	21.93%	20.54%
− Not re-aged: 0-30 days in A/R	68.29%	57.23%	57.50%
− Not re-aged: 31-60 days in A/R	9.64%	13.03%	13.01%
− Not re-aged: 61-90 days in A/R	7.00%	6.88%	6.89%
− Not re-aged: 91-120 days in A/R	3.41%	4.48%	4.22%
− Not re-aged: 120+ days in A/R	12.00%	18.04%	17.18%
Total A/R per FTE physician	$198,593	$268,731	$263,602
Charges			
∞ Months gross FFS charges in A/R	1.04	1.37	1.32
Days gross FFS charges in A/R	31.64	41.75	40.17
Gross FFS charges per FTE physician	$2,417,103	$2,397,786	$2,409,478
Gross FFS collection percentage	46.76%	41.78%	42.92%
Adjustments to FFS charges per FTE physician	$1,300,838	$1,283,007	$1,295,665
Adjusted FFS charges per FTE physician	$1,071,574	$1,056,597	$1,056,993
Collections			
∞ Adjusted FFS collection percentage	100.00%	97.22%	97.81%
Bad debts due to FFS activity per FTE physician	$11,482	$39,849	$29,731
Staffing			
Patient accounting support staff per FTE physician	0.68	0.84	0.79
General accounting support staff per FTE physician	0.08	0.10	0.10
Patient accounting support staff cost per FTE physician	$22,056	$25,834	$25,727
General accounting support staff cost per FTE physician	$3,266	$4,999	$4,273
Revenue			
∞ Total medical revenue per FTE physician	$1,102,057	$1,027,678	$1,028,721
Total medical revenue after operating cost per FTE physician	$592,518	$514,322	$521,454
Total medical revenue after operating and NPP cost per FTE physician	$583,305	$489,810	$497,699

∞—⚓ Key Indicator

Figure V.C.4	Accounts receivable and collections indicators			

Orthopedic surgery

	Better Performers	Others	All
Accounts receivable management			
☐ Percent of total A/R 120+ days	14.11%	21.32%	19.55%
Percent of total A/R 0-30 days	58.88%	45.06%	47.43%
Percent of total A/R 31-60 days	14.86%	17.35%	16.74%
Percent of total A/R 61-90 days	7.25%	8.48%	8.40%
Percent of total A/R 91-120 days	4.25%	5.36%	5.23%
− Re-aged: 0-30 days in A/R	65.46%	47.47%	49.50%
− Re-aged: 31-60 days in A/R	14.84%	17.81%	17.23%
− Re-aged: 61-90 days in A/R	5.81%	8.41%	7.74%
− Re-aged: 91-120 days in A/R	3.06%	4.87%	4.50%
− Re-aged: 120+ days in A/R	10.43%	18.30%	18.09%
− Not re-aged: 0-30 days in A/R	55.10%	44.24%	47.02%
− Not re-aged: 31-60 days in A/R	15.40%	17.01%	16.24%
− Not re-aged: 61-90 days in A/R	8.14%	8.77%	8.67%
− Not re-aged: 91-120 days in A/R	4.83%	5.61%	5.31%
− Not re-aged: 120+ days in A/R	14.65%	22.12%	20.10%
Total A/R per FTE physician	$307,725	$358,271	$330,635
Charges			
☐ Months gross FFS charges in A/R	1.50	1.92	1.78
Days gross FFS charges in A/R	45.55	58.52	54.21
Gross FFS charges per FTE physician	$2,321,577	$2,166,454	$2,188,061
Gross FFS collection percentage	48.99%	45.63%	45.68%
Adjustments to FFS charges per FTE physician	$1,296,153	$1,065,057	$1,100,471
Adjusted FFS charges per FTE physician	$1,110,466	$1,052,006	$1,055,350
Collections			
☐ Adjusted FFS collection percentage	98.65%	96.17%	97.28%
Bad debts due to FFS activity per FTE physician	$18,754	$37,582	$28,966
Staffing			
Patient accounting support staff per FTE physician	0.95	0.89	0.89
General accounting support staff per FTE physician	0.13	0.11	0.11
Patient accounting support staff cost per FTE physician	$26,013	$26,352	$26,352
General accounting support staff cost per FTE physician	$3,965	$4,683	$4,528
Revenue			
☐ Total medical revenue per FTE physician	$1,117,275	$1,019,930	$1,032,830
Total medical revenue after operating cost per FTE physician	$631,081	$532,613	$560,833
Total medical revenue after operating and NPP cost per FTE physician	$660,671	$490,005	$508,329

8——* Key Indicator

Figure V.C.5	Accounts receivable and collections indicators

Multispecialty, primary and specialty care, not hospital-owned

	Better Performers	Others	All
Accounts receivable management			
↻ Percent of total A/R 120+ days	11.27%	20.78%	18.27%
Percent of total A/R 0-30 days	61.36%	49.92%	52.40%
Percent of total A/R 31-60 days	14.58%	14.37%	14.40%
Percent of total A/R 61-90 days	7.00%	7.22%	7.18%
Percent of total A/R 91-120 days	4.12%	4.87%	4.82%
– Re-aged: 0-30 days in A/R	66.38%	52.40%	55.94%
– Re-aged: 31-60 days in A/R	14.71%	12.72%	12.94%
– Re-aged: 61-90 days in A/R	5.61%	6.27%	6.24%
– Re-aged: 91-120 days in A/R	3.76%	4.35%	4.29%
– Re-aged: 120+ days in A/R	9.96%	20.48%	18.70%
– Not re-aged: 0-30 days in A/R	59.91%	48.93%	50.54%
– Not re-aged: 31-60 days in A/R	14.35%	14.81%	14.68%
– Not re-aged: 61-90 days in A/R	7.15%	7.66%	7.65%
– Not re-aged: 91-120 days in A/R	4.50%	5.22%	5.20%
– Not re-aged: 120+ days in A/R	13.42%	21.20%	18.13%
Total A/R per FTE physician	$86,975	$154,041	$140,290
Charges			
↻ Months gross FFS charges in A/R	1.21	1.64	1.54
Days gross FFS charges in A/R	36.68	49.92	46.94
Gross FFS charges per FTE physician	$935,588	$1,112,927	$1,067,787
Gross FFS collection percentage	64.22%	59.05%	59.69%
Adjustments to FFS charges per FTE physician	$334,772	$409,312	$381,165
Adjusted FFS charges per FTE physician	$607,222	$680,767	$660,166
Collections			
↻ Adjusted FFS collection percentage	99.29%	97.38%	97.81%
Bad debts due to FFS activity per FTE physician	$6,544	$21,485	$16,547
Staffing			
Patient accounting support staff per FTE physician	0.53	0.72	0.66
General accounting support staff per FTE physician	0.07	0.08	0.08
Patient accounting support staff cost per FTE physician	$16,152	$20,407	$19,620
General accounting support staff cost per FTE physician	$2,709	$3,069	$3,012
Revenue			
↻ Total medical revenue per FTE physician	$637,617	$729,600	$713,722
Total medical revenue after operating cost per FTE physician	$267,806	$289,446	$286,218
Total medical revenue after operating and NPP cost per FTE physician	$244,159	$275,303	$266,579

ᴏ—ᴋ Key Indicator

Figure V.C.6	Accounts receivable and collections indicators

Primary care single specialties

	Better Performers	Others	All
Accounts receivable management			
♔ Percent of total A/R 120+ days	8.48%	16.17%	14.42%
┗ Percent of total A/R 0-30 days	72.37%	55.29%	56.61%
Percent of total A/R 31-60 days	13.18%	14.68%	14.58%
Percent of total A/R 61-90 days	5.42%	7.29%	7.15%
Percent of total A/R 91-120 days	2.68%	4.54%	4.22%
– Re-aged: 0-30 days in A/R	65.45%	57.65%	58.82%
– Re-aged: 31-60 days in A/R	18.23%	13.24%	13.45%
– Re-aged: 61-90 days in A/R	9.37%	5.85%	5.87%
– Re-aged: 91-120 days in A/R	3.07%	3.62%	3.61%
– Re-aged: 120+ days in A/R	2.35%	13.57%	13.15%
– Not re-aged: 0-30 days in A/R	73.97%	54.47%	55.62%
– Not re-aged: 31-60 days in A/R	12.47%	15.26%	14.74%
– Not re-aged: 61-90 days in A/R	5.28%	7.98%	7.52%
– Not re-aged: 91-120 days in A/R	2.61%	4.97%	4.83%
– Not re-aged: 120+ days in A/R	9.01%	16.67%	14.84%
Total A/R per FTE physician	$54,644	$76,611	$73,796
Charges			
♔ Months gross FFS charges in A/R	1.01	1.32	1.26
┗ Days gross FFS charges in A/R	30.63	40.03	38.30
Gross FFS charges per FTE physician	$688,363	$683,327	$683,327
Gross FFS collection percentage	70.57%	68.83%	69.14%
Adjustments to FFS charges per FTE physician	$195,392	$185,279	$187,067
Adjusted FFS charges per FTE physician	$496,873	$484,212	$484,622
Collections			
♔ Adjusted FFS collection percentage	100.00%	98.96%	99.12%
┗ Bad debts due to FFS activity per FTE physician	$1,542	$6,050	$5,709
Staffing			
Patient accounting support staff per FTE physician	0.85	0.62	0.64
General accounting support staff per FTE physician	0.13	0.12	0.12
Patient accounting support staff cost per FTE physician	$21,585	$17,618	$17,883
General accounting support staff cost per FTE physician	$4,812	$4,407	$4,544
Revenue			
♔ Total medical revenue per FTE physician	$506,887	$491,353	$498,780
┗ Total medical revenue after operating cost per FTE physician	$170,648	$199,775	$196,657
Total medical revenue after operating and NPP cost per FTE physician	$163,129	$188,478	$187,630

ð——ⵜ Key Indicator

From the *Performance and Practices of Successful Medical Groups, 2005 Report Based on 2004 Data.*
Reprinted with permission from the Medical Group Management Association, 104 Inverness Terrace East,
Englewood, Colorado 80112. www.mgma.com. Copyright 2005. Pages 184–194.

Figure **V.C.7**	Accounts receivable and collections indicators			

Medicine single specialty, excluding general internal medicine

	Better Performers	Others	All
Accounts receivable management			
☉ Percent of total A/R 120+ days	8.29%	17.88%	16.41%
Percent of total A/R 0-30 days	67.61%	54.06%	56.01%
Percent of total A/R 31-60 days	13.97%	14.51%	14.46%
Percent of total A/R 61-90 days	6.08%	7.23%	7.00%
Percent of total A/R 91-120 days	3.69%	4.80%	4.53%
− Re-aged: 0-30 days in A/R	65.05%	53.79%	56.66%
− Re-aged: 31-60 days in A/R	15.91%	12.40%	13.63%
− Re-aged: 61-90 days in A/R	6.46%	6.80%	6.80%
− Re-aged: 91-120 days in A/R	3.35%	4.80%	4.44%
− Re-aged: 120+ days in A/R	7.81%	18.24%	13.99%
− Not re-aged: 0-30 days in A/R	68.29%	54.22%	55.36%
− Not re-aged: 31-60 days in A/R	12.76%	14.81%	14.73%
− Not re-aged: 61-90 days in A/R	5.28%	7.47%	7.24%
− Not re-aged: 91-120 days in A/R	3.50%	4.81%	4.56%
− Not re-aged: 120+ days in A/R	8.88%	17.87%	16.74%
Total A/R per FTE physician	$188,087	$224,791	$217,026
Charges			
☉ Months gross FFS charges in A/R	1.05	1.48	1.37
Days gross FFS charges in A/R	32.03	45.11	41.56
Gross FFS charges per FTE physician	$2,017,189	$1,809,251	$1,849,636
Gross FFS collection percentage	48.77%	46.47%	46.77%
Adjustments to FFS charges per FTE physician	$949,398	$944,248	$944,248
Adjusted FFS charges per FTE physician	$948,106	$890,633	$897,770
Collections			
☉ Adjusted FFS collection percentage	100.00%	97.05%	97.62%
Bad debts due to FFS activity per FTE physician	$11,683	$28,928	$26,058
Staffing			
Patient accounting support staff per FTE physician	0.72	0.75	0.75
General accounting support staff per FTE physician	0.14	0.11	0.11
Patient accounting support staff cost per FTE physician	$23,483	$22,953	$23,029
General accounting support staff cost per FTE physician	$6,857	$5,248	$5,442
Revenue			
☉ Total medical revenue per FTE physician	$1,064,857	$880,808	$908,622
Total medical revenue after operating cost per FTE physician	$587,103	$454,868	$475,014
Total medical revenue after operating and NPP cost per FTE physician	$579,805	$440,552	$459,511

☉━ᴹ Key Indicator

Figure V.C.8	Accounts receivable and collections indicators			

Surgical single specialty

	Better Performers	Others	All
Accounts receivable management			
Percent of total A/R 120+ days	8.62%	18.32%	17.07%
Percent of total A/R 0-30 days	68.25%	49.53%	51.23%
Percent of total A/R 31-60 days	14.46%	16.45%	16.04%
Percent of total A/R 61-90 days	5.90%	8.29%	7.84%
Percent of total A/R 91-120 days	3.23%	5.19%	4.86%
– Re-aged: 0-30 days in A/R	70.97%	49.77%	52.07%
– Re-aged: 31-60 days in A/R	10.68%	17.23%	16.38%
– Re-aged: 61-90 days in A/R	5.53%	7.51%	7.04%
– Re-aged: 91-120 days in A/R	3.02%	4.81%	4.44%
– Re-aged: 120+ days in A/R	7.70%	18.04%	15.63%
– Not re-aged: 0-30 days in A/R	66.35%	49.35%	51.20%
– Not re-aged: 31-60 days in A/R	15.08%	16.21%	15.92%
– Not re-aged: 61-90 days in A/R	6.44%	8.46%	8.26%
– Not re-aged: 91-120 days in A/R	3.23%	5.28%	5.04%
– Not re-aged: 120+ days in A/R	9.79%	18.59%	17.30%
Total A/R per FTE physician	$169,081	$269,603	$242,607
Charges			
Months gross FFS charges in A/R	1.18	1.65	1.55
Days gross FFS charges in A/R	35.99	50.25	47.12
Gross FFS charges per FTE physician	$1,771,373	$1,832,888	$1,817,494
Gross FFS collection percentage	52.88%	46.60%	48.09%
Adjustments to FFS charges per FTE physician	$866,537	$930,200	$925,420
Adjusted FFS charges per FTE physician	$927,453	$925,322	$927,453
Collections			
Adjusted FFS collection percentage	99.48%	97.12%	97.87%
Bad debts due to FFS activity per FTE physician	$9,597	$25,950	$21,298
Staffing			
Patient accounting support staff per FTE physician	0.66	0.77	0.75
General accounting support staff per FTE physician	0.13	0.13	0.13
Patient accounting support staff cost per FTE physician	$22,697	$23,273	$23,231
General accounting support staff cost per FTE physician	$4,867	$4,702	$4,784
Revenue			
Total medical revenue per FTE physician	$949,758	$936,605	$936,715
Total medical revenue after operating cost per FTE physician	$480,349	$496,183	$493,804
Total medical revenue after operating and NPP cost per FTE physician	$448,557	$476,254	$468,956

8——* Key Indicator

Figure V.C.9	Accounts receivable and collections indicators			

Multispecialty, all owners

	Better Performers	Others	All
Accounts receivable management			
Percent of total A/R 120+ days	10.48%	20.23%	17.89%
Percent of total A/R 0-30 days	63.56%	49.13%	52.39%
Percent of total A/R 31-60 days	13.75%	14.83%	14.68%
Percent of total A/R 61-90 days	7.00%	7.76%	7.60%
Percent of total A/R 91-120 days	4.49%	5.34%	5.11%
– Re-aged: 0-30 days in A/R	64.92%	50.40%	55.94%
– Re-aged: 31-60 days in A/R	13.05%	13.92%	13.57%
– Re-aged: 61-90 days in A/R	6.26%	6.84%	6.81%
– Re-aged: 91-120 days in A/R	3.98%	4.52%	4.44%
– Re-aged: 120+ days in A/R	10.90%	19.91%	17.48%
– Not re-aged: 0-30 days in A/R	61.32%	49.01%	51.11%
– Not re-aged: 31-60 days in A/R	14.28%	15.34%	15.08%
– Not re-aged: 61-90 days in A/R	7.26%	8.19%	7.97%
– Not re-aged: 91-120 days in A/R	4.83%	5.51%	5.35%
– Not re-aged: 120+ days in A/R	10.03%	20.75%	17.98%
Total A/R per FTE physician	$73,623	$118,538	$107,380
Charges			
Months gross FFS charges in A/R	1.19	1.62	1.48
Days gross FFS charges in A/R	36.11	49.19	45.11
Gross FFS charges per FTE physician	$778,992	$881,066	$857,010
Gross FFS collection percentage	65.04%	60.29%	61.54%
Adjustments to FFS charges per FTE physician	$243,082	$316,601	$311,278
Adjusted FFS charges per FTE physician	$483,230	$562,066	$543,355
Collections			
Adjusted FFS collection percentage	99.02%	97.16%	97.67%
Bad debts due to FFS activity per FTE physician	$6,338	$16,315	$14,492
Staffing			
Patient accounting support staff per FTE physician	0.58	0.63	0.62
General accounting support staff per FTE physician	0.07	0.08	0.08
Patient accounting support staff cost per FTE physician	$17,241	$18,008	$17,761
General accounting support staff cost per FTE physician	$2,694	$2,989	$2,982
Revenue			
Total medical revenue per FTE physician	$525,902	$602,168	$582,307
Total medical revenue after operating cost per FTE physician	$221,619	$240,350	$236,021
Total medical revenue after operating and NPP cost per FTE physician	$206,741	$222,362	$217,069

◖—ᴊ Key Indicator

Patient Satisfaction

This appendix contains articles and data from MGMA's *Performance and Practices of Successful Medical Groups* reports on patient satisfaction:

- Patient Satisfaction: Achieving Results (from P*erformance and Practices of Successful Medical Groups: 2004 Report Based on 2003 Data*, pages 109–112)

- Six Steps to Customer Satisfaction: From Patient Survey to Action Plan (from *Performance and Practices of Successful Medical Groups: 2004 Report Based on 2003 Data*, pages 39–41)

- MGMA Benchmarks: Better Performing Practices Comparison Exhibits (from *Performance and Practices of Successful Medical Groups: 2005 Report Based on 2004 Data*, pages 196–197)

Patient Satisfaction: Achieving Results

Introduction and summary

The following information describes implementing a patient satisfaction program and creating a plan that can lead to improved practice performance and profit.

Medical groups across the country may employ a variety of successful patient satisfaction processes and all should be able to apply some segment of the information presented on the next few pages to those processes. The intent of this information is to provide useful insights into one possible process that other medical groups may incorporate into their patient satisfaction activities.

Objectives

- Implement a successful patient satisfaction program
- Create a measurement tool that provides actionable data
- Create an action plan based on the data captured
- Measure results and improve operations
- Reduce malpractice risk and dissatisfied patients
- Benefit from pay-for-performance measures when applicable

Challenges

- Realizing that you are measuring patient perception
- Managing the process
- Engaging staff to take ownership of action plans
- Changing physician and staff behavior

Philosophy and helpful considerations

- Use and apply patient satisfaction information to help identify potential issues before they become problems
- Act on the information provided to contribute to improving many aspects of the practice — clinical, payer relations, patient referrals and physician referrals
- Reward achievements and recognize staff who go above and beyond to satisfy patients
- Use the information to identify the practice's strengths and weaknesses
- Decide on the frequency of surveying the patients
- Define the action plan to implement the changes needed

(Continued on next page)

- Create a quality assurance committee as a driving force for patient satisfaction within the practice

Key metrics

- Ease of making an appointment
- Facility access
- Waiting time
- Staff courtesy
- Physician treatment of patients
- Quality of medical care

Body of Knowledge reference

- Business and Clinical Operations
- Planning and Marketing
- Risk Management

Key audiences

- Patients
- Practice physicians
- Staff

Involved staff

- Administrator/CEO
- Managing partner/president
- Practice physicians
- Staff

Industry applicability

Most if not all practices will benefit from this best practice idea.

Management difficulty

Medium / High — the initial gathering of information must be managed along with tabulating the results. Defining action plans based on initiatives takes careful management and follow through. Once the program is established, operational difficulty will decrease.

Process duration and time factors

Three to 12 months

Key obstacles to avoid

- Ignoring the information given by patients
- Avoiding follow through on action items
- Surveying the patients too frequently and not providing time to fix the issues
- Leaving out staff when creating the action plans
- Neglecting to set specific goals
- Neglecting to hold people accountable for not following through on action plans

Key organizational attitudes

- Devote time to the process and reward successes
- Listen to patients and staff to achieve maximum results

(Continued on next page)

The process outlined below will help the practice think through the development of a program, its implementation and the actions required for improvement.

Getting started

- Determine the areas to be measured:
  - Appointment ease and availability
  - Courtesy and professionalism of the staff
  - Quality of communication
  - The visit experience
  - The facility
  - Overall satisfaction with the practice and quality of medical care
  - Willingness to refer other patients
- Define which program approach will best serve your practice:
  - In-house development and program management
  - Adoption of a commercially available survey
  - Outsourcing of the program to commercial vendors — one advantage to outsourcing is the ability to compare to other practices

- Determine the method and frequency of survey distribution:
  - Mailed surveys
  - On-site surveys
  - Phone surveys
  - Internet surveys

Survey content and design

If you choose to design your own survey:

- Include survey questions that address the performance measures agreed upon above:
  - Ease and timeliness of the appointment scheduling
  - Attitude and professionalism of staff
  - Physician communication, listening and bedside manner
  - Wait time
  - Cleanliness and aesthetics of facilities
- Keep survey short to increase response rates.
- Use clear and specific questions.
- Allow patients to be anonymous but provide room for contact information.
- Use a 5-point likert scale for question responses.

Data gathering and report results

- Designate a staff person or a quality assurance committee member to gather responses at a specific time (monthly, quarterly, etc.).
- Compile results on a regular basis — small practices may find one time per year sufficient, while larger and more complex practices may benefit from an on-going program throughout the year.
- Use spreadsheet or database programs such as Microsoft® Excel or Access to enter data and create reports of the results. Or, hire a service to measure results and create reports for you.
- Share collective survey results with physicians and staff regularly.
- Share individualized results with providers.
- Identify issues and repeat complaints and create an action plan to address them.
- Reward employees for positive patient feedback.
- Provide customer service education and training for employees to change and improve behavior.
- Compare data to previous surveys and identify trends in performance over time.

(Continued on next page)

From the *Performance and Practices of Successful Medical Groups, 2004 Report Based on 2003 Data.*
Reprinted with permission from the Medical Group Management Association, 104 Inverness Terrace East, Englewood, Colorado 80112. www.mgma.com. Copyright 2004. Pages 109–112.

Creating an action plan

- ☐ Determine each initiative addressing the areas that scored low.
- ☐ Create goals, tasks and timelines for each initiative in a simple decision tree format.
- ☐ Execute the action plan.
- ☐ Review the plan at regular intervals.
- ☐ Keep momentum behind the initiatives.
- ☐ Evaluate the success of the action plans with subsequent surveys.

Other things to consider

- ☐ Target new patients to get first-impression data.
- ☐ Conduct training workshops.
- ☐ Schedule regular meetings with employees.

Content contributors

David N. Gans, FACMPE and Kevin Sullivan, *Using Patient Satisfaction Information to Measure Performance and Improve Practice Profit*, Medical Group Management Association audio conference, May 2004.

Medical Group Management Association *Performance and Practices of Successful Medical Groups: 2003 Report Based on 2002 Data*, 2004, p. 158 – 160.

Notes:

Six Steps to Customer Satisfaction — From Patient Survey to Action Plan

By Kevin W. Sullivan

Practice leaders understand the need to be the provider of choice in their service area. However, a difference exists between practices that achieve best in market prominence and those whose results fall short of expectations. This article summarizes the experience of small and large medical groups and identifies the strategies that mark providers of choice in competitive markets nationwide.

System vs. sermon

In health care, you can manage performance two ways. Clinical, technical and procedural expectations are carefully defined, closely managed and not optional. Service expectations are too often loosely defined, managed through in-service pep-talks, and left to the discretion of physicians and employees.

As a consequence, performance varies among departments and practice sites — particularly when medical professionals go on autopilot in the face of heavier workloads, demanding patients, lean staffing and limited resources.

Many Medical Group Management Association members use a more formal and businesslike process for measuring their strengths and weaknesses and convert the findings into workable action plans that produce immediate improvement and ongoing results.

Figure II.B.6 illustrates a six-step process used by best-practice organizations — single- and multispecialty groups as well as independent practice association provider networks — to analyze strengths and weaknesses, define service standards, monitor performance, hold people accountable for results and recognize top contributors.

Step 1 — Service assessment

To build a business plan to protect your existing revenue base and generate new market share, you need to take the first step and know how customers perceive your service strengths and weaknesses.

Use a patient survey as your tool to obtain feedback from a large number of people who offer a customer's perspective on how it feels to access your services. All questions should have a positive statistical correlation with overall satisfaction, which

means that any increase in scores will improve your market position.

More detailed information can be found in mystery patient visits in which an experienced observer can spot strengths and weaknesses in the specific performance areas that affect patient loyalty and referrals.

Finally, surveying and interviewing your inside customers — board members, physicians, managers and staff — not only produces essential feedback, but also builds stronger support for your action plan among people who are consulted beforehand.

Figure II.B.6	The six-step customer service initiative

1. Conduct a baseline service assessment
- Patient satisfaction survey
- Mystery patient visits
- Physician, supervisor, staff surveys
- Key-leader interviews

2. Leadership involvement (buy-in and objectives)
- Review service assessment
- Set quantifiable goals
- Form customer service committee
- Develop action plan

3. Develop service standards
- Develop customer-centered performance standards
- Incorporate into job descriptions
- Integrate into the performance appraisal process

4. Conduct training workshops
- Physicians and mid-levels
- Managers and supervisors
- Clinical and support staff

5. Track performance (benchmark)
- Use dashboard monitoring and reporting
- Monitor progress
- Provide support to departments

6. Momentum strategy
- Ongoing communication program
- Booster meetings
- Recognize top performers

(Continued on next page)

Figure II.B.7	Patient survey findings			
		Mean score	Percentile ranking	90th percentile
	A1. Ease of making appointments by phone	4.56	67.7%	4.76
	A2. Appointment available in a reasonable amount of time	4.47	73.0%	4.70
	A3. The efficiency of the check-in process	4.54	60.2%	4.73
	A4. Waiting time in the reception area	4.08	57.6%	4.47
	A5. Waiting time in the exam room	4.06	60.6%	4.44
	A6. Keeping you informed if appointment time was delayed	4.10	53.1%	4.58

Step 2 – Leadership involvement

Every provider needs to perform as if customer satisfaction is the key to protecting the existing revenue base and generating new market share. Furthermore, research has proven that satisfied patients don't litigate, and that happy employees surpass those who clock in for a paycheck. In terms of medical quality, there is a direct correlation between patients who are satisfied with provider communication and compliance with treatment plans, which leads to improved medical outcomes.

Convene a meeting of board members, physicians and managers — all the people who will be involved in implementing the action plan. Review the findings of the service assessment and ask the group to help set improvement priorities for the coming year. This is also a good time to formalize responsibility for coordinating the implementation process through a customer service committee comprised of physicians, managers and employees — with at least one board member in an ex-officio capacity.

Bristol Park Medical Group Costa Mesa, Calif., took a unique approach to building its customer service action plan. In a half-day meeting, 44 board and committee members, medical directors, administration and department heads reviewed the assessment, set priorities and goals and assigned responsibilities to designated task groups. The leadership team reviewed progress at every monthly partner meeting and modified strategies as needed.

You can use patient survey findings to set improvement priorities. Figure II.B.7 shows how survey scores can be viewed in terms of their percentage rankings. You can use the percentile rankings to determine which areas to address as well as the score you'll need to rank in the top 10 percent of the database.

In Figure II.B.7, the mean score for question A1 ranks at the 67.7 percentile of the benchmark database. A score of 4.76 must be reached to rank in the top 10 percent of the database.

In taking this approach, your practice will have quantifiable goals to measure progress. With specific goals, the customer service committee can now brainstorm strategies for raising the score from 4.56 to 4.76 by the next time you survey your patients.

Step 3 – Service standards

Service performance needs the same careful definition as clinical and procedural criteria — not only for employees but also for physicians and nonphysician providers who are part of the delivered product. Successful practices connect improving scores on specific survey questions with job descriptions and annual performance appraisals.

Physician standards should reflect the four phases of the patient encounter: establishing rapport, eliciting information, educating the patient and ensuring compliance. The standards should also include issues related to staff relations, peer

relations and partnership or professional criteria.

Employees must address customer service as a priority, not an option or an ideal to be pursued only on good days. Rather, exceeding customer expectations must become a part of the practice's mission and values — as important to professionals as medical quality and technical expertise. Staff performance standards should include making a great first impression, using appropriate telephone etiquette, handling patient complaints and creating a team environment within and among departments (See Figure II.B.8).

Rockwood Clinic, Spokane, Wash., made its service standards the centerpiece of physician seminars, manager development and staff workshops. To ensure the effectiveness of the training, the customer service committee began a series of self-directed mystery patient visits and engaged consultants to conduct shadow coaching encounters for low-scoring physicians.

Step 4 – Skills training

Once you publish and understand the standards, conduct training seminars to enable everyone in your practice to meet or exceed the standards. As an example, patient surveys usually contain a question about the amount of time the physician spends with a patient. Your doctors need to understand that answers to this question have nothing to do with actual minutes spent in the exam room. Top ratings go to physicians who know the techniques

(Continued on next page)

From the *Performance and Practices of Successful Medical Groups, 2004 Report Based on 2003 Data.*
Reprinted with permission from the Medical Group Management Association, 104 Inverness Terrace East,
Englewood, Colorado 80112. www.mgma.com. Copyright 2004. Pages 39–41.

Figure II.B.8 — Customer service standard (Staff)

Make a great first impression

1. Acknowledge patients immediately; use eye contact and smile

2. Let patients know of expected delays; keep them informed of their status

3. Use the patient's last name until you sense using first names is appropriate

4. Use layperson's language whenever possible

5. Be an active listener; pay attention to what the patient is saying

6. Be helpful to patients who need help finding their way around the facility

7. Give clear directions; answer all questions with patience and professional concern

8. Reassure anxious patients; ask what you can do to make things easier

9. Conclude with a friendly thank you

Once you've trained front- and back-office people in customer-pleasing techniques, a special effort should be made to improve the leadership skills of those responsible for medical and staff management. A formal manager training program will emphasize skills for team building, conflict resolution, correcting unsatisfactory performance, preparing and conducting objective performance reviews and other key subjects.

Step 5 — Tracking mechanisms

Establish tracking mechanisms to measure progress and keep customer service at the top of everyone's agenda. Use follow-up patient surveys, referrer and insider surveys, requests for records transfer, exit interviews of departing physicians and staff members and number and source of complaints. Develop monthly reports and reserve a portion of each partner-management meeting to review them.

Step 6 — Momentum strategy

The final step in your action plan involves momentum — promotional activities that keep customer service in the minds of every member of the practice and recognition programs that reward top performers. Small and large practices can use a variety of strategies to encourage top-level performance by rewarding those who excel at customer satisfaction.

Some practices establish programs in which service stars receive public recognition; others install bonus formulas in which high-scores on customer surveys equate to monetary awards. In any case, these programs help practice managers reinforce their commitment to customer satisfaction.

Enhance momentum by publishing the results of regular patient surveys and referring-physician surveys for single-specialty practices that depend on referrals for a major portion of new patients.

In addition, many best-practice groups maintain a continuing schedule of mystery patient assessments, where trained observers use first-hand observations to look beyond the survey data, identify specific performance areas and recommend practical strategies for improving the survey scores.

Bright Medical Associates, Whittier Calif., uses monthly reports from mystery patient visits and telephone calls to help physician-manager teams spot deficiencies in daily operations or performance and develop fast-track action plans to improve customer satisfaction.

Many practices use shadow coaching as an effective strategy to improve customer satisfaction. A trained consultant dons a lab coat, poses as a writer doing a story, and follows the physician through a day's encounters — after which the low-scoring doctor receives direct, one-on-one feedback on how he/she interacted with patients seen during the day.

Putting it all together

The six-step process closes the disconnect that often exists between leadership plans and front-line performance. It produces a cultural change in meeting and exceeding customers' service expectations. The process emphasizes that service is not an option and holds each member of the practice accountable for making internal and external customers feel valued and important.

Your practice benefits by gaining greater patient loyalty and more patient referrals.

that make patients feel that the limited encounter time was well spent. Body language, eye contact, active listening and other validating behaviors produce satisfied patients and high survey scores.

Similarly, staff members can learn and practice techniques that enhance patient satisfaction. When rooming the patient, for example, medical assistants get high marks when they make congenial small talk and use the patient's name.

Figure V.D.1

Practices and procedures survey results — patient satisfaction

	Profitability and cost management	Productivity, capacity and staffing	Accounts receivable management	Patient satisfaction	Better performance status		
	Better Performers	Better Performers	Better Performers	Better Performers	All Better Performers	Others	All
Employee satisfaction surveys							
Never	36.67%	30.65%	33.33%	22.47%	31.19%	40.24%	36.63%
Less than once per year	31.67%	33.87%	25.00%	34.83%	30.28%	20.73%	24.54%
Once per year	26.67%	33.87%	36.11%	38.20%	33.94%	32.93%	33.33%
Twice per year	1.67%	1.61%	2.78%	2.25%	1.83%	4.88%	3.66%
Quarterly	3.33%	0.00%	2.78%	2.25%	2.75%	0.61%	1.47%
Monthly or more often	0.00%	0.00%	0.00%	0.00%	0.00%	0.61%	0.37%
Patient satisfaction surveys							
Never	18.03%	19.05%	25.00%	0.00%	18.18%	28.48%	24.36%
Less than once per year	27.87%	23.81%	22.22%	30.00%	24.55%	24.85%	24.73%
Once per year	16.39%	17.46%	19.44%	23.33%	19.09%	18.79%	18.91%
Twice per year	13.11%	15.87%	8.33%	15.56%	12.73%	12.12%	12.36%
Quarterly	9.84%	6.35%	8.33%	11.11%	9.09%	5.45%	6.91%
Monthly or more often	14.75%	17.46%	16.67%	20.00%	16.36%	10.30%	12.73%
Physician satisfaction surveys							
Never	66.67%	67.21%	60.00%	59.09%	64.81%	60.00%	61.94%
Less than once per year	18.33%	18.03%	22.86%	21.59%	17.59%	14.38%	15.67%
Once per year	11.67%	13.11%	11.43%	14.77%	12.96%	19.38%	16.79%
Twice per year	0.00%	0.00%	2.86%	1.14%	0.93%	1.88%	1.49%
Quarterly	0.00%	1.64%	0.00%	1.14%	0.93%	1.25%	1.12%
Monthly or more often	3.33%	0.00%	2.86%	2.27%	2.78%	3.13%	2.99%
Referral physician satisfaction surveys							
Never	66.10%	65.00%	71.43%	58.62%	64.49%	59.63%	61.57%
Less than once per year	16.95%	18.33%	17.14%	22.99%	18.69%	23.60%	21.64%
Once per year	15.25%	11.67%	8.57%	13.79%	13.08%	13.04%	13.06%
Twice per year	1.69%	1.67%	0.00%	1.15%	0.93%	0.62%	0.75%
Quarterly	0.00%	1.67%	2.86%	2.30%	1.87%	2.48%	2.24%
Monthly or more often	0.00%	1.67%	0.00%	1.15%	0.93%	0.62%	0.75%

(Continued on next page)

From the *Performance and Practices of Successful Medical Groups, 2005 Report Based on 2004 Data*.
Reprinted with permission from the Medical Group Management Association, 104 Inverness Terrace East,
Englewood, Colorado 80112. www.mgma.com. Copyright 2005. Pages 196–197.

Figure V.D.1

Practice and procedures survey results — patient satisfaction (continued)

	Profitability and cost management	Productivity, capacity and staffing	Accounts receivable management	Patient satisfaction	Better performance status		
	Better Performers	Better Performers	Better Performers	Better Performers	All Better Performers	Others	All
Elements of patient satisfaction surveys							
Appointment availability	62.50%	53.75%	60.98%	90.00%	59.56%	48.94%	53.40%
Bedside manner	40.28%	31.25%	34.15%	55.56%	36.76%	36.17%	36.42%
Cleanliness/comfort of facilities	54.17%	45.00%	51.22%	77.78%	51.47%	48.40%	49.69%
Confidentiality	23.61%	21.25%	12.20%	32.22%	21.32%	21.28%	21.30%
Overall exposure	58.33%	55.00%	56.10%	87.78%	58.09%	56.38%	57.10%
Patient name	11.11%	11.25%	9.76%	15.56%	10.29%	11.70%	11.11%
Physician communication style	36.11%	42.50%	36.59%	58.89%	38.97%	34.57%	36.42%
Professionalism of the staff	63.89%	57.50%	65.85%	93.33%	61.76%	52.66%	56.48%
Quality of care	56.94%	50.00%	58.54%	85.56%	56.62%	51.60%	53.70%
Recommendation of practice to others	44.44%	42.50%	43.90%	71.11%	47.06%	40.96%	43.52%
Unique appointment time code	4.17%	3.75%	4.88%	6.67%	4.41%	1.60%	2.78%
Unique provider code	6.94%	10.00%	7.32%	13.33%	8.82%	10.11%	9.57%
Unique service line	1.39%	2.50%	0.00%	3.33%	2.21%	2.13%	2.16%
Wait time	56.94%	50.00%	58.54%	82.22%	54.41%	47.34%	50.31%
Other element	4.17%	3.75%	2.44%	5.56%	4.41%	3.19%	3.70%
How survey results are used							
Benchmark to other practices	12.50%	10.00%	7.32%	17.78%	11.76%	14.89%	13.58%
Contracting purposes	5.56%	8.75%	7.32%	12.22%	8.09%	7.45%	7.72%
Educate physicians about behavior	56.94%	53.75%	63.41%	87.78%	58.09%	53.72%	55.56%
Educate staff about behavior	61.11%	55.00%	60.98%	88.89%	58.82%	52.13%	54.94%
Evaluate and improve practice operations	62.50%	58.75%	65.85%	93.33%	61.76%	54.26%	57.41%
Liability risk management	22.22%	17.50%	17.07%	28.89%	19.12%	17.02%	17.90%
Marketing and promotional purposes	11.11%	13.75%	24.39%	23.33%	15.44%	12.77%	13.89%
Part of physician compensation formula	0.00%	1.25%	2.44%	3.33%	2.21%	5.85%	4.32%
Reward outstanding customer service	8.33%	6.25%	7.32%	11.11%	7.35%	6.38%	6.79%
Staff incentive/bonus	5.56%	7.50%	4.88%	10.00%	6.62%	2.66%	4.32%
Staff performance reviews	6.94%	15.00%	17.07%	21.11%	13.97%	8.51%	10.80%
Other use of results	0.00%	2.50%	4.88%	1.11%	1.47%	3.72%	2.78%

Managed Care

This appendix contains articles and data from MGMA's *Performance and Practices of Successful Medical Groups* reports on managed care:

- The Practices of Successful Medical Groups (from *Performance and Practices of Successful Medical Groups: 2003 Report Based on 2002 Data*, pages 176–177)

- MGMA Benchmarks: Better Performing Practices Comparison Exhibits (from *Performance and Practices of Successful Medical Groups: 2004 Report Based on 2003 Data*, pages 192–193)

The Practices of Successful Medical Groups

" Better performing medical groups proactively direct managed care activities... to ensure that they remain viable and continue to meet the health care needs of their communities. "

Deborah L. Walker, MBA, FACMPE

Despite the negative images associated with managed care, better performing practices continuously seek innovative and effective approaches to the delivery of health care under capitation arrangements. Better performers retain control of managed care operations by negotiating a range of delegated arrangements, such as claims payment, utilization review/ management and credentialing. This administrative ownership leads to a holistic patient care approach; increased patient care quality and profits; and decreased medical costs. A fundamental component of successful practice management includes managing the complete patient experience. Better performing practices use early intervention programs to assist patients in navigating the managed care delivery model and seeking services.

Through research and analysis, MGMA has identified managed care performance criteria from the MGMA *Cost Survey Report* data to select better performing medical groups. To be acknowledged as a better performer in Managed Care Operations, a practice must meet the following performance indicators:

■ Greater than 10 percent net capitation revenue as a percentage of total medical revenue;

■ Greater than the median for net capitation revenue to gross capitation charges ratio; and

■ Greater than the median for revenue after operating cost per FTE physician.

Practices achieving this designation possess similar operational methods, often deeply rooted in the organizations' value systems. Common values noted among better performing groups are:

• Supporting managed care objectives by providing preventative and qualitative patient care;

• Improving patient outcomes through a variety of chronic disease management programs;

• Establishing and monitoring performance goals;

• Reviewing and managing contracts; and

• Addressing operational problems that delay timely access to care.

Successful medical groups also exhibit a number of specific behaviors in the administration of managed care patients. To more deeply understand these cultural and operational indicators, MGMA has conducted a five-year qualitative analysis of better performing practices. Following are characteristics reported by these better performing medical groups in their pursuit of best practice level results under Managed Care Operations.

(Continued on next page)

From the *Performance and Practices of Successful Medical Groups, 2003 Report Based on 2002 Data.*
Reprinted with permission from the Medical Group Management Association, 104 Inverness Terrace East,
Englewood, Colorado 80112. www.mgma.com. Copyright 2003. Pages 176–177.

Clinical and Referral Processes

☐ Establish well coordinated and efficient referral processes and systems

☐ Remain flexible and responsive to patients through individual referral management

☐ Establish a referral network of comprehensive primary and specialty care physicians

☐ Use referral data to predict demand for health care services and access to physicians

☐ Expand internal expertise and physician competencies through increased physician subspecialties

☐ Offer case management and disease management programs

Physician Involvement

☐ Increase physician involvement and dedication to managed care objectives

☐ Clearly communicate practice philosophy to employed and contracted physicians

☐ Offer one-on-one meetings between primary care and single-specialty physicians

☐ Use physician profiling to identify cost trends on a per provider basis for physician education on cost containment strategies

☐ Contract and hire physicians who fit with your organization's cost and quality goals

Perform Regular Contract Reviews

☐ Set a predetermined contract rate for out-of-area and out-of-network referrals

☐ Work with insurance companies to establish reimbursement for quality goals

☐ Conduct contract performance analysis by payer

☐ Build into contracts per member per month (PMPM) inflation factors for growth

☐ Conduct regular fee-for-service comparative analysis to make sure the practice is remaining profitable with PMPM reimbursement

☐ Clearly identify risk pool arrangements for inpatient and pharmacy risk arrangements

Other Ideas

☐ Form strategic partnerships with employer groups and health plans

☐ Implement stop-loss programs through reinsurance

☐ Implement special programs — such as hospitalists, after-hours care and urgent care centers — to curtail ER and inpatient overusage

☐ Bring services in-house to capitalize on PMPM dollars

☐ Ensure that the practice's information system can combine and track claims and encounter data for analysis

☐ Use patient satisfaction data to learn how patients view their health care quality

☐ Track member dropout factors and complaints to better grasp PMPM dollars

Key Managed Care Measurements

• Net capitation revenue as percent of gross capitation charges

• Number of visits by per member per month (PMPM)

• Number of referrals per 1000 members

• Number of bed days per 1000 members

• Relative Value Units (RVUs) per physician

• Cost per visit, per case and per covered life

• Patient panel size per physician

• Charges by payer type

• Revenue by payer type

Other Standards

☐ _____
_____
_____

☐ _____
_____
_____

Notes

Figure **IV.E.1**	Managed care operations demographic profile				

Practice type

	Single specialty		Multispecialty	
	Better Performers	All	Better Performers	All
Practice description				
Number of organizations	3	27	13	50
Total provider FTE	18.75	16.51	31.73	57.25
Total physician FTE	6.00	12.00	31.70	52.00
Total nonphysician provider FTE	6.00	3.60	6.08	8.50
Total support staff FTE	33.90	61.86	221.00	278.06
Number of branch clinics	8	6	9	9
Square footage of all facilities	11,233	18,936	82,168	98,343
Payer mix				
Net capitation revenue	27.71%	19.51%	32.84%	24.92%
Medicare: fee-for-service	32.00%	11.51%	14.27%	17.09%
Medicare: managed care FFS	1.95%	0.00%	0.00%	0.00%
Medicare: capitation	0.00%	0.00%	7.26%	0.00%
Medicaid: fee-for-service	1.00%	1.30%	1.81%	2.72%
Medicaid: managed care FFS	0.00%	0.00%	0.00%	0.00%
Medicaid: capitation	0.00%	0.00%	2.00%	0.00%
Commercial: fee-for-service	6.00%	25.46%	32.80%	32.76%
Commercial: managed care FFS	35.67%	22.57%	0.00%	0.00%
Commercial: capitation	11.06%	15.54%	16.47%	15.65%
Workers' compensation	0.10%	0.00%	0.71%	0.61%
Charity care and prof courtesy	0.00%	0.00%	0.00%	0.00%
Self-pay	1.39%	2.50%	4.00%	3.30%
Other federal government payers	0.00%	0.00%	0.00%	0.00%
Location				
Eastern section	3.70%	29.63%	2.00%	18.00%
Midwest section	3.70%	25.93%	4.00%	28.00%
Southern section	3.70%	18.52%	2.00%	12.00%
Western section	*	25.93%	18.00%	42.00%

Figure IV.E.2	Managed care operations indicators		

Multispecialty

	Better Performers	All
Revenue		
Net capitation revenue as a percent of total medical revenue	32.84%	24.92%
Net capitation revenue as a percent of gross capitation charges	89.71%	78.52%
Total medical revenue per FTE physician	$686,320	$629,088
Total medical revenue after operating cost per FTE physician	$289,094	$232,576
Net capitation revenue per FTE physician	$243,343	$158,492
Capitation revenue per FTE physician	$360,622	$206,330
Productivity		
Gross capitation charges per FTE physician	$216,970	$192,010
Total gross charges per FTE physician	$789,947	$798,060
Patients per FTE physician	1,579	1,579
Total procedures per FTE physician	10,959	10,558
Square feet per FTE physician	1,794	1,863
Purchased services for capitation patients per FTE physician	$168,474	$165,972
Staffing		
Total nonphysician providers per FTE physician	0.30	0.20
Total employed support staff per FTE physician	5.73	5.17

○—✘ Key Indicator

Sources of Benchmarking and Operations Improvement Information

Austin, C. and S. Boxerman. *Quantitative Analysis for Health Services Administration*. Ann Arbor, MI: Association of University Programs in Health Administration Press and the Foundation of the American College of Healthcare Executives, 1995.

Balestracci, D. and J. Barlow. *Quality Improvement: Practical Applications for Medical Group Practice*, 2nd ed. Englewood, CO: Medical Group Management Association (MGMA), 1996.

Bluman, A. *Elementary Statistics: A Step by Step Approach*, 4th ed. Boston: McGraw-Hill, 2001.

Costello, J., J. Reiboldt, M. Reiboldt, K. Solinsky and K. Stanley. *Physician Ancillary Services: Evaluation, Implementation, and Management of New Practice Opportunities*. Sudbury, MA: Jones and Bartlett Publishers, 2006.

Daniel, W. *Biostatistics: A Foundation for Analysis in the Health Sciences*, 7th ed. New York: John Wiley & Sons, Inc., 1999.

Delio, S. *The Efficient Physician: 7 Guiding Principles for a Tech-Savvy Practice*, 2nd ed. Englewood, CO: MGMA, 2005.

Gift, R. and D. Mosel. *Benchmarking in Healthcare*. Chicago: American Hospital Publishing, Inc., 1994.

Griffith, J. and K. White. *The Well-Managed Healthcare Organization*, 5th ed. Chicago: Association of University Programs in Health Administration Press, 2002.

Gulko, E. *Business and Clinical Operations*. Vol. 2, Body of Knowledge Review. Englewood, CO: MGMA, 2006.

Hajny, T. *Looking for the Cashcow: Action Steps to Improve Cash Flow in Medical Group Practices*. Englewood, CO: MGMA, 2000.

Johnson, B., D. Schryver and D. Stech. *Building Practice Revenue: A Guide to Developing New Services*. Englewood, CO: MGMA, 2003.

Kelley, D. *Measurement and Quality Improvement Methods*. Thousand Oaks, CA: SAGE Publishing, 1999.

Lutz, S. and PricewaterhouseCoopers. *Physician Group Management at the Crossroads: Developing, Operating, and Growing Physician and Dental Groups.* New York: McGraw-Hill, 1999.

McDowell, I. and C. Newell. *Measuring Health: A Guide to Rating Scales and Questionnaires*, 2nd ed. New York: Oxford University Press, 1996.

MGMA. *Cost Survey for Multispecialty Practices: 2006 Report Based on 2005 Data.* Englewood, CO: MGMA, 2006.

MGMA. *Performance and Practices of Successful Medical Groups, 2006 to 1998 Report Based on 2005 to 1997 Data.* Englewood, CO: MGMA, 2006.

Miller, G. and M. Whicker. *Handbook of Research Methods in Public Administration.* New York: Marcel Dekker, 1999.

Ott, R. *An Introduction to Statistical Methods and Data Analysis*, 4th ed. Belmont, CA: Duxbury Press, 1993.

Pavlock, E. *Financial Management for Medical Groups*, 2nd ed. Englewood, CO: MGMA, 2000.

Rosner, B. *Fundamentals of Biostatistics*, 3rd ed. Boston: PWS-Kent Publishing Co., 1990.

Rothstein, J. and J. Echternach. *Primer on Measurement: An Introductory Guide to Measurement Issues.* Alexandria, VA: American Physical Therapy Association, 1993.

Streiner, D. and G. Norman. *Health Measurement Scales: A Practical Guide to Their Development and Use*, 3rd ed. New York: Oxford University Press, 2003.

Tabachnick, B. and L. Fidell. *Using Multivariate Statistics*, 4th ed. Boston: Allyn and Bacon, 2001.

Walker, D., S. Larch and E .Woodcock. *The Physician Billing Process: Avoiding Potholes in the Road to Getting Paid.* Englewood, CO: MGMA, 2004.

Warn, B. and E. Woodcock. *Operating Policies and Procedures Manual for Medical Practices*, 2nd ed. Englewood, CO: MGMA, 2001.

Wolper, L. *Physician Practice Management.* Sudbury, MA: Jones and Bartlett Publishers, 2005.

Glossary

A **Accounting methods: cash** An accounting system in which revenues are recorded when cash is received and costs are recorded when cash is paid out. Receivables, payables, accruals and deferrals arising from operations are ignored. On a pure cash basis, long-lived (fixed) assets are expensed when acquired, leaving cash and investments as the only assets, and borrowings and payroll withholds as the only liabilities.

Accounting methods: accrual An accounting system in which revenues are recorded as earned when services are performed rather than when cash is received. Cost is recorded in the period during which it is incurred; that is, when the asset or service is used, regardless of when cash is paid. Costs for goods and services that will be used to produce revenues in the future are reported as assets and recorded as costs in future periods. The accrual system balance sheet includes not only the assets and liabilities from the cash basis balance sheet but also the receivables from patients, prepayments and deferrals of costs, accruals of costs and revenues, and payables to suppliers.

Accounting methods: income tax A system used to file an income tax return and based on federal tax laws.

Accounting methods: modified cash An accounting system that is primarily a cash basis system but allows the cost of long-lived (fixed) assets to be expensed through depreciation. The modified cash system recognizes inventories of goods intended for resale as assets. Under a modified cash system, purchases of buildings and equipment, leasehold improvements and payments of insurance premiums applicable to more than one accounting period are normally recorded as assets. Costs for these assets are allocated to accounting periods in a systematic manner over the length of time the practice benefits from the assets.

accounts receivable current to 30 days Amounts owed to the practice by patients, third-party payers, employer groups and unions for fee-for-service activities before adjustments for anticipated payment reductions or allowances for adjustments or bad debts. Amounts assigned to accounts receivable (A/R) are due to "gross fee for service charges." Assignment of a charge into A/R is initiated at the time an invoice is submitted to a payer or patient for payment. For example, if an obstetrics practice establishes an open account for accumulation of charges when a patient is accepted into a prenatal program and the account will not be invoiced until after delivery, then A/R will not reflect these charges until an invoice is created. Deletion of charges from A/R is done when the account is paid, turned over to a collection agency or written off as bad debt. "Accounts payable to patients and payers" are subtracted from A/R before reporting A/R. This is the net amount owed after patient refunds. Do not include capitation payments owed to the practice by HMOs.

adjusted RVU values for modifier usage Modifiers that cause adjustments to RVU values include those for additional complexity or multiple procedures such as -21, -22, -51, -80, and modifiers for technical and professional component billing such as -26, -TC (technical component).

administrative supplies and services cost This consists of cost of printing, postage, books, subscriptions, administrative and medical forms, stationery, bank processing fees and other administrative supplies and services. This should also include purchased medical transcription services.

ambulatory surgery center Freestanding entity that is specifically licensed to provide surgery services performed on a same-day outpatient basis.

ASA units American Society of Anesthesiology relative units.

average Measure of central tendency and the arithmetic mean of a dataset (or mathematical center; also known as the mean).

adjusted charges See *adjustments to fee-for-service charges.*

adjustments to fee-for-service charges Difference between "gross fee-for-service charges" and the amount expected to be paid by patients or third-party payers. This represents the value of services performed for which payment is not expected. This should also include: (1) Medicare and Medicaid charge restrictions (the difference between the practice's full, undiscounted charge and the Medicare limiting charge); (2) third-party payer contractual adjustments (commercial insurance and/or managed care organization); (3) charitable, professional courtesy or employee adjustments; and (4) the difference between a gross charge and the Federally Qualified Health Center payment.

B **bad debts due to fee-for-service activity** Difference between adjusted fee-for-service charges and the amount actually collected. This should also include: (1) losses on settlements for less than the billed amount; (2) accounts written off as not collectible; (3) accounts assigned to collection agencies; and (4) the provision for bad debts, in the case of accrual accounting.

bell-shaped curve See *normal distribution.*

benchmarking Continual process of measuring and comparing key work process indicators with those of best performers. The overall objective is to facilitate organizational improvement by identifying best processes and practices through accurate and relevant measurement. In other words, successful benchmarking demonstrates to organizations how to improve their performance and profitability through evidence-based management.

best practices Proven services, functions or processes that have been shown to produce superior outcomes or results in benchmarks that meet or set a new standard. However, there is no single best practice or "silver bullet." Instead, "best" refers to what is optimal for a particular organization, given its patients, mission, community, culture and external environment.

billing and collections purchased services When a medical practice decides to purchase billing and collections services from an outside organization as opposed to hiring and developing its own employed staff to conduct billing and collections activities, the cost for such purchased services should be considered "billing and collections purchased services." This should also include claims clearinghouse cost.

branch or satellite clinic Smaller clinical facility for which the practice incurs occupancy costs, such as lease, depreciation and utilities. A branch is in a separate location from the practice's principal facility. Merely having physicians practice in another location does not qualify that location as a branch or satellite clinic. For example, if a physician sees patients in a hospital, this would not normally be counted as a branch or satellite clinic unless the practice pays rent for the space.

building and occupancy cost Cost of general operation of buildings and grounds. Includes: (1) rental, operating lease and leasehold improvements for buildings and grounds; (2) depreciation cost for buildings and grounds; (3) interest paid on loans for real estate used in practice operations; (4) cost of utilities such as water, electric power and space heating fuels; (5) cost of supplies and materials used in housekeeping and maintenance; and (6) other costs such as building repairs and security systems. Does not include: (1) interest paid on short-term loans, which is included in "miscellaneous operating cost"; (2) interest paid on loans for real estate not used in practice operations such as nonmedical office space in practice-owned properties (such interest is included in nonmedical costs); or (3) cost of producing revenue from sources such as parking lots or leased office space from practice-owned properties.

business corporation For-profit organization recognized by law as a business entity separate and distinct from its shareholders. Shareholders need not be licensed in the profession practiced by the corporation.

C   capacity See *throughput*.

capitation Process when a provider organization receives a fixed, previously negotiated periodic payment per member covered by the health plan in exchange for delivering specified health care services to the members for a specified length of time regardless of how many or how few services are actually required or rendered. Per member per month is the commonplace calculation unit for such capitation payments.

capitation contract Contract in which the practice agrees to provide medical services to a defined population for a fixed price per beneficiary per month, regardless of actual services provided. Capitation contracts always contain an element of risk.

centralized administrative department Provides leadership and has the authority and responsibility for the operations of the various physician practices within the entity. This department provides oversight and encompasses many or all of the following types of activities: establishing policies, negotiating managed care agreements, strategic planning, physician contracting, approving expenditures and affording any other resources required to manage the physician practices.

central tendency Center of the distribution of data, which consists of the mean, median and mode.

charity care and professional courtesy Charity patients are those not covered by either commercial insurance or federal, state or local governmental health care programs and who do not have the resources to pay for services. Charity patients must be identified at the time that service is provided so that a bill for service is not prepared. Professional courtesy charges are included in this category. Fee-for-service gross charges, at the practice's undiscounted rates, for all services provided to charity patients.

clinical laboratory and pathology procedures This consists of: (1) 36415 and 36416, venous and capillary blood collection; (2) 80048–89356, a panel of tests represented by a single Current Procedural Terminology (CPT®) code and considered to be one procedure; (3) HCPCS P codes; (4) all clinical laboratory and pathology procedures conducted by laboratories outside of the practice's facilities as long as the practice pays the outside laboratory directly for the procedures and the procedures are only for the practice's fee-for-service patients. The cost for these purchased laboratory services should be reported as a subset of "clinical laboratory"; and (5) all procedures done either at the practice (where the practice bills at a global rate for both the technical and professional components) or procedures done at an outside facility (where the practice bills at a professional rate only). This should not include purchased laboratory services from external providers and facilities on behalf of the practice's capitation patients for which costs are reported as "purchased services for capitation patients."

clinical laboratory cost This consists of cost of clinical laboratory and pathology procedures defined by CPT codes 80048–89356, 36415 and 36416. This should also include: (1) rental and/or depreciation cost of major furniture and equipment subject to capitalization; (2) repair and maintenance contract cost; (3) cost of supplies and minor equipment not subject to capitalization; (4) other costs unique to the clinical laboratory; and (5) cost of purchased laboratory technical services for fee-for-service patients. This should not include cost of purchased laboratory technical services for capitation patients. Such cost should be reported as purchased services for capitation patients.

clinical laboratory FTE This consists of procedures for clinical laboratory and pathology CPT codes 80048–89356, 36415 and 36416. This should also include: (1) FTE and cost of support staff such as nurses, secretaries and technicians; and (2) FTE and cost of department director or manager.

clinical science department A unit of organization in a medical school with an independent chair and a single budget. The department's mission is to conduct teaching, research and/or clinical activities related to the entire spectrum of health care delivery to humans, from prevention through treatment.

clinical support staff Registered nurses, licensed practical nurses, medical assistants and nurse's aides.

commercial — capitation Fee-for-service (FFS) equivalent gross charges, at the practice's undiscounted rates, for all services provided to patients under a commercial capitated contract. This should not include: (1) charges for FFS patients; or (2) charges for patients covered under discounted FFS contract arrangements.

commercial — fee-for-service Fee-for-service gross charges, at the practice's undiscounted rates, for all services provided to fee-for-service patients who are covered by commercial contracts that do not include a withhold but may or may not include a performance-based incentive. A commercial contract is any contract that is not Medicare, Medicaid or workers' compensation. This should not include charges for: (1) Medicare patients; (2) Medicaid patients; (3) capitation patients; (4) patients covered by a managed care plan; (5) workers' compensation patients; (6) charity or professional courtesy patients; or (7) self-pay patients.

commercial — managed care fee-for-service Fee-for-service gross charges, at the practice's undiscounted rates, for all services provided to patients who are covered by managed care contracts that include a withhold and may or may not include a performance-based incentive. A commercial contract is any contract that is not Medicare, Medicaid or workers' compensation. This should also include charges for patients covered under discounted fee-for-service contract arrangements. This should not include charges for: (1) Medicare patients; (2) Medicaid patients; (3) capitation patients; (4) workers' compensation patients; (5) charity or professional courtesy patients; or (6) self-pay patients.

continuous data Data that can be divided and subdivided into equal-sized subunits (for example, a meter can be subdivided into centimeters, which can be subdivided into millimeters, and so on). For the opposite of continuous data, see *discrete data.*

cost Amount of resources used to acquire an asset.

cost allocated to medical practice from parent organization When a medical practice is owned by a hospital, integrated delivery system or other entity, the parent organization often allocates indirect costs to the medical practice. These indirect costs may have different names depending on the situation; for example, "shared services costs" or "uncontrollable costs." These costs may be arbitrarily assigned to the medical practice, may be the result of negotiations between the practice and the parent organization or the result of some sort of cost accounting system. Often, these indirect costs include a portion of the salaries of the senior management team of the parent organization, a portion of corporate human resources costs or a portion of corporate marketing costs. Depending on the type of cost, the cost may be allocated to the medical practice as a function of the ratio of medical practice FTE to total system FTE, the ratio of medical practice square footage to total system square footage or the ratio of medical practice gross charges to total system gross charges. Depending on the culture of the integrated system, these indirect costs may or may not show up on the financial statements of the medical practice. This should not include cash loans made to subsidiaries.

cost of sales and/or cost of other medical activities Cost of activities that generate revenue included in "revenue from the sale of medical goods and services," as long as this cost is not also included in total operating cost or nonmedical cost. This should also include cost of pharmaceuticals, medical supplies and equipment sold to patients primarily for use outside the practice. Examples include prescription drugs, hearing aids, optical goods and orthopedic supplies. This should not include: (1) cost of drugs used in providing services, including vaccinations, allergy injections, immunizations, chemotherapy and antinausea drugs (such cost is included in "drug supply"); or (2) cost of supplies and instruments used in providing medical and surgical services (such cost is included in "medical and surgical supply").

current assets Cash and other assets expected to be converted to cash, sold or consumed in the normal course of operations within one year.

current liabilities This consists of: (1) payables such as liabilities that mature and require payment from current assets or through the creation of other liabilities within one year; (2) payroll liabilities such as amounts withheld from employees or otherwise accrued; and (3) other current liabilities such as accrued nonpayroll liabilities, advances from settlements due to third-party agencies, patient deposits, estimated contract claims payable (incurred but not reported claims), deferred revenue and deferred income taxes.

D **diagnostic radiology and imaging procedures** This consists of: (1) 70010–76499, diagnostic radiology; (2) 76506–76999, diagnostic ultrasound; (3) 78000–78999, diagnostic nuclear medicine; (4) all diagnostic radiology and imaging procedures conducted by laboratories outside of the practice's facilities as long as the practice pays the outside laboratory directly for the procedures and the procedures are only for the practice's fee-for-service patients; and (5) all procedures done either at the practice (where the practice bills at a global rate for both the technical and professional components) or procedures done at an outside facility (where the practice bills at a professional rate only). This should not include: (1) 77261–77799, radiation oncology; (2) 79000–79999, therapeutic nuclear medicine (radiation oncology and therapeutic nuclear medicine activity is included in "medical procedures" on line 111 or 112, depending on location code); or (3) purchased radiology services from external providers and facilities on behalf of the practice's capitation patients, for which costs are reported as "purchased services for capitation patients."

discrete data Unlike continuous data, discrete data cannot be divided or subdivided into equal-sized subunits (e.g., people are nondivisible entities and cannot be subdivided; if there is a group of 10 people, subdividing the group in half and then in half again would result in 2.5 people, and it is not possible to have 0.5 of a person). See *continuous data*.

drug supply cost Cost of drugs purchased for general practice use. This should also include cost of chemotherapy drugs, allergy drugs and vaccines used in providing medical and surgical services. This should not include: (1) cost of specialized supplies dedicated for exclusive use in the departments of clinical laboratory, radiology and imaging, or other ancillary services departments; or (2) cost of pharmaceuticals sold to patients primarily for use outside the practice and not used in providing medical and surgical services; for example, prescription drugs (such cost is included in "cost of sales and/or cost of other medical activities").

E **encounter** See *patient encounters*.

expense Resources consumed by the practice when generating revenue.

extraordinary nonmedical cost Cost unusual in nature and infrequent in occurrence. This should also include: (1) legal settlement cost; and (2) environmental disaster recovery cost.

extraordinary nonmedical revenue Revenue unusual in nature and infrequent in occurrence. This should also include: (1) legal settlement receipts; and (2) environmental disaster recovery funds.

F **faculty practice plan** Formal framework that structures the clinical practice activities of the medical school faculty. The plan performs a range of services, including billing, collections, contract negotiations and the distribution of income. Plans may form a separate legal organization or may be affiliated with the medical school through a clinical science department or teaching hospital. Faculty associated with the plan must provide patient care as part of a teaching or research program.

financial support for operating costs Operational support received from a parent organization such as a hospital, integrated delivery system or other entity. This should also include operating subsidies received from a hospital, health system, physician practice management company or management services organization.

freestanding ambulatory surgery center See *ambulatory surgery center;* a freestanding ambulatory surgery center does not employ physicians.

full-time-equivalent (FTE) physicians Primary care physicians, nonsurgical specialty physicians and surgical specialty physicians. A full-time physician works whatever number of hours the practice considers to be the minimum for a normal work week, which could be 37.5, 40, 50 hours or some other standard. To compute the FTE of a part-time physician, divide the total hours worked by the number of hours that your practice considers to be a normal work week. A physician working 30 hours compared to a normal work week of 40 hours would be 0.75 FTE (30 hours divided by 40 hours). A physician working full-time for three months during a year would be 0.25 FTE (3 months divided by 12 months). A medical director devoting 50 percent effort to clinical activity would be 0.5 FTE. A physician cannot be counted as more than 1.0 FTE regardless of the number of hours worked. This should also include: (1) practice physicians such as shareholders and partners, salaried associates, employed and contracted physicians and locum tenens; (2) residents and fellows working at the practice; and (3) only physicians involved in clinical care. This should not include full-time physician administrators or the time that a physician devotes to medical director activities. The FTE and cost for such activities should be included as "general administrative."

furniture and equipment cost Cost of furniture and equipment in general use in the practice. This should also include: (1) rental and/or depreciation cost of furniture and equipment used in reception areas, patient treatment and exam rooms, physician offices and administrative areas; and (2) other costs related to clinic furniture and equipment such as maintenance cost. This should not include cost of specialized furniture and equipment dedicated for exclusive use in the information technology, clinical laboratory, radiology and imaging, or other ancillary services departments.

G   **general accounting**   FTE and cost of general accounting office staff, such as department supervisor, controller and financial accounting manager; and accounts payable, payroll, bookkeeping and financial accounting input staff.

general administrative FTE and cost   FTE and cost of general administrative and practice management staff, supporting secretaries and administrative assistants. This should include FTE and cost of executive staff such as administrator, assistant administrator, chief financial officer, medical director and site and branch office managers; and human resources, marketing, credentialing and purchasing department staff. This should not include FTE and cost of directors of departments, such as information technology director, medical records director, laboratory director and radiology director. Credentialing staff as they pertain to managed care departments, such FTE and cost, should be accounted for as "managed care administrative."

general operating cost   This should not include costs: (1) for sales and/or other medical activities; (2) for support staff; (3) for nonphysician providers; (4) included in "purchased services for capitation patients"; and (5) for nonmedical.

goodwill amortization   When an integrated delivery system, hospital or physician practice management company purchases a medical practice, the purchase price can be thought of as having two components: (1) the value of the tangible assets; and (2) the value of the goodwill. Goodwill is the premium paid in excess of the value of the tangible assets and may be amortized over a period of time. The tangible assets are depreciated over a period of time. This should not include depreciation of tangible assets, such as the building or equipment. These depreciation costs are reported as a component of costs for information technology, building and occupancy, furniture and equipment, clinical laboratory, radiology and imaging, and other ancillary services.

government-owned practice   Ownership by a governmental organization at the federal, state or local level. Government funding is not a sufficient criterion for ownership. An example would be a medical clinic at a federal, state or county correctional facility.

gross capitation revenue Revenue received in a fixed per member payment, usually on a prospective and monthly basis, to pay for all covered goods and services due to capitation patients. This should include: (1) per member per month capitation payments including those received from an HMO, Medicare AAPCC (average annual per capita cost), the state for Medicaid beneficiaries and other medical groups; (2) portions of the capitation withholds returned to a practice as part of a risk-sharing arrangement; (3) bonuses and incentive payments paid to a practice for good capitation contract performance; (4) patient copayments or other direct payments made by capitation patients; (5) payments received due to a coordination of benefits and/or reinsurance recovery situation for capitation patients; and (6) payments made by other payers for care provided to capitation patients. This should not include payments paid to a practice by an HMO under the terms of a discounted fee-for-service managed care contract. Such payments should be included in "net fee-for-service collections/revenue."

gross charges for patients covered by capitation contracts Full value, at a practice's undiscounted rates, of all covered services provided to patients covered by all capitation contracts, regardless of payer (also known as fee-for-service equivalent gross charges). Includes fee-for-service equivalent gross charges for all services covered under the terms of the practice's capitation contracts, such as: (1) professional services provided by physicians, nonphysician providers and other physician extenders such as nurses and medical assistants; (2) both the professional and technical components of laboratory, radiology, medical diagnostic and surgical procedures; (3) drug charges, including vaccinations, allergy injections, immunizations, chemotherapy and antinausea drugs; (4) charges for supplies consumed during a patient encounter inside the practice's facilities (charges for supplies sold to patients for consumption outside the practice's facilities are reported as a subset of "revenue from the sale of medical goods and services"); and (5) facility fees, including for the operation of an ambulatory surgery unit or of a medical practice owned by a hospital where split billing for professional and facility services is utilized. This should not include: (1) pharmaceuticals, medical supplies and equipment sold to patients primarily for use outside the practice, including prescription drugs, hearing aids, optical goods and orthopedic supplies (if such goods are not covered under the capitation contract, the revenue from these charges is included in "revenue from the sale of medical goods and services"); (2) the value of purchased services from external providers and facilities on behalf of the practice's capitation patients (cost of these purchased services is included in "purchased services for capitation patients"); (3) charges for fee-for-service activity allowed under the terms of capitation contracts (such charges are reported as "gross fee-for-service charges"); or (4) capitation revenue (if capitation charges are not tracked, leave space blank).

gross fee-for-service charges Full value, at the practice's undiscounted rates, of all services provided to fee-for-service (FFS), discounted FFS and noncapitated patients for all payers. This should include: (1) professional services provided by physicians, nonphysician providers and other physician extenders such as nurses and medical assistants; (2) both the professional and technical components of laboratory, radiology, medical diagnostic and surgical procedures; (3) contractual adjustments such as Medicare charge restrictions, third-party payer contractual adjustments, charitable adjustments and professional courtesy adjustments; (4) drug charges, including vaccinations, allergy injections, immunizations, chemotherapy and antianusea drugs; (5) charges for supplies consumed during a patient encounter inside the practice's facilities and charges for supplies sold to patients for consumption outside the practice's facilities, reported as a subset of "revenue from the sale of medical goods and services"; (6) facility fees, including for the operation of an ambulatory surgery unit or of a medical practice owned by a hospital where split billing for professional and facility services is utilized; (7) charges for FFS allowed under the terms of capitation contracts; (8) charges for professional services provided on a case-rate reimbursement basis; and (9) charges for purchased services for FFS patients, defined as services that are purchased by the practice from external providers and facilities on behalf of the practice's FFS patients. For purchased services, note the following: (1) the revenue for such services should be included in "net fee-for-service collections revenue"; (2) the cost for such services should be included, as appropriate, in "clinical laboratory," "radiology and imaging," "other ancillary services" and/or "provider consultant cost"; and (3) the count of the number of purchased procedures for FFS patients should be included in "number of procedures." This should not include: (1) charges for services provided to capitation patients, which are included in "gross charges for patients covered by capitation contracts"; (2) charges for pharmaceuticals, medical supplies and equipment sold to patients primarily for use outside the practice, including prescription drugs, hearing aids, optical goods and orthopedic supplies (revenue generated by such charges is included in "revenue from the sale of medical goods and services"); or (3) charges for any other activities that generate the revenue reported in "revenue from the sale of medical goods and services."

gross revenue from other medical activities In general, this consists of revenue generated from ancillary services and indirect patient care activities. This should not include: (1) interest income, which is reported as "nonmedical revenue"; (2) income from practice nonmedical property such as parking areas or commercial real estate, which is reported as "nonmedical revenue"; (3) income from business ventures such as a billing service or parking lot, which is reported as "nonmedical revenue"; (4) onetime gains from the sale of equipment or property, which is reported as "nonmedical revenue"; and (5) cash received from loans.

gross square footage Total number of finished and occupied square feet within outside walls for all the facilities (both administrative and clinical) that comprise the practice, including hallways, closets, elevators and stairways. For anesthesia practices, any leased or rented administrative office space, regardless of whether inside or outside a hospital setting, should be included.

H **health maintenance organization (HMO)** Insurance company that accepts responsibility for providing and delivering a predetermined set of comprehensive health maintenance and treatment services to a voluntarily enrolled population for a negotiated and fixed periodic premium.

hospital Inpatient facility that admits patients for overnight stays, incurs nursing care costs and generates bed–day revenues.

housekeeping, maintenance, security This consists of FTE and cost of housekeeping, maintenance and security staff. This should not include: FTE and cost of parking attendants if parking generates revenue, which is reported as "nonmedical revenue." The cost of parking attendants should be included as "nonmedical cost."

I **incurred but not reported liability accounts (IBNR)** Special liability accounts used by medical practices with capitation contracts to keep track of amounts owed to providers outside the practice for services provided to the practice's capitated patients.

independent practice association (IPA) Association or network of licensed providers and/or medical practices. An IPA is usually a unique legal entity, most often operating on a for-profit basis. Typically, the primary purpose of the IPA is to secure and maintain contractual relationships between providers and health plans.

individual patient Person who received at least one service from the practice during the 12-month reporting period, regardless of the number of encounters or procedures received by that person. If a person was a patient two years ago but did not receive any services at all last year, that person would not be counted as a patient for last year. A patient is not the same as a covered life. The number of capitated patients, for example, could be less than the number of capitated covered lives if a subset of the covered lives did not utilize any services during the 12-month reporting period.

information technology cost Cost of practice-wide data processing, computer, telephone and telecommunications services. This should include: (1) cost of local and long-distance telephone, radio paging and answering services; (2) rental and/or depreciation cost of major data processing, computer and telecommunications furniture, equipment, hardware and software subject to capitalization; (3) hardware and software repair and maintenance contract cost; (4) cost of data-processing services purchased from an outside service bureau; and (5) cost of data-processing supplies and minor software and equipment not subject to capitalization. This should not include cost of specialized information services equipment dedicated for exclusive use in the departments of clinical laboratory, radiology and imaging, or other ancillary services departments.

information technology FTE FTE staff such as data processing, computer programming, telecommunications and department director or manager.

in-house professional procedures Medical, surgery and anesthesia procedures conducted inside the practice's facilities.

in-house professional gross charges Medical, surgery and anesthesia gross charges conducted inside the practice's facilities.

intangibles and other assets Organization costs (legal, accounting and fees), goodwill and deposits.

integrated delivery system (IDS) Network of organizations that provide or coordinate and arrange for the provision of a continuum of health care services to consumers and are willing to be held clinically and fiscally responsible for the outcomes and the health status of the populations served. Generally consists of hospitals, physician groups, health plans, home health agencies, hospices, skilled nursing facilities or other provider entities; these networks may be built through "virtual" integration processes encompassing contractual arrangements and strategic alliances as well as through direct ownership.

insurance company Organization that indemnifies an insured party against a specified loss in return for premiums paid, as stipulated by a contract.

investments and long-term receivables Investments meant for purposes that do not include supporting current operations (e.g., long-term receivables, long-term investments, investments in affiliates, and property held for future use).

K **kurtosis** Measures the "peakedness" of a data distribution. If the kurtosis is clearly different than zero, then the distribution is either flatter or more peaked than normal; the kurtosis of a normal distribution is zero. Kurtosis values above zero (positive) indicate a distribution that is too peaked, with short, thick tails, whereas values less than zero (negative) indicate a distribution that is too flat, with too many data points in the tails.

L **levels of measurement** Categories of numerical values related to the aspects of the objects, items or events they represent (also known as scales of measurement); the levels of measurement are nominal, ordinal (categorical), interval and ratio.

licensed practical nurses This consists of FTE and cost of licensed practical nurses functioning in clinical/direct patient care capacities. This should not include: FTE and cost of licensed practical nurses who worked exclusively in the departments of clinical laboratory, radiology and imaging, or other ancillary departments.

limited liability company (LLC) Legal entity that is a hybrid between a corporation and a partnership, because it provides limited liability to owners such as a corporation while passing profits and losses through to owners such as a partnership.

locum tenens Temporary employees who typically consist of temporary providers and physicians hired specifically as employees for a specific period of time (for example, gap fill).

M **managed care** System in which the provider of care is given incentives to establish mechanisms to contain costs, control utilization and deliver services in the most appropriate settings. There are three key factors: (1) controlling the utilization of medical services; (2) shifting financial risk to the provider; and (3) reducing the use of resources in rendering treatments to patients.

managed care administrative FTE and cost of managed care administrative staff, such as supporting secretaries and administrative assistants. This should include health maintenance organization and preferred provider organization contract administrators; case management staff; actuaries; managed care medical directors; and managed care marketing, quality assurance, referral coordinators, utilization review and credentialing staff.

management fees paid to a management services organization (MSO) or physician practice management company (PPMC) Fees paid for management or other services from an MSO, PPMC, hospital or other parent organization. The fee could be a contracted fixed amount, a percentage of collections or any other mutually agreed-upon arrangement. This should include: (1) fees paid to an MSO/PPMC, hospital or parent organization for management services, including management, administrative and/or related support services; and (2) the cost of support staff employed by the MSO or PPMC. If FTE data for the MSO or PPMC support staff is accurate and easily obtainable, it is preferable to report the MSO/PPMC support staff FTE and cost. If the FTE counts are not known, it is suggested that the support staff cost be treated as a purchased service and be reported. This should not include the cost of support staff employed by the MSO or PPMC.

management services organization (MSO) Entity organized to provide various forms of practice management and administrative support services to health care providers. These services may include centralized billing and collections services, management information services and other components of the managed care infrastructure. MSOs, which do not actually deliver health care services, may be jointly or solely owned and sponsored by physicians, hospitals or other parties. Some MSOs also purchase assets of affiliated physicians and enter into long-term management service arrangements with a provider network. Some expand their ownership base by involving outside investors to help capitalize the development of such practice infrastructure.

mean See *average.*

median Data point in the true center of the dataset.

Medicaid — capitation Fee-for-service equivalent gross charges, at the practice's undiscounted rates, for all services provided to Medicaid or similar state health care program patients under a capitated contract. This should not include: (1) charges for fee-for-service patients; or (2) charges for patients covered under discounted fee-for-service contract arrangements.

Medicaid — fee-for-service Fee-for-service (FFS) gross charges, at the practice's established undiscounted rates, for all services provided to Medicaid or similar state health care program patients on a FFS basis. This should not include: (1) FFS equivalent gross charges for services provided to Medicaid or other state health care program patients under capitated, prepaid or other "at-risk" arrangements; (2) charges for patients covered under discounted FFS contract arrangements.

Medicaid — managed care fee-for-service Fee-for-service (FFS) gross charges, at the practice's established undiscounted rates, for all services provided to Medicaid or similar state health care program patients under a managed care plan. If patients are covered by both Medicare and Medicaid or a similar state health care plan on an FFS basis, all charges for such patients should be included as Medicare FFS charges. This should also include charges for patients covered under discounted FFS contract arrangements. This should not include: (1) charges for FFS patients; or (2) FFS equivalent gross charges for services provided to patients under capitated, prepaid arrangements.

medical assistants and nurse's aides FTE and cost of medical assistants and nurse's aides. This should not include FTE and cost of medical assistants and nurse's aides who worked exclusively in the departments of clinical laboratory, radiology and imaging, or other ancillary departments.

medical procedures conducted inside the practice's facilities This consists of evaluation and management (E&M) services and Current Procedural Terminology (CPT) (given an appropriate location code: (1) 99201–99215, office or other outpatient services; (2) 99241–99245, office or other outpatient consultations; (3) 99271–99275, confirmatory consultations; (4) 99354–99360, prolonged and standby services; (5) 99361–99373, case management services; (6) 99374–99380, care plan oversight services; (7) 99381–99429, preventive medicine services; (8) 99431–99432, newborn care; (9) 99450–99375, special evaluation and management services, radiology services (given an appropriate location code); (10) 77261–77799, radiation oncology; (11) 79000–79999, therapeutic nuclear medicine, medicine services (given an appropriate location code); and (12) 90281–99090; and (13) 99170–99199. This should not include: (1) 10021–69990, surgery procedures, which are reported as "surgery and anesthesia procedures"; (2) 70010–76499, diagnostic radiology, which are reported as "diagnostic radiology and imaging procedures"; (3) 76506–76999, diagnostic ultrasound; (4) 78000–78999, diagnostic nuclear medicine; and (5) 80048–89399, clinical laboratory and pathology, which are reported as "clinical laboratory and pathology procedures."

medical procedures conducted outside the practice's facilities This consists of: (1) 99217–99220, hospital observation services; (2) 99221–99239, hospital inpatient services; (3) 99251–99255, initial inpatient consultations; (4) 99261–99263, follow-up inpatient consultations; (5) 99281–99290, emergency services; (6) 99291–99292, critical care services; (7) 99293–99294, pediatric critical care services; (8) 99295–99299, neonatal intensive care services; (9) 99301–99316, nursing facility services; (10) 99321–99333, custodial care services; (11) 99354–99360, prolonged services; (12) 99341–99350, home services; (13) 99431–99440, newborn care; and (14) 99500–99602, home health services.

medical receptionists FTE and cost of medical receptionist staff such as switchboard operators, schedulers and appointment staff. This should not include FTE and cost of medical receptionists who worked exclusively in the departments of clinical laboratory, radiology and imaging, or other ancillary departments.

medical records FTE and cost of medical records staff such as medical records clerks and department director or manager. This should not include FTE and cost of medical records and coding staff who worked exclusively in the departments of clinical laboratory, radiology and imaging, or other ancillary departments.

medical school Institution that trains physicians and awards medical and osteopathic degrees.

medical secretaries and transcribers This consists of FTE and cost of medical secretaries and transcribers. This should not include: FTE and cost of medical secretaries and transcribers who worked exclusively in the departments of clinical laboratory, radiology and imaging, or other ancillary departments.

medical and surgical supply cost Cost of supplies purchased for general practice use. This should include: (1) cost of medical and surgical supplies and instruments used in providing medical and surgical services; and (2) cost of laundry and linens. This should not include: (1) cost of specialized supplies dedicated for exclusive use in the departments of clinical laboratory, radiology and imaging, or other ancillary services departments; (2) cost of pharmaceuticals, medical supplies and equipment sold to patients primarily for use outside the practice and not used in providing medical or surgical services; for example, prescription drugs, hearing aids, optical goods and orthopedic supplies (such cost is included in "cost of sales and/or cost of other medical activities)"; or (3) the cost of any equipment subject to depreciation.

Medicare — capitation Fee-for-service (FFS) equivalent gross charges, at the practice's undiscounted rates, for all services provided to patients under Medicare/TEFRA (Tax Equity and Fiscal Responsibility Act), received from a capitated contract. This should not include: (1) charges for FFS patients; or (2) charges for patients covered under discounted FFS contract arrangements.

Medicare — fee-for-service Fee-for-service (FFS) gross charges, at the practice's established undiscounted rates, for all services provided to Medicare patients on an FFS basis. If patients are covered by both Medicare and Medicaid or a similar state health care plan, all charges for such patients should be included as Medicare FFS charges. This should not include: (1) FFS equivalent gross charges for services provided to Medicare/TEFRA (Tax Equity and Fiscal Responsibility Act) patients under capitated, prepaid or other "at-risk" arrangements; or (2) charges for patients covered under discounted FFS contract arrangements.

Medicare — managed care fee-for-service Fee-for-service (FFS) gross charges, at the practice's established undiscounted rates, for all services provided to Medicare patients through a managed care plan. If patients are covered by both Medicare and Medicaid or a similar state health care plan on an FFS basis, all charges for such patients should be included as Medicare FFS charges. This should include charges for patients covered under discounted FFS contract arrangements. This should not include FFS equivalent gross charges for services provided to Medicare/TEFRA

(Tax Equity and Fiscal Responsibility Act) patients under capitated, prepaid arrangements.

Military Health System (MHS) Health care system of the U.S. Department of Defense consisting of medical services from the Army, Navy and Air Force. The system consists of a multibillion dollar budget; millions of beneficiaries; outpatient and inpatient services covering the entire continuum of health care services; and large number of medical centers, hospitals and clinics. The Coast Guard is not part of the MHS because it is part of the Department of Homeland Defense.

miscellaneous operating cost Operating cost not stated in other operating cost categories, such as charitable contributions; employee relations dinners and picnics; entertainment; uniforms; business transportation; interest on loans; health, business and property taxes; recruiting cost; job position classified advertising; moving cost; and payouts to retired physicians from accounts receivable. This should not include: (1) federal or state income taxes, which are included in "nonmedical cost"; or (2) principal paid on loans.

mode Value that occurs most frequently in the dataset.

multispecialty with primary and specialty care Medical practice that consists of physicians practicing in different specialties, including at least one of the following primary care specialties: family practice — general with or without obstetrics, sports medicine, urgent care; geriatrics; internal medicine — general and urgent care; and pediatrics — adolescent medicine, general and sports medicine.

multispecialty with primary care only Medical practice that consists of physicians practicing in more than one of the primary care specialties listed in multispecialty with primary and specialty care or the surgical specialties of obstetrics/gynecology, gynecology (only) or obstetrics (only).

multispecialty with specialty care only Medical practice that consists of physicians practicing in different specialties, none of which are the following primary care specialties: family practice — general, sports medicine, urgent care, and with or without obstetrics; geriatrics; internal medicine — general and urgent care; and pediatrics — adolescent medicine, general or sports medicine.

N   **net collections** Revenue received from all payers.

net fee-for-service charges See *gross fee-for-service charges*.

net fee-for-service collections and revenue Revenue collected from patients and third-party payers for services provided to fee-for-service (FFS), discounted FFS and noncapitated Medicare and Medicaid patients. This is the revenue remaining after patient refunds and checks returned to patients. If the practice used accrual basis accounting, "net fee-for-service collections and revenue" should equal "gross fee-for-service charges" minus "adjustments to fee-for-service charges" minus "bad debts due to fee-for-service activity." This should also include: (1) portions of the withholds returned to a practice as part of a risk-sharing arrangement; (2) bonuses and incentive payments paid to a practice for good performance; (3) patient copayments; (4) payments received due to a coordination of benefits and/or reinsurance recovery situation; and (5) revenue due to purchased services (i.e., purchased by the practice from external providers and facilities on behalf of the practice's patients) for FFS patients.

noncurrent and all other assets This should include: (1) investments and long-term receivables such as long-term investments in securities, restricted cash, property not used for operations and receivables due beyond one year (assets recorded in these accounts are not used to finance operations); (2) noncurrent tangible assets such as long-lived tangible assets used in practice operations (assets recorded in these accounts generally have a useful life in excess of one year); and (3) intangible and other assets such as cost of property rights without physical substance that benefits future operations (such assets are purchased from external sources, provide future benefit and are relatively long lived). Other assets include long-term prepayments, deferred charges and assets not included in other categories.

noncurrent and all other liabilities Long-term liabilities that mature and require payment at some time beyond one year.

nonmedical cost This should include: (1) income taxes based on net profit that is paid to federal, state or local government (for cash basis accounting, income taxes equal the cash payment or refund for the tax year paid or received in following tax year plus periodic withholding paid; for accrual accounting, the income tax equals the total tax liability regardless of when the tax was paid or refunds were received); (2) all costs required to maintain the productivity of income-producing rental property and parking lots; (3) losses on the sale of real estate or equipment, and from the sale of marketable securities; (4) other nonmedical cost; (5) all direct costs related to business ventures such as rental property, parking lots or billing services, for which gross revenue is reported as "nonmedical revenue," as long as these costs are not also included in "total operating cost"; and (6) state taxes on medical revenue.

nonmedical revenue This should include: (1) interest and investment revenue such as interest, dividends and/or capital gains earned on savings accounts, certificates of deposit, securities, stocks, bonds and other short-term or long-term investments; (2) gross rental revenue such as rent or lease income earned from practice-owned property not used in practice operations; (3) capital gains on the sale of practice real estate or equipment; (4) interest paid by insurance companies for failure to pay claims on time; (5) bounced check charges paid by patients; and (6) gross revenue from business ventures such as a billing service or parking lot (the direct costs of such ventures should be reported as "nonmedical cost"). This should not include cash received from loans.

nonphysician provider benefit cost This should include: (1) employer's share of FICA, payroll and unemployment insurance taxes; (2) employer's share of health, disability, life and workers' compensation insurance; (3) employer payments to defined benefit and contribution, 401(k), 403(b) and nonqualified retirement plans; (4) deferred compensation paid or expensed during the year; (5) dues and memberships in professional organizations and state and local license fees; (6) allowances for education, professional meetings, travel and automobile; and (7) entertainment, country and athletic club membership, and travel for spouse. This should not include: (1) voluntary employee salary deductions used as contributions to 401(k) and 403(b) plans; and (2) expense reimbursements.

nonphysician provider compensation Nonphysician providers are specially trained and licensed providers who can provide medical care and billable services. Examples of nonphysician providers include audiologists, certified registered nurse anesthetists, dieticians and nutritionists, midwives, nurse practitioners, occupational therapists, optometrists, physical therapists, physician assistants, psychologists, social workers, speech therapists and surgeon's assistants. This should include the total compensation paid to nonphysician providers who comprise the count of "total nonphysician provider" cost column. This should also include: (1) compensation for both employed and contracted nonphysician providers; (2) compensation for full-time and part-time nonphysician providers; (3) salaries, bonuses, incentive payments, research contract revenue, honoraria and profit distributions; and (4) voluntary employee salary deductions used as contributions to 401(k), 403(b) or Section 125 plans. Do not include: (1) amounts included in "nonphysician provider benefit cost"; or (2) expense reimbursements.

nonprocedural gross charges This should include: (1) facility fee charges for the operation of an ambulatory surgery unit; (2) facility fee charges in a hospital-affiliated practice that utilizes a split billing system where both facility fees and professional charges are billed; (3) charges for drugs and medications administered inside the practice's facilities, such as chemotherapy drugs; and (4) charges for HCPCS A, J, R and V codes. This should not include charges for the sale of medical goods and services.

normal distribution Also known as a Poisson distribution, a normal curve or a bell-shaped curve.

not-for-profit corporation or foundation Organization that has obtained special exemption under Section 501c of the Internal Revenue Service code that qualifies the organization to be exempt from federal income taxes. To qualify as a tax-exempt organization, a practice or faculty practice plan would have to provide evidence of a charitable, educational or research purpose.

0 **objective** Measurement not affected by the person taking the measurement. No emotional or personal interpretations affect the result; in general, the more objective a measurement, the more reliable.

operating expenses Expense generated by the practice when engaged in medical revenue-producing activities.

other administrative support FTE and cost of other administrative staff such as shipping and receiving, cafeteria, mailroom and laundry staff.

other ancillary services Operating costs for all ancillary services departments except clinical laboratory and radiology and imaging. This should include: (1) operating costs for departments such as physical therapy, optical, ambulatory surgery, radiation oncology and therapeutic nuclear medicine; (2) rental and/or depreciation cost of major furniture and equipment subject to capitalization; (3) repair and maintenance cost; (4) cost of supplies and minor equipment not subject to capitalization; (5) other costs unique to the ancillary services departments; and (6) cost of purchased "other ancillary" technical services for fee-for-service patients. This should not include: (1) cost of purchased "other ancillary" technical services for capitation patients, which should be reported as "purchased services for capitation patients"; (2) cost of physical therapy and orthopedic items such as crutches and braces sold to patients, which should be included in "cost of sales and/or cost of other medical activities"; or (3) cost of optical items such as eyeglasses and contact lenses sold to patients, which is included in "cost of sales and/or cost of other medical activities."

other federal government payers Fee-for-service gross charges, at the practice's undiscounted rates, for all services provided to patients who are covered by other federal government payers other than Medicare. This should include charges for TRICARE patients. This should not include charges for Medicare and Medicaid patients.

other insurance premiums Cost of other policies such as fire, flood, theft, casualty, general liability, officers' and directors' liability, and reinsurance.

other medical revenue Grants, honoraria, research contract revenues, government support payments and educational subsidies. This should include: (1) federal, state, or local government or private foundation grants to provide indigent patient care or for case management of the frail and elderly; (2) honoraria income for practice participation in educational programs; (3) research contract revenues for activities such as pharmaceutical studies; and (4) educational subsidies used to train residents. This should not include: (1) charges for the delivery of services made possible by subsidies or grants (such charges are included in "gross fee-for-service charges" and/or "gross charges for patients covered by capitation contracts"); or (2) the value of operating subsidies from parent organizations such as hospitals or integrated systems (such subsidies should be included in "financial support for operating costs").

other medical support services FTE and cost of support staff in any ancillary services department other than clinical laboratory and radiology and imaging. This should include: (1) FTE and cost of support staff who provide assistance to patients such as patient relations staff or lay counselors; (2) FTE and cost of support staff such as nurses, secretaries, technicians, physical therapy aides and assistants in ancillary services departments such as physical therapy, optical, ambulatory surgery, radiation oncology, therapeutic nuclear medicine, clinical research, pharmacists and pharmacy support staff; and (3) FTE and cost of the department directors and managers in these ancillary services departments. This should not include nonphysician providers such as nurse practitioners, physician's assistants and physical therapists.

output measures When calculating procedure counts and gross charges for practice activities, it is necessary to identify whether the activity occurred inside or outside the practice's facilities. This inside/outside distinction enables the proper assignment of operating costs to develop cost per unit output statistics. The Centers for Medicare and Medicaid Services' "place of service" codes are used to make this inside/outside distinction. While one place-of-service code, the "office" code (11), indicates activity inside the practice's facilities, all other place-of-service codes are for activities occurring outside the practice's facilities. Examples of "outside" locations are the patient's home, inpatient or outpatient hospital, psychiatric or rehabilitation facility, emergency room, freestanding ambulatory surgery center, birthing center, skilled nursing or custodial care facility, hospice, ambulance, independent laboratory, radiology and imaging center, and ambulatory emergency center. This should include: (1) procedures performed by all practice physicians, nonphysician providers and other health care professionals such as nurses, medical assistants and technicians; and (2) purchased procedures from external providers and facilities on behalf of the practice's fee-for-service patients for which revenue is reported as a subset of "net fee-for-service collections/ revenue" and for which costs are reported as a subset of "clinical laboratory," "radiology and imaging," "other ancillary services" and/or "provider consultant cost." This should not include purchased procedures from external providers and facilities on behalf of the practice's capitation patients, for which costs are reported as "purchased services for capitation patients."

outside professional fees Fees for professional services performed on a one-time or sporadic basis. This should include: (1) fees for legal and accounting services; and (2) fees for management, financial and actuarial consultants. This should not include: (1) information services, architectural and public relations consultant fees (such costs are included in "information technology," "building and occupancy" and "promotion and marketing"); and (2) cost for contracted support staff, which is reported as "total contracted support staff."

P   **partnership** An unincorporated organization where two or more individuals have agreed to share profits, losses, assets and liabilities, although not necessarily on an equal basis. The partnership agreement may or may not be formalized in writing.

patient accounting FTE and cost of patient accounting (billing and collections) staff such as department supervisor, billing/accounts receivable manager, coding, charge entry, insurance, billing, collections, payment posting, refund, adjustment and cashiering staff.

patient encounters Documented, face-to-face contact between a patient and a provider who exercises independent judgment in the provision of services to the individual. If a patient with the same diagnosis sees two different providers on the same day, it is one encounter. If a patient sees two different providers on the same day for two different diagnoses, then it is considered two encounters. The total number of patient encounters should include only procedures from the evaluation and management chapter (CPT codes 99201–99375) or the medicine chapter (CPT codes 90800–99199) of the Physicians' Current Procedural Terminology (4th edition, copyrighted by the American Medical Association). This should include: (1) pre- and postoperative visits and other visits associated with a global charge; (2) for diagnostic radiologists, the total number of procedures or reads; (3) for obstetric care, if a single CPT-4 code is used for a global service, each ambulatory contact, such as a prenatal and postnatal visit, is a separate ambulatory encounter, whereas the delivery is a single surgical case; (4) administration of chemotherapy drugs; (5) administration of immunizations; (6) ambulatory encounters attributed to nonphysician providers; and (7) visits where there is no identifiable contact between a patient and a physician or nonphysician provider (for example, a patient comes into the practice solely for an injection, vein puncture, EKG, EEG, etc., administered by an RN or technician). This should not include: (1) encounters for the physician specialties of pathology or diagnostic radiology; (2) encounters that include procedures from surgery (CPT codes 10040–69979) or anesthesia (CPT codes 00100–01999); or

(3) number of procedures, because a single encounter can generate multiple procedures.

percentile Provides indication of the relative position with respect to other data points and is simply a value indicating the percent of values less than or equal to the percentile.

physician Any doctor of medicine (MD) or doctor of osteopathy (DO) who is duly licensed and qualified under the law of jurisdiction in which treatment is received.

physician practice management company (PPMC) Usually a publicly held or entrepreneurial directed enterprise that acquires total or partial ownership interests in physician organizations. PPMC is a type of management services organization (MSO), although the motivations, goals, strategies and structures arising from its unequivocal ownership character — development of growth and profits for its investors rather than for the participating providers — differentiate it from other MSO models.

physician work relative value units (RVUs) This should include: (1) RVUs for the "physician work RVUs" only; (2) physician work RVUs for all professional medical and surgical services performed by physicians, nonphysician providers and other physician extenders, such as nurses and medical assistants; (3) physician work RVUs for the professional component of laboratory, radiology, medical diagnostic and surgical procedures; (4) physician work RVUs for all procedures performed by the medical practice (for procedures with either no listed CPT code or with an RVU value of zero, RVUs can be estimated by dividing the total gross charges for the unlisted or unvalued procedures by the practice's known average charge per RVU for all procedures that are listed and valued); (5) physician work RVUs for procedures for both fee-for-service and capitation patients; (6) physician work RVUs for all payers, not just Medicare; and (7) physician work RVUs for purchased procedures from external providers on behalf of the practice's fee-for-service patients. This should not include: (1) RVUs for "malpractice RVUs" or "nonfacility practice expense RVUs"; (2) RVUs for the technical components of laboratory, radiology, medical diagnostic and surgical procedures; (3) RVUs for other scales, such as McGraw-Hill and California; (4) RVUs for purchased procedures from external providers on behalf of the practice's capitation patients; (5) RVUs that have been weighted by a conversion factor (do not weigh the RVUs by a conversion factor); and (6) RVUs where the geographic practice cost index (GPCI) equals any value other than 1 (GPCI must be set to 1.000 [neutral]).

population designation: nonmetropolitan (less than 50,000) The community in which the practice is located is generally referred to as "rural." It is located outside of a "metropolitan statistical area" (MSA), as defined by the U.S. Office of Management and Budget, and has a population less than 50,000.

population designation: metropolitan (50,000 to 250,000) The community in which the practice is located is an MSA or Census Bureau–defined urbanized area with a population of 50,000 to 250,000.

population designation: metropolitan (250,001 to 1,000,000) The community in which the practice is located is an MSA or Census Bureau–defined urbanized area with a population of 250,001 to 1,000,000.

population designation: metropolitan (more than 1,000,000) The community in which the practice is located is a "primary metropolitan statistical area" (PMSA) with a population more than 1,000,000.

practice affiliated with a medical school This consists of clinicians from the medical group practice who hold nontenured appointments as medical school faculty and/or are part of a health system that is associated with a medical school that grants a doctor of medicine degree; or practices that have a legal standing with a medical school, faculty practice plan or clinical science department. Practices that provide residency rotations but do not meet these criteria should not be considered affiliated with a medical school.

primary clinic location This consists of clinic with the most FTE physicians of all the practice branches.

professional corporation or association This consists of for-profit organization recognized by law as a business entity separate and distinct from its shareholders. Shareholders must be licensed in the profession practiced by the organization.

professional gross charges This consists of medical, surgery and anesthesia gross charges for procedures conducted inside the practice's facilities and medical, surgery and anesthesia gross charges conducted outside the practice's facilities

professional liability insurance premiums This consists of premiums paid or self-insurance cost for malpractice and professional liability insurance for practice physicians, nonphysician providers and employees.

professional procedures This consists of medical, surgery and anesthesia procedures conducted inside the practice's facilities and medical, surgery and anesthesia procedures conducted outside the practice's facilities.

promotion and marketing This consists of cost of promotion, advertising and marketing activities, including patient newsletters, information booklets, fliers, brochures, Yellow Page listings and public relations consultants.

property, furniture, fixtures and equipment This consists of tangible, long-lived assets used in practice operations (for example, land, land improvements, buildings, furniture, fixtures, equipment and capital leases).

provider consultant cost This consists of fee-for-service fees paid to consulting pathologists, radiologists and other consulting physicians and/or nonphysician providers who are not included in the count of "total physician" or the count of "total nonphysician provider." This should not include: costs for purchased physician and/or nonphysician provider consultation services for capitation patients. Such costs are included in "purchased services for capitation patients."

purchased services for capitation patients Fees paid to health care providers and organizations external to the practice for services provided to capitation patients under the terms of capitation contracts. This should include: (1) payments to providers outside the practice for physician professional, nonphysician professional, clinical laboratory, radiology and imaging, hospital inpatient and emergency, ambulance, out-of-area emergency and pharmacy services; and (2) accrued expenses for "incurred but not reported" claims for purchased services for capitation patients for which invoices have not been received.

Q **quartile** Provides indication of the relative position with respect to the other data points (similar to percentile) and is simply the 25th (25 percent), 50th (50 percent or median), or 75th (75 percent) percentiles.

R **radiology and imaging cost** Cost of diagnostic radiology and imaging procedures defined by diagnostic radiology CPT codes 70010–76499, diagnostic ultrasound CPT codes 76506–76999, diagnostic nuclear medicine CPT codes 78000–78999, echocardiography CPT codes 93303–93350, noninvasive vascular diagnostic studies CPT codes 93825–93990, and electrocardiograph CPT codes 93300–93350. This should also include: (1) rental and/or depreciation cost of major furniture and equipment subject to capitalization; (2) repair and maintenance contract cost; (3) cost of radiological diagnostics (isotopes); (4) cost of supplies and minor equipment not subject to capitalization (this amount is the net after subtracting the revenue from silver recovery from X-ray film and processing fixer); (5) other costs unique to the radiology and imaging department; and (6) cost of purchased radiology technical services for fee-for-service patients. This should not include: (1) cost of purchased radiology technical services for capitation patients, which should be reported as "purchased services for capitation patients"; or (2) cost of procedures for radiation oncology CPT codes 77261–77799 or therapeutic nuclear medicine CPT codes 79000–79999, which are included in "other ancillary services."

radiology and imaging FTE Film library staff and the diagnostic radiology and imaging department that conducts procedures for diagnostic radiology CPT codes 70010–76499, diagnostic ultrasound CPT codes 76506–76999, diagnostic nuclear medicine CPT codes 78000–78999, echocardiography CPT codes 93303–93350, noninvasive vascular diagnostic studies CPT codes 93875–93990, and electrocardiograph CPT codes 93000–93350. This should also include: (1) FTE and cost of support staff such as nurses, secretaries and technicians; and (2) FTE and cost of department director or manager. This should not include FTE and staff cost for radiation oncology CPT codes 77261–77799 or therapeutic nuclear medicine CPT codes 79000–79999, which are included as "other medical support services."

registered nurses This consists of FTE and cost of registered nurse staff and registered nurses working as frontline managers or lead nurses. This should not include: (1) FTE and cost of nonphysician providers such as nurse practitioners, certified registered nurse anesthetists or nurse midwives; or (2) FTE and cost of registered nurses who worked exclusively in the departments of clinical laboratory, radiology and imaging, or other ancillary departments.

relative value unit (RVU) Nonmonetary standard unit of measure that indicates the value of services provided by physicians, nonphysician providers and other health care professionals. RVUs are associated with procedural codes performed by medical providers and are used for reimbursement purposes. RVU tables (procedural codes and their associated RVU weight) are published by the Centers for Medicare and Medicaid on a calendar year basis. RVUs consist of three components: (1) physician work (includes physician time, mental effort, technical skill, judgment, stress and amortization of the physician's education); (2) practice expense (direct expenses such as supplies, nonphysician labor, equipment expenses and indirect expenses); and (3) malpractice expense. RVUs do not include a component for clinical outcomes, quality or severity.

relative weighted product (RWP) Similar to relative value unit and used by the Military Health System for inpatient services.

reliability Consistency across repeated measures.

resource based relative value scale (RBRVS) This consists of total and physician work relative value units (RVUs) and/or American Society of Anesthesiologists (ASA) units. Report the RVUs, as measured by the RBRVS, not weighted by a conversion factor, attributed to all professional services. The RVU system is explained in detail in the Nov. 7, 2003, *Federal Register*, pages 63,261–63,386. Total RVUs for a given procedure consist of three components: (1) physician work RVUs; (2) practice expense (PE) RVUs; and (3) malpractice RVUs. Thus, total RVUs = physician work

RVUs + PE RVUs + malpractice RVUs. There are two different types of PE RVUs: (1) fully implemented nonfacility PE RVUs; and (2) fully implemented facility PE RVUs. "Nonfacility" refers to RVUs associated with a medical practice that is not affiliated with a hospital and does not utilize a split billing system that itemizes facility (hospital) charges and professional charges. "Nonfacility" also applies to services performed in settings other than a hospital, skilled nursing facility or ambulatory surgery center. "Facility" refers to RVUs associated with a hospital-affiliated medical practice that utilizes a split billing fee schedule where facility (hospital) charges and professional charges are billed separately. "Facility" also refers to services performed in a hospital, skilled nursing facility or ambulatory surgery center. This should not include total RVUs that are a function of "facility" practice expense RVUs. To summarize, there are two different types of total RVUs: (1) fully implemented nonfacility total RVUs; and (2) fully implemented facility total RVUs. If you are a hospital affiliated medical practice that utilizes a split billing fee schedule, total RVUs should be calculated as if you were a medical practice not affiliated with a hospital.

revenue Income generated from the delivery of products and services.

revenue from the sale of medical goods and services This consists of: (1) revenue from pharmaceuticals, medical supplies and equipment sold to patients primarily for use outside the practice, including prescription drugs, hearing aids, optical goods and orthopedic supplies (this amount should be net of write-offs and discounts); (2) compensation paid by a hospital to a practice physician for services as a medical director; (3) hourly wages of physicians working in a hospital emergency room; (4) contract revenue from a hospital for physician services in staffing a hospital indigent care clinic or emergency room; (5) contract revenue from a school district for physician services in conducting physical exams for high school athletes; (6) revenue from the preparation of court depositions, expert testimony, postmortem reports and other special reports; and (7) fees received from patients for the photocopying of patient medical records. This should not include capitation revenue used to pay for covered goods and services for capitation patients (such revenue is included in "gross capitation revenue").

S   **self-pay** Fee-for-service gross charges, at the practice's undiscounted rates, for all services provided to patients who pay the medical practice directly. Note that these patients may or may not have insurance. This should include: (1) charges for patients who have no insurance but have the resources to pay for their own care and do so; and (2) charges for patients who have insurance but choose to pay for their own care and submit claims to their insurance company directly. Because the practice may or may not be aware of this situation, all charges paid directly by the patient should be considered as self-pay.

single specialty Medical practice that focuses its clinical work in one specialty. The determining factor for classifying the type of specialty is the focus of clinical work and not necessarily the specialties of the physicians in the practice. For example, a single specialty neurosurgery practice may include a neurologist and a radiologist. Practices that include only the subspecialties of internal medicine should be classified as a single specialty internal medicine practice. Internal medicine subspecialties include: allergy and immunology; cardiology; endocrinology/metabolism; gastroenterology; hematology/oncology; infectious disease; nephrology; pulmonary disease; and rheumatology.

skew Skewness measures the deviation of the distribution from symmetry. If the skewness is clearly different from zero, then that distribution is asymmetrical, while normal distributions are perfectly symmetrical. If skewness is greater than zero (positive), then a large number of data points are to the right and the left tail is too long. If skewness is less than zero (negative), then a large number of data points are to the left and the right tail is too long.

sole proprietorship Organization with a single owner who is responsible for all profit, losses, assets and liabilities.

standard deviation Measure of variation or dispersion, which represents the spread of the data around the mean.

subjective Measurement affected by the person taking the measurement. Emotional or personal interpretations affects the result; in general, the more subjective a measurement, the less reliable.

support staffing This consists of: (1) FTE for all support staff employed by all the legal entities working in support of the medical practice; (2) FTE for both full-time and part-time support staff. (To compute FTE, add the number of full-time [1.0 FTE] support staff to the FTE count for the part-time support staff. A full-time support staff employee works whatever number of hours the practice considers to be the minimum for a normal work week, which could be 37.5, 40, 50 hours or some other standard. To compute the FTE of a part-time support staff employee, divide the total hours worked in an average week by the number of hours that your practice considers to be a normal work week. An employee working 30 hours compared to a normal work week of 40 hours would be 0.75 FTE [30 divided by 40 hours]. An employee working full-time for three months during a year would be 0.25 FTE [3 divided by 12 months]. A support staff employee cannot be counted as more than 1.0 FTE regardless of the number of hours worked.); and (3) the allocated FTE where the practice consists of multiple legal entities. (For example, a management services organization managing two medical practices and employing one billing clerk who devotes an equal amount of time to each practice would add 0.5 FTE to the total FTE count in "patient accounting" for each managed practice. This should not include the FTE of contracted support staff, which should be reported as "total contracted support staff.")

support staff cost This consists of: (1) salaries, bonuses, incentive payments, honoraria and profit distributions; (2) voluntary employee salary deductions used as contributions to 401(k), 403(b) or Section 125 plans; (3) compensation paid to the total FTE count; (4) compensation for all support staff employed by all of the legal entities working in support of the medical practice; (5) the allocated support staff cost where the practice consists of multiple legal entities (for example, a management services organization managing two medical practices and employing one billing clerk who devotes an equal amount of time to each practice would add 50 percent of the one billing clerk's compensation to the total cost of "patient accounting" for each managed practice); and (6) compensation for both full-time and part-time employed support staff. This should not include: (1) nonphysician provider cost; (2) any benefits for employed support staff, which should be reported as "total employed support staff benefit cost"; (3) expense reimbursements; and (4) any benefits or the cost of contracted support staff who do not work for any of the legal entities that comprise the medical practice (these costs should be reported as "total contracted support staff").

surgery and anesthesia procedures conducted inside the practice's facilities This consists of: (1) 00100–01999, anesthesia procedures; (2) 10021–36410, 36420–69990, surgery procedures; (3) 99100–99142, anesthesia procedures; and (4) surgery and anesthesia procedures performed in the practice's own ambulatory surgery unit. This should not include 36415 and 36416, venous and capillary blood collection.

surgery and anesthesia procedures conducted outside the practice's facilities This consists of surgery and anesthesia procedures performed in an inpatient hospital or a freestanding ambulatory surgery center. This should not include 36415 and 36416, venous and capillary blood collection.

T **throughput** Often synonymous with "capacity," throughput is typically an amount of something per unit time that processes into and out of a system. In the case of a typical medical practice, throughput refers to the practice's (system) ability to handle/treat patients (process) from the time a patient enters until he/she leaves the facility.

total contracted support staff (temporary) Represents all the staff hired on a contract basis that are not employed by any of the legal entities that comprise the medical practice. The utilization of contracted support staff occurs when the medical practice (including all the associated legal entities that comprise the medical practice) contracts to have full-time and/or ongoing support staff activities conducted by contracted staff. A defining characteristic of contracted support staff is that the hours worked (hence, the FTE) by the contracted support staff are easily identified and reported. If the hours worked are not easily identified and reported, then the FTE count cannot be accurately reported. One example of this type of cost would be purchased services for billing and collections activities. When a practice decides to hire a billing company to conduct billing activities, it is often not possible to track the hours that the billing company devotes to the given practice. Such cost should be reported as "billing and collections purchased services." Includes temporary staff working for temporary agencies. Do not include: (1) the FTE and cost of support staff employed directly by the practice or any of the legal entities comprising the medical practice; or (2) the FTE and cost for legal, accounting, management and/or other consultants for services performed on a one-time or sporadic basis (the costs for these types of consultants are reported as "outside professional fees").

total employed support staff benefit cost This consists of: (1) employer's share of FICA payroll and unemployment insurance taxes; (2) employer's share of health, disability, life and workers' compensation insurance; (3) employer payments to defined benefit and contribution, 401(k), 403(b) and nonqualified retirement plans; (4) deferred compensation paid or expensed during the year; (5) dues and memberships in professional organizations and state and local license fees; (6) allowances for education, professional meetings, travel and automobile; and (7) entertainment, country and athletic club membership, and travel for spouse. This should not include: (1) voluntary employee salary deductions used as contributions to 401(k) and 403(b) plans; or (2) expense reimbursements.

total nonphysician provider FTE A full-time nonphysician provider works whatever number of hours the practice considers to be the minimum for a normal work week, which could be 37.5, 40, 50 hours or some other standard. To compute "total nonphysician provider" FTE, add the number of full-time (1.0 FTE) nonphysician providers to the FTE count for part-time nonphysician providers. To compute the FTE of a part-time nonphysician provider, divide the total hours worked by the number of hours that your practice considers to be a normal work week. A nonphysician provider working 30 hours compared to a normal work week of 40 hours would be 0.75 FTE (30 hours divided by 40 hours). A nonphysician provider working full-time for three months during a year would be 0.25 FTE (3 months divided by 12 months). A nonphysician provider cannot be counted as more than 1.0 FTE regardless of the number of hours worked.

total operating expense Expenses incurred by the practice while earning medical revenue, consisting of employee salaries and fringe benefits (does not include physicians and mid-level providers); services and general expenses (for example, office and administrative expenses, depreciation, pharmaceuticals, medical supplies and occupancy costs such as rent and utilities); purchased services; and provider-related expenses (physician salaries, taxes, health insurance, licenses and other costs associated with physician and mid-level provider compensation).

total physician benefit cost Total benefits paid to physicians who comprise "total physician" FTE. This should include: (1) employer's share of FICA payroll and unemployment insurance taxes; (2) employer's share of health, disability, life and workers' compensation insurance; (3) employer payments to defined benefit and contribution, 401(k), 403(b) and non-qualified retirement plans; (4) deferred compensation paid or expensed during the year; (5) dues and memberships in professional organizations and state and local license fees; (6) allowances for education, professional meetings, travel and automobile; and (7) entertainment, country and athletic club membership, and travel for spouse. This should not include: (1) voluntary employee salary deductions used as contributions to 401(k) and 403(b) plans; or (2) expense reimbursements.

total physician compensation Total compensation paid to physicians who comprise "total physician" FTE. This should include: (1) compensation for shareholders and partners, salaried associates, employed physicians, contract physicians, locum tenens, residents and fellows; (2) compensation for full-time and part-time physicians; (3) salaries, bonuses, incentive payments, research contract revenue, honoraria and profit distributions; (4) voluntary employee salary deductions used as contributions to 401(k), 403(b) or Section 125 plans; and (5) compensation attributable to activities related to revenue in "nonmedical revenue." This should not include: (1) amounts included in "provider consultant cost"; (2) amounts included in "total physician benefit cost"; or (3) expense reimbursements.

total RVUs This consists of RVUs for: (1) "physician work RVUs," "malpractice RVUs" and "nonfacility practice expense RVUs"; (2) all professional medical and surgical services performed by physicians, nonphysician providers and other physician extenders such as nurses and medical assistants; (3) the professional component of laboratory, radiology, medical diagnostic and surgical procedures; (4) the technical components of laboratory, radiology, medical diagnostic and surgical procedures; (5) all procedures performed by the medical practice (for procedures with either no listed CPT code or with an RVU value of zero, RVUs can be estimated by dividing the total gross charges for the unlisted or unvalued procedures by the practice's known average charge per RVU for all procedures that are listed and valued); (6) procedures for both fee-for-service and capitation patients; (7) all payers, not just Medicare; and (8) purchased procedures from external providers on behalf of the practice's fee-for-service patients. This should not include RVUs: (1) for other scales such as McGraw-Hill and California; (2) for purchased procedures from external providers on behalf of the practice's capitation patients; (3) that have been weighted by a conversion factor (do not weigh the RVUs by a conversion factor); and (4) where the geographic practice cost index (GPCI) equals any value other than 1. The GPCI must be set to 1.000 (neutral).

U   **university** Institution of higher learning with teaching and research facilities comprising undergraduate, graduate and professional schools.

V   **validity** Meaningfulness within a generally accepted theoretical basis; that is, does the measure or metric mean what it's suppose to?

variance Indicator of how large or small the difference is in the values (in nonstatistical terms). Standard deviation, like variance, is a measure of variability or dispersion.

visit See *patient encounters.*

W   **workload** Generic term or measure for work that can be represented as visits, encounters or RVUs.

workers' compensation Fee-for-service gross charges, at the practice's undiscounted rates, for all services provided to patients covered by workers' compensation insurance. This should not include charges for: (1) Medicare patients; (2) Medicaid patients; (3) charity or professional courtesy patients; or (4) self-pay patients.

Acronyms and Geographic Sections

A/R	accounts receivable
ASA	American Society of Anesthesiologists
CMS	Centers for Medicare & Medicaid Services
DO	doctor of osteopathy
EHR	electronic health record
FFS	fee-for-service
FTE	full-time-equivalent
HMO	health maintenance organization
IBNR	incurred but not reported
IDS	integrated delivery system
MD	doctor of medicine
MGMA	Medical Group Management Association
MSO	management services organization
OB/GYN	obstetrics/gynecology
PhD	doctor of philosophy
PPMC	physician practice management company
RBRVS	resource based relative value scale
RVU	relative value unit(s)
TC	technical component

Eastern Section	Midwest Section	Southern Section	Western Section
Connecticut	Illinois	Alabama	Alaska
Delaware	Indiana	Arkansas	Arizona
District of Columbia	Iowa	Florida	California
Maine	Michigan	Georgia	Colorado
Maryland	Minnesota	Kansas	Hawaii
Massachusetts	Nebraska	Kentucky	Idaho
New Hampshire	North Dakota	Louisiana	Montana
New Jersey	Ohio	Mississippi	Nevada
New York	South Dakota	Missouri	New Mexico
North Carolina	Wisconsin	Oklahoma	Oregon
Pennsylvania		South Carolina	Utah
Rhode Island		Tennessee	Washington
Vermont		Texas	Wyoming
Virginia			
West Virginia			

Physician Categories

Primary care physicians include:

Family practice: general
Family practice: sports medicine
Family practice: urgent care
Family practice: with obstetrics
Family practice: without obstetrics
Geriatrics

Internal medicine: general
Internal medicine: urgent care
Pediatrics: adolescent medicine
Pediatrics: general
Pediatrics: sports medicine

Nonsurgical specialty physicians include:

Allergy/immunology
Cardiology
Cardiology: electrophysiology
Cardiology: invasive
Cardiology: invasive/interventional
Cardiology: noninvasive
Critical care: intensivist
Dentistry
Dermatology
Emergency medicine
Endocrinology/metabolism
Gastroenterology
Gastroenterology: hepatology
Genetics
Hematology/oncology
Hospitalist
Infectious disease
Maternal and fetal medicine
Nephrology
Neurology
Nuclear medicine
Occupational medicine

Oncology (only)
Orthopedics: nonsurgical
Pathology: anatomic
Pathology: anatomic and clinical
Pathology: clinical
Pathology: general
Pediatrics: allergy and immunology
Pediatrics: cardiology
Pediatrics: child development
Pediatrics: clinical and lab
  immunology
Pediatrics: critical care intensivist
Pediatrics: emergency medicine
Pediatrics: endocrinology
Pediatrics: gastroenterology
Pediatrics: genetics
Pediatrics: hematology/oncology
Pediatrics: hospitalist
Pediatrics: infectious disease
Pediatrics: neonatal medicine
Pediatrics: nephrology
Pediatrics: neurology

Pediatrics: pulmonology

Pediatrics: rheumatology

Physical medicine and
  rehabilitation (physiatry)

Podiatry: general

Psychiatry: child and adolescent

Psychiatry: forensic

Psychiatry: general

Psychiatry: geriatric

Public health

Pulmonary medicine

Pulmonary medicine: critical care

Radiation oncology

Radiology: diagnostic-invasive

Radiology: diagnostic-noninvasive

Radiology: nuclear medicine

Reproductive endocrinology

Rheumatology

Surgical specialty physicians include:

Anesthesiology

Anesthesiology: pain management

Anesthesiology: pediatric

Dermatology: MOHS surgery

Gynecology (only)

Gynecological oncology

Obstetrics

Obstetrics/gynecology

Ophthalmology

Ophthalmology: pediatric

Ophthalmology: retina

Otorhinolaryngology

Otorhinolaryngology: pediatric

Podiatry: surgical foot and ankle

Podiatry: surgical forefoot only

Surgery: cardiovascular

Surgery: cardiovascular pediatric

Surgery: colon and rectal

Surgery: general

Surgery: neurological

Surgery: oncology

Surgery: oral

Surgery: orthopedic

Surgery: orthopedic (foot and
  ankle)

Surgery: orthopedic (hand)

Surgery: orthopedic (hip and joint)

Surgery: orthopedic (oncology)

Surgery: orthopedic (pediatric)

Surgery: orthopedic (spine)

Surgery: orthopedic (sports
  medicine)

Surgery: orthopedic (trauma)

Surgery: pediatric

Surgery: plastic and reconstruction

Surgery: plastic and reconstruction,
  hand

Surgery: plastic and reconstruction,
  pediatric

Surgery: thoracic

Surgery: transplant

Surgery: trauma

Surgery: trauma, burn

Surgery: vascular

Urology

Urology: pediatric

About the Authors

Gregory S. Feltenberger, MBA, FACMPE, FACHE, CPHIMS, has over 14 years of operational health care experience and is an active duty Medical Service Corps officer (health services administrator) in the U.S. Air Force. Currently, he is the chief of performance improvement tool development at the Office of the Air Force Surgeon General, Air Force Medical Support Agency, Data Modeling & Analysis Office in Falls Church, Va. In addition to his jobs as a chief information officer, chief of information management, group practice manager and medical control center team chief, Greg was competitively selected and completed a 10-month fellowship in Survey Development, Analysis, and Performance Measurement at MGMA. He has experience in the use of bivariate and multivariate statistics, sampling methodologies, quantitative and qualitative research methods, and statistical software.

Greg is a PhD student at Old Dominion University in the Health Services Research program, and has an MBA in information systems from Kent State University, a BA in specialized studies (summa cum laude) and an associate degree in engineering technology in biomedical equipment technology from Edinboro University of Pennsylvania. He is a Fellow in the American College of Medical Practice Executives (ACMPE), the standard-setting and certification body of the MGMA; a Fellow in the American College of Healthcare Executives; a Certified Medical Practice Executive in ACMPE; a certified health care executive in the American College of Healthcare Executives; and a certified professional in health care information and management systems in the Healthcare Information and Management Systems Society. Greg has taught several online courses, authored several research posters and articles, and presented at national and military health care management conferences.

Finally, he is a principal and co-founder of SmHart, Inc. (www.SmHart.net), an education, training and organizational improvement firm specializing in Webcasts and online training; survey development, administration and analysis; organizational and needs assessments; and financial (P&L) evaluations and business valuations. Greg can be reached at gsf@SmHart.net.

David N. Gans, MHSA, FACMPE, is vice president of Practice Management Resources at MGMA in Englewood, Colo., where he is the MGMA staff expert on medical group practice management. He is an educational program speaker, author of a monthly column in *MGMA Connexion*, and he provides technical assistance to the Association's staff and members on topic areas of benchmarking, use of survey data, financial management, cost efficiency, physician compensation and productivity, managerial compensation, the resource based relative value scale, employee staffing, cost accounting, medical group organization and emergency preparedness. He is a retired colonel in the United States Army Reserve.

Dave earned an undergraduate degree in government at the University of Notre Dame, a master's degree in education from the University of Southern California and a master's degree in health administration from the University of Colorado. He is a Fellow in ACMPE and a certified medical practice executive in the American College of Medical Practice Executives. Dave can be reached at dng@mgma.com.

Index

Note: *ex.* indicates exhibit; *f.* indicates figure.